iPad®

FOR

DUMMIES®

2ND EDITION

by Edward C. Baig
and Bob "Dr. Mac" LeVitus

WILEY

Wiley Publishing, Inc.

iPad® For Dummies®, 2nd Edition

Published by
Wiley Publishing, Inc.
111 River Street
Hoboken, NJ 07030-5774

www.wiley.com

Copyright © 2011 by Wiley Publishing, Inc., Indianapolis, Indiana

Published by Wiley Publishing, Inc., Indianapolis, Indiana

Published simultaneously in Canada

For general information on our other products and services, please contact our Customer Care Department within the U.S. at 877-762-2974, outside the U.S. at 317-572-3993, or fax 317-572-4002.

For technical support, please visit www.wiley.com/techsupport.

Wiley also publishes its books in a variety of electronic formats. Some content that appears in print may not be available in electronic books.

Library of Congress Control Number is available from the Publisher upon request.

ISBN: 978-1-118-02444-7

Manufactured in the United States of America

10 9 8 7 6 5 4 3 2

WILEY

About the Authors

Edward C. Baig writes the weekly Personal Technology column in *USA TODAY* and is cohost of *USA TODAY*'s Talking Tech podcast with Jefferson Graham. Ed is also the author of *Macs For Dummies,* 11th Edition. (Wiley Publishing) and cowriter of *iPhone For Dummies.* Before joining *USA TODAY* as a columnist and reporter in 1999, Ed spent six years at *Business Week,* where he wrote and edited stories about consumer tech, personal finance, collectibles, travel, and wine tasting, among other topics. He received the Medill School of Journalism 1999 Financial Writers and Editors Award for contributions to the "*Business Week* Investor Guide to Online Investing." That followed a three-year stint at *U.S. News & World Report,* where Ed was the lead tech writer for the News You Can Use section but also dabbled in numerous other subjects.

Ed began his journalist career at *Fortune* magazine, gaining the best basic training imaginable during his early years as a fact checker and contributor to the Fortune 500. Through the dozen years he worked at the magazine, Ed covered leisure-time industries, penned features on the lucrative "dating" market and the effect of religion on corporate managers, and was heavily involved in the Most Admired Companies project. Ed also started up *Fortune*'s Products to Watch column, a venue for low- and high-tech items.

Bob LeVitus, often referred to as "Dr. Mac," has written or cowritten nearly 60 popular computer books, with millions of copies in print. His titles include *Mac OS X For Dummies, iPhone For Dummies, Incredible iPhone Apps For Dummies,* and *Microsoft Office 2008 For Mac For Dummies* for Wiley Publishing, Inc.; *Stupid Mac Tricks* and *Dr. Macintosh* for Addison-Wesley; and *The Little iTunes Book*, 3rd Edition and *The Little iDVD Book*, 2nd Edition for Peachpit Press.

Bob has also penned the popular Dr. Mac column for the *Houston Chronicle* for more than 12 years and has been published in pretty much every magazine that ever used the word *Mac* in its title. His achievements have been documented in major media around the world. (Yes, that was him juggling a keyboard in *USA TODAY* a few years back!)

Bob is known for his expertise, trademark humorous style, and ability to translate techie jargon into usable and fun advice for regular folks. Bob is also a prolific public speaker, presenting more than 100 Macworld Expo training sessions in the United States and abroad, keynote addresses in three countries, and Macintosh training seminars in many U.S. cities.

Dedications

I dedicate this book to my beautiful wife, Janie, for inspiring me in myriad ways; every day I am with her. And to my incredible kids: my adorable little girl, Sydney (one of her first words was *iPod*) and my little boy, Sammy (who is all smiles from the moment he wakes up in the morning). My kids are already hooked on the iPad. This book is also dedicated to the memory of my "canine" son, Eddie Jr. I am madly in love with you all. —Ed Baig

This book is dedicated to my wife, Lisa, who taught me almost everything I know about almost everything except computers. And to my children, Allison and Jacob, who love my iPad almost as much as I love them (my kids, not my iPad). Last but certainly not least, to my dear friend Robyn Ray, who just ordered an iPad 2: This one's for you, kid. —Bob LeVitus

Authors' Acknowledgments

Special thanks to everyone at Apple who helped us turn this book around so quickly: Katie Cotton, Natalie Kerris, Natalie Harrison, Teresa Brewer, Janette Barrios, Keri Walker, Jennifer Bowcock, Jason Roth, and everyone else who lent a hand from the mothership out in Cupertino. We couldn't have done it without you.

Big-time thanks to the gang at Wiley: Bob "Can't you work any faster?" Woerner, Rebecca Huehls, John Edwards, Andy "The Boss" Cummings, Jen Riggs, and our incredible technical editor Dennis R. Cohen, who did a rocking job in record time as always. Finally, thanks to everyone at Wiley we don't know by name. If you helped with this project in any way, you have our ever-lasting thanks.

Ed adds: Thanks to my agent Matt Wagner for again turning me into a For Dummies author. Matt had the right instincts to push this book, even back when we were calling the first edition of the book Project X For Dummies. I'd also like to thank Jim Henderson, Geri Tucker and Nancy Blair, and all my *USA TODAY* friends and colleagues for your continuing support and encouragement of such projects. Most of all, thanks to my loving family for understanding my nightly (and weekend) disappearances as we raced to get this project completed on time. You are quite simply the greatest.

And Bob says: Extra special thanks to my agent, Carole "Swifty" Jelen, who has guided my writing career for more than 20 years and is still the best in the business. Here's to 20 more years of friendship and success together.

Publisher's Acknowledgments

We're proud of this book; please send us your comments at http://dummies.custhelp.com. For other comments, please contact our Customer Care Department within the U.S. at 877-762-2974, outside the U.S. at 317-572-3993, or fax 317-572-4002.

Some of the people who helped bring this book to market include the following:

Acquisitions and Editorial

Project Editor: Rebecca Huehls

Executive Editor: Bob Woerner

Copy Editor: Jen Riggs

Technical Editor: Dennis Cohen

Sr. Editorial Manager: Leah P. Cameron

Editorial Assistant: Amanda Graham

Sr. Editorial Assistant: Cherie Case

Cartoons: Rich Tennant (www.the5thwave.com)

Composition Services

Project Coordinator: Patrick Redmond

Layout and Graphics: Samantha K. Cherolis, Joyce Haughey

Proofreader: Susan Hobbs

Indexer: BIM Indexing & Proofreading Services

Special Art: Credits for chapter opener art are as follows:

Corbis Digital Stock — pages 63, 79, 245, 295, 305

Image Source — page 317

iStockPhoto.com — Ronen, page 41; Matt Jeacock, page 103; HannahmariaH, page 151; Vasko Miokovic, page 187

PhotoDisc, Inc. — page 267

PhotoDisc/Getty Images — pages 169, 205, 223

Publishing and Editorial for Technology Dummies

Richard Swadley, Vice President and Executive Group Publisher

Andy Cummings, Vice President and Publisher

Mary Bednarek, Executive Acquisitions Director

Mary C. Corder, Editorial Director

Publishing for Consumer Dummies

Diane Graves Steele, Vice President and Publisher

Composition Services

Debbie Stailey, Director of Composition Services

Table of Contents

Introduction

A s Yogi Berra would say, "It was déjà vu all over again": Front-page treatment, top billing on network TV and cable, and diehards lining up days in advance to ensure landing a highly lusted-after product from Apple. Only the product generating the remarkable buzz this time around wasn't the iPhone or even the first iPad. This time around it was iPad 2. We trust you didn't pick up this book to read yet another account about how the iPhone launch followed by the iPad launch followed by the iPad 2 launch were epochal events. We trust you *did* buy the book to find out how to get the very most out of your remarkable device, and that goes for the original iPad as well as its successor. Our goal is to deliver that information in a light and breezy fashion. We expect you to have fun using your iPad or iPad 2. We equally hope that you have fun spending time with us.

About This Book

We need to get one thing out of the way right from the get-go. We think you're pretty darn smart for buying a *For Dummies* book. That says to us that you have the confidence and intelligence to know what you don't know. The *For Dummies* franchise is built around the core notion that everyone feels insecure about certain topics when tackling them for the first time, especially when those topics have to do with technology.

As with most Apple products, iPads are beautifully designed and intuitive to use. And though our editors may not want us to reveal this dirty little secret (especially on the first page, for goodness sake), the truth is you'll get pretty far just by exploring the iPad's many functions and features on your own, without the help of this (or any other) book.

Okay, now that we spilled the beans, we'll tell you why you shouldn't run back to the bookstore and request a refund. This book is chock-full of useful tips, advice, and other nuggets that should make your iPad experience all the more pleasurable. We'd even go so far as to say you wouldn't find some of these nuggets anywhere else. So keep this book nearby and consult it often.

Conventions Used in This Book

First, we want to tell you how we go about our business. *iPad For Dummies* makes generous use of numbered steps, bullet lists, and pictures. Web addresses are shown in a special monofont typeface, `like this`.

We also include a few sidebars with information that isn't required reading (not that any of this book is) but that we hope will provide a richer understanding of certain subjects. Overall, we aim to keep technical jargon to a minimum, under the guiding principle that with rare exceptions, you need not know what any of it really means.

How This Book Is Organized

Here's something we imagine you've heard before: Most books have a beginning, a middle, and an end, and you do well to adhere to that linear structure — unless you're one of those knuckleheads out to ruin it for the rest of us by revealing that the butler did it.

Fortunately, there is no ending to spoil in a *For Dummies* book. So although you may want to digest this book from start to finish — and we hope you do — we won't penalize you for skipping ahead or jumping around. Having said that, we organized *iPad For Dummies* in an order that we think makes the most sense, as follows.

Part I: Getting to Know Your iPad

In the introductory chapters of Part I, you tour the iPad inside and out, find out what all those buttons and other nonvirtual doodads do, as well as get some hands-on (or, more precisely, fingers-on) experience with the iPad's unique virtual multitouch display. And, of course, you'll see how easy it is to synchronize stuff on your Mac or PC with your dynamic device.

Part II: The Internet iPad

Part II is all about getting connected with your iPad. Along the way, you discover how to surf the web with the Safari web browser; set up mail accounts; send and receive mail; work with maps, YouTube, and social media apps; and buy and use apps from the iTunes App Store.

Part III: The iPad at Work and Play

Part III is where the fun truly begins as well as where we show you how to get serious about using your iPad for work. You discover how to use your iPad for music, video, movies, and photos, as well as how to buy and read iBooks from the iBookstore. If you have an iPad 2, this is the part where you read all about the tablet's front and rear cameras. You also spend quality time with your Calendar and Contacts apps and find out just a bit about Apple's (optional) productivity iWork apps — Pages, Numbers, and Keynote.

Part IV: The Undiscovered iPad

In Part IV, you find out how to apply your preferences through the iPad's internal settings, discover where to go for troubleshooting assistance if your iPad should misbehave, and find out about some must-have accessories you may want to consider.

Part V: The Part of Tens

The Part of Tens: Otherwise known as the *For Dummies* answer to David Letterman (which, as it happens, both have close ties to Indianapolis). The lists presented in Part V steer you to some of our favorite iPad apps as well as some very handy tips and shortcuts.

Icons Used in This Book

Little round pictures (or *icons*) appear in the left margins throughout this book. Consider these icons as miniature road signs, telling you something extra about the topic at hand or hammering a point home.

Here's what the five icons used in this book look like and mean.

These are the juicy morsels, shortcuts, and recommendations that might make the task at hand faster or easier.

This icon emphasizes the stuff we think you ought to retain. You may even jot down a note to yourself in the iPad.

Put on your propeller beanie hat and pocket protector; this text includes the truly geeky stuff. You can safely ignore this material, but if it weren't interesting or informative, we wouldn't have bothered to write it.

You wouldn't intentionally run a stop sign, would you? In the same fashion, ignoring warnings may be hazardous to your iPad and (by extension) your wallet. There, you now know how these warning icons work, for you have just received your very first warning!

We put a New icon next to anything that's new since last edition, including hardware updates for iPad 2 as well as software updates, extra accessories, or anything else that's new for either version of the iPad.

Where to Go from Here

Why straight to Chapter 1, of course (without passing Go).

In all seriousness, we wrote this book for you, so please let us know what you think. If we screwed up, confused you, left out something, or — heaven forbid — made you angry, drop us a note. And if we hit you with one pun too many, it helps to know that as well.

Because writers are people too (believe it or not), we also encourage positive feedback if you think it's warranted. So kindly send e-mail to Ed at `baigdummies@aol.com` and to Bob at `iPadLeVitus@boblevitus.com`. We do our best to respond to reasonably polite e-mail in a timely fashion.

Most of all, we want to thank you for buying our book. Please enjoy it along with your new iPad.

Note: At the time we wrote this book, all the information it contained was accurate for the Wi-Fi and Wi-Fi + 3G iPads and iPad 2s, version 4.3 of the iOS (operating system) used by the iPad, and version 10.2.1 of iTunes. Apple is likely to introduce new iPad models and new versions of iOS and iTunes between book editions. If you've bought a new iPad and its hardware, user interface, or the version of iTunes on your computer looks a little different, be sure to check out what Apple has to say at `www.apple.com/ipad`. You'll no doubt find updates on the company's latest releases. When a change is very substantial, we may add an update or bonus information that you can download at this book's companion web site, `www.dummies.com/go/ipad`.

Part I
Getting to Know Your iPad

The 5th Wave   By Rich Tennant

"Other than this little glitch with the landscape view, I really love my iPad."

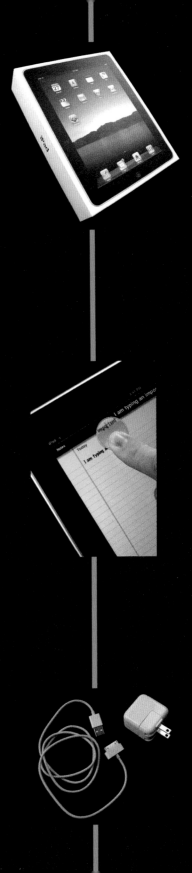

In this part . . .

You have to crawl before you walk, so consider this part basic training for crawling. The three chapters that make up Part I serve as a gentle introduction to your iPad.

We start out nice and easy in Chapter 1, with a big-picture overview, even letting you know what's in the box (if you haven't already peeked). Then we examine just some of the cool things your iPad can do. We finish things off with a quick-and-dirty tour of the hardware and the software so that you'll know where things are when you need them.

Next, after you're somewhat familiar with where things are and what they do, we move right along to a bunch of useful iPad skills, such as turning the darn thing on and off (which is very important) and locking and unlocking your iPad (which is also very important). Chapter 2 covers useful tips and tricks to help you master the iPad's unique multitouch interface so that you can use it effectively and efficiently.

Then, in Chapter 3, we explore the process of synchronization and how to get data — contacts, appointments, movies, songs, podcasts, books, and so on — from your computer into your iPad, quickly and painlessly.

Unveiling the iPad

Congratulations! You've selected one of the most incredible handheld devices we've ever seen. Of course, the iPad is a combination of a killer audio and video iPod, an e-book reader, a powerful Internet communications device, a superb handheld gaming device, a still and video camera (iPad 2 only), and a platform for over 150,000 apps at the time this was written — and probably a lot more by the time you read this.

In this chapter, we offer a gentle introduction to all the pieces that make up your iPad, plus overviews of its revolutionary hardware and software features.

Exploring the iPad's Big Picture

The iPad has many best-of-class features, but perhaps its most unusual feature is the lack of a physical keyboard or stylus. Instead, it has a 9.7-inch super-high-resolution touchscreen (132 pixels per inch, if you care about such things) that you operate using a pointing device you're already intimately familiar with: your finger.

And what a display it is. We venture that you've never seen a more beautiful screen on a handheld device other than the iPhone 4.

Another feature that knocked our socks off was the iPad's built-in sensors. An accelerometer detects when you rotate the device from portrait to landscape mode and instantly adjusts what's on the display accordingly.

What's in the box

Somehow we think you've already opened the handsome box that the iPad came in. But if you didn't, here's what you can expect to find inside:

- **Dock connector–to–USB cable:** Use this handy cable to sync or charge your iPad. You can plug the USB connector into your Mac or PC to sync or plug it into the USB power adapter, which we describe next.

Note: If you connect the USB cable to USB ports on your keyboard, USB hub, display, or other external device, or even the USB ports on an older Mac or PC, you may be able to sync, but more than likely can't charge the battery. For the most part, only your computer's built-in USB ports (and only recent vintage computers at that) have enough juice to recharge the battery. If you use an external USB port, you probably see a Not Charging message next to the Battery icon at the top of the screen.

- **USB power adapter:** Use this adapter to recharge your iPad from a standard AC power outlet.

- **Some Apple logo decals:** Of course.

- **iPad instruction sheet:** Unfortunately (or fortunately if you're the author of a book about using the iPad), this little one-page, two-sided "manual" offers precious little useful information about the new object of your affection.

- **Important Product Information Guide pamphlet:** Well, it must be important because it says so right on the cover. You'll find basic safety warnings, a bunch of legalese, warranty information, and info on how to dispose of or recycle the iPad. *What! You're getting rid of it already?* A few other pieces of advice: Don't drop the iPad if you can help it, keep the thing dry, and — as with all handheld electronic devices — give full attention to the road while driving (or walking, for that matter).

- **SIM eject tool (iPad 2 with 3G only):** A little metal doohickey that does just what its name implies. Most people go through their entire lives without ever ejecting a SIM card, but at least now you know.

Tip: Original iPad with 3G owners can use a straightened paper clip to eject the SIM card. Not as cool as a special tool, but it works.

- **iPad:** You were starting to worry. Yes, the iPad itself is also in the box.

What's not in the box is a stereo headset. If you want to use a headset for music, video, games, or anything else, you have to find one elsewhere. Might we suggest you find one that includes a built-in microphone? Although the iPad doesn't come with the VoiceNotes app found on the iPhone, it can record to many of the apps that are available in the App Store, such as the free iTalk Recorder app from Griffin Technology or the Voice Memos for iPad app from KendiTech, Inc.

The aforementioned iPhone headset works great with the iPad as will any other headset that works with an iPhone. If you use one with your iPhone, give it a try with your iPad.

The screen rotates, that is, unless the Screen Rotation Lock is engaged. We tell you more about this feature shortly.

And a light sensor adjusts the display's brightness in response to the current ambient lighting conditions.

In addition to the aforementioned sensors, the iPad 2 also has a three-axis gyro sensor that works in conjunction with the accelerometer and built-in compass. Although all iPads can sense their orientation and direction, the iPad 2 senses such things even better and faster.

In the following sections, we're not just gawking over the wonderful screen. We take a brief look at some of the iPad's features, broken down by product category.

The iPad as an iPod

We agree with Steve Jobs on this one: The iPad is magical — and without a doubt, the best iPod Apple has ever produced. You can enjoy all your existing iPod content — music, audiobooks, audio and video podcasts, music videos, television shows, and movies — on the iPad's gorgeous high-resolution color display, which is bigger, brighter, and richer than any iPod or iPhone display that came before it.

Bottom line: If you can get the content — be it video, audio, or whatever — into iTunes on your Mac or PC, you can synchronize it and watch or listen to it on your iPad.

Chapter 3 is all about syncing, but for now, just know that some video content may need to be converted to an iPad-compatible format (with proper resolution, frame rate, bit rate, and file format) to play on your iPad. If you try to sync an incompatible video file, iTunes alerts you that there's an issue.

If you get an error message about an incompatible video file, select the file in iTunes and choose Advanced⇨Create iPad or Apple TV Version. When the conversion is finished, sync again. Chapter 9 covers video and video compatibility in more detail.

The iPad as an Internet communications device

But wait — there's more! Not only is the iPad a stellar iPod, but it's also a full-featured Internet communications device with — we're about to drop a bit of industry jargon on you — a rich HTML e-mail client that's compatible with most POP and IMAP mail services, with support for Microsoft Exchange

ActiveSync. (For more on this topic, see Chapter 5.) Also onboard is a world-class web browser (Safari) that, unlike on many mobile devices, makes web surfing fun and easy on the eyes. Chapter 4 explains how to surf the web using Safari.

Another cool Internet feature is *Maps,* a killer mapping application based on Google Maps. By using GPS (Wi-Fi + 3G model) or triangulation (Wi-Fi model), the iPad can determine your location, let you view maps and satellite imagery, and obtain driving directions and traffic information regardless of where you happen to be. (See Chapter 6 for the scoop on Maps.) You can also find businesses, such as gas stations, pizza restaurants, hospitals, and Apple Stores, with just a few taps.

We daresay that the Internet experience on an iPad is far superior to the Internet experience on any other handheld device.

The iPad as an e-book reader

Download the free iBooks app or any of the excellent (and free) third-party e-book readers such as the Kindle and Nook apps and you'll discover a whole new way of finding and reading books. The iBookstore, covered in Chapter 11, is chock-full of good reading at prices that are lower than a hardcover copy. Better still, when you read an e-book, you're helping the environment and saving trees. And best of all, a great number of books are absolutely free. If you've never read a book on your iPad, give it a try. We think you'll like (or love) it.

The iPad as a multimedia powerhouse

The spectacular screen found on both iPad models is superb for personal video viewing. Add an adapter cable as discussed in Chapter 15 and it turns into a superb device for watching video on an HDTV (or even a non-HD TV), with support for output resolutions up to 1080p (iPad 2).

 And the iPad 2, with its pair of cameras and FaceTime video chatting app, takes iPad's multimedia acumen to new heights. Chapter 9 gets you started with FaceTime.

The iPad as a platform for third-party apps

Over 300,000 iPhone apps are available at this writing, in categories that include games, business, education, entertainment, healthcare and fitness, music, photography, productivity, travel, sports, and many more. The cool thing is that most of those iPhone apps run flawlessly on the iPad.

Meanwhile, at the time we wrote this, the App Store offered more than 65,000 apps designed specifically for the iPad's large screen, with many more on the way. Chapter 7 helps you fill your iPad with all the cool apps your heart desires. We share our favorite free and for-sale apps in Chapters 16 and 17, respectively.

What do you need to use an iPad?

To actually *use* your iPad, only a few simple things are required. Here's a list of everything you need:

- An iPad
- An iTunes Store account (assuming you want to acquire apps, videos, music, iBooks, podcasts, and the like, which you almost certainly do)
- Internet access — broadband wireless Internet access recommended

Plus you need *one* of the following:

- A Mac with a USB 2.0 port, Mac OS X version 10.5.8 or later, and iTunes 10.2.1 or later
- A PC with a USB 2.0 port; Windows 7, Windows Vista, or Windows XP Home or Professional with Service Pack 3 or later; and iTunes 10.2.1 or later

Touring the iPad Exterior

The iPad is a harmonious combination of hardware and software. In the following sections, we take a brief look at the hardware — what's on the outside.

On the top

On the top of your iPad, you find the headphone jack, and the Sleep/Wake button, as shown in Figure 1-1:

- **Sleep/Wake button:** This button is used to put your iPad's screen to sleep or to wake it up. It's also how you turn your iPad on or off. To put it to sleep or wake it up, just press the button. To turn it on or off, press and hold the button for a few seconds.

  Your iPad's battery will run down faster when your iPad is awake, so we suggest that you make a habit of putting it to sleep when you're not using it.

When your iPad is sleeping, nothing happens if you touch its screen. To wake it up, merely press the button again or press the Home button on the front of the device (as described in a moment).

iPad 2 owners with an Apple Smart Cover can just open the cover to wake their iPad and close the cover to put iPad 2 to sleep.

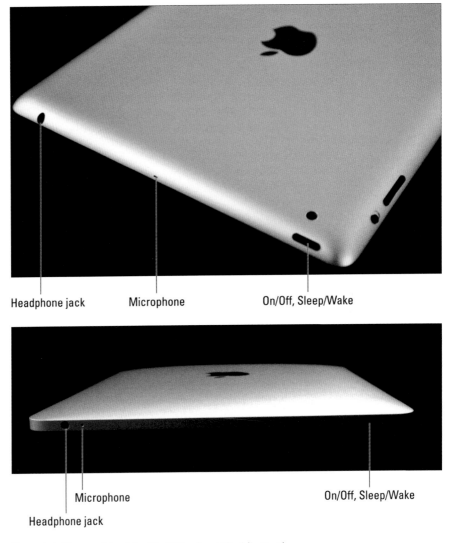

Headphone jack   Microphone   On/Off, Sleep/Wake

Microphone   On/Off, Sleep/Wake

Headphone jack

Figure 1-1: The top side of the iPad 2 (top) and iPad (bottom).

Find out how to make your iPad go to sleep automatically after a period of inactivity in Chapter 13.

✔ **Headphone jack:** This jack lets you plug in a headset. You can use the Apple headsets or headphones that came with your iPhone or iPod. Or, you can use pretty much any headphones or headset that plugs into a 3.5-mm stereo headphone jack.

Throughout this book, we use the words *headphones, earphones,* and *headset* interchangeably. Strictly speaking, a headset includes a microphone so that you can talk (or record) as well as listen; headphones or earphones are for listening only. Either type works with your iPad.

✔ **Microphone:** The tiny dot next to the headphone jack on the original iPad and in the middle of the top on the iPad 2 is actually a pretty good microphone.

Although your iPad doesn't include the VoiceNotes app that comes with the iPhone, the App Store offers several free voice-recording apps for the iPad and/or iPhone.

On the bottom

On the bottom of your iPad are the speaker and dock connector, as shown in Figure 1-2:

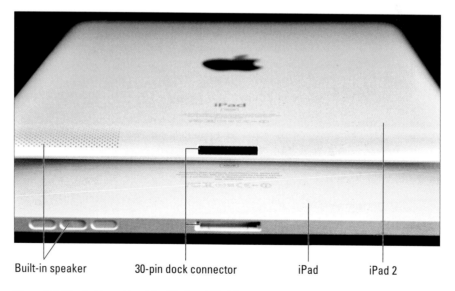

Built-in speaker   30-pin dock connector   iPad   iPad 2

Figure 1-2: The bottom side of the iPad and iPad 2.

✔ **Speaker:** The speaker plays audio — music or video soundtracks — if no headset is plugged in.

✔ **30-pin dock connector:** This connector has two purposes. One, you can use it to recharge your iPad's battery: Simply connect one end of the included dock connector–to–USB cable to the dock connector and the other end to the USB power adapter. Two, you can use the dock connector to recharge your iPad's battery as well as to synchronize: Connect one end of the same cable to the dock connector and the other end to a USB port on your Mac or PC.

In the "What's in the box" sidebar earlier in this chapter, reread the note about using the USB ports on anything other than your Mac or PC including keyboards, displays, and hubs.

On the right side

On the right side of your iPad are the Volume Up/Down control and Mute switch, as shown in Figure 1-3:

✔ **Mute switch:** When the switch is set to Silent mode — the down position, with an orange dot visible on the switch — your iPad doesn't make any sound when you receive new mail or an alert pops up on the screen. Note that the Mute switch doesn't silence what we think of as "expected" sounds, which are sounds you expect to hear in a particular app. Therefore, it doesn't silence the iTunes or Videos apps, nor will it mute games and other apps that emit noises. About the only thing the Mute switch will mute are "unexpected" sounds, such as those associated with notifications from apps or the iPad operating system (iOS).

If the switch doesn't mute your notification sounds when engaged (that is, you can see the little orange dot on the switch), look for a little No Rotation icon (shown here in the margin) to the left of the Battery icon near the top of your screen.

If you see this icon when you flick the Mute switch, there are two possible reasons. Reason 1: Your iPad is running an older version (version 3) of iOS. Reason 2: Your iPad is running version 4 or higher of iOS, and you have selected the Lock Rotation option in the Settings app's General pane.

Reason 1 occurs because iOS 3 treats the switch as a rotation lock, period, with no option for you to use it as a Mute switch. If that's the case, may we suggest you connect your iPad to your computer and use iTunes to upgrade your iPad to the current version by clicking the Check for Updates button on the Summary tab (as described in Chapter 3) and following the instructions for updating your iPad.

The current version of iOS 4 treats it as a Mute switch by default, but you can change it to a Rotation Lock in the Settings app's General pane.

✔ **Volume Up/Down control:** The Volume Up/Down control is a single button that's just below the Screen Rotation Lock. The upper part of the button increases the volume; the lower part decreases it.

iPad 2

Mute

Volume Up/Down

iPad

Volume Up/Down

Screen rotation lock

Figure 1-3: The right side has two buttons.

On the front and back

On the front of your iPad, you find the following (labeled in Figure 1-4):

Front camera

Back camera

Touchscreen

Application buttons

Home

Figure 1-4: The front of the iPad is a study in elegant simplicity.

- **Touchscreen:** You find out how to use the iPad's gorgeous high-resolution color touchscreen in Chapter 2. All we have to say at this time is . . . try not to drool all over it.

- **Home button:** No matter what you're doing, you can press the Home button at any time to display the Home screen, as shown in Figure 1-3.

- **Front camera (iPad 2 only):** It's not the greatest still camera on earth, but it's serviceable and captures decent video.

- **Application buttons:** Each of the 14 (17 on the iPad 2) buttons (icons) shown on the screen in Figure 1-3 launches an included iPad application. You read more about these applications later in this chapter and throughout the rest of the book.

Finally, if you have an iPad 2, you have a second camera just below the Sleep/Wake on the back side.

Status bar

The status bar, which is at the top of the screen, displays tiny icons that provide a variety of information about the current state of your iPad:

- **Airplane mode (Wi-Fi + 3G models only):** You're allowed to use your iPod on a plane after the captain gives the word. But you can't use a cellphone or iPad Wi-Fi + 3G except when the plane is in the gate area before takeoff or after landing. Fortunately, your iPad offers an Airplane mode, which turns off all wireless features of your iPad — the cellular, 3G, GPRS (General Packet Radio Service), and EDGE networks; Wi-Fi; and Bluetooth — and makes it possible to enjoy music or video during your flight.

- **3G (Wi-Fi + 3G models only):** This icon informs you that the high-speed 3G data network from your wireless carrier (that's AT&T or Verizon in the United States) is available and that your iPad can connect to the Internet via 3G. (Wondering what 3G and these other data networks are? Check out the nearby sidebar, "Comparing Wi-Fi, 3G, GPRS, and EDGE.")

- **GPRS (Wi-Fi + 3G models only):** This icon says that your wireless carrier's GPRS data network is available and that your iPad can use it to connect to the Internet.

- **EDGE (Wi-Fi + 3G models only):** This icon tells you that your wireless carrier's EDGE network is available and you can use it to connect to the Internet.

- **Wi-Fi:** If you see the Wi-Fi icon, your iPad is connected to the Internet over a Wi-Fi network. The more semicircular lines you see (up to three), the stronger the Wi-Fi signal. If you have only one or two semicircles of Wi-Fi strength, try moving around a bit. If you don't see the Wi-Fi icon in the status bar, Internet access is not currently available.

✓ **Activity:** This icon tells you that some network or other activity is occurring, such as over-the-air synchronization, sending or receiving e-mail, or loading a web page. Some third-party applications also use this icon to indicate network or other activity.

 ✓ **VPN:** This icon shows that you are currently connected to a virtual private network (VPN).

 ✓ **Lock:** This icon tells you when your iPad is locked. See Chapter 2 for information on locking and unlocking your iPad.

 ✓ **Screen Orientation Lock:** This icon appears when the Screen Rotation Lock is engaged.

 ✓ **Play:** This icon informs you that a song is currently playing. You find out more about playing songs in Chapter 8.

 ✓ **Bluetooth:** This icon indicates the current state of your iPad's Bluetooth connection. If you see this icon in the status bar, Bluetooth is on and a device (such as a wireless headset or keyboard) is connected. If the icon is gray (as shown on the right in the picture in the margin), Bluetooth is turned on but no device is connected. If the icon is white (as shown on the left in the picture in the margin), Bluetooth is on and one (or more) device is connected. If you don't see a Bluetooth icon at all, Bluetooth is turned off. Chapter 13 goes into more detail about Bluetooth.

 ✓ **Battery:** This icon reflects the level of your battery's charge. It's completely filled when you aren't connected to a power source and your battery is fully charged (as shown in the margin). It then empties as your battery becomes depleted. The icon shows when you're connected to a power source, and when the battery is fully charged or is currently charging. You see an onscreen message when the charge drops to 20 percent or below and another when it reaches 10 percent.

Comparing Wi-Fi, 3G, GPRS, and EDGE

Wireless (that is, cellular) carriers may offer one of three data networks. The fastest is a 3G data network, which as you probably guessed, is available only on the iPads with 3G. The device first looks for a 3G network and then, if it can't find one, looks for a slower EDGE or GPRS data network.

Wi-Fi networks, however, are even faster than any cellular data network — 3G, EDGE, or GPRS.

So all iPads connect to a Wi-Fi network if one is available, even if a 3G, GPRS, or EDGE network is also available.

Last but not least, if you don't see one of these icons — 3G, GPRS, EDGE, or Wi-Fi — you don't currently have Internet access. Chapter 2 offers more details about these different networks.

The iPad's Fabulous 14 or Superb 17: Discovering the Home Screen Icons

The Home screen offers 14 icons on both the original iPad and iPad 2, each representing a different built-in application or function. If you have an iPad 2, you have three additional apps — FaceTime, Camera, and Photo Booth — for a total of 17. Because the rest of the book covers each and every one of these babies in full and loving detail, we merely provide brief descriptions here.

To get to your Home screen, tap the Home button. If your iPad is asleep when you tap, the unlock screen appears. After your iPad is unlocked, you see whichever page of icons was on the screen when it went to sleep. If that happens to have been the Home screen, you're golden. If it wasn't, merely tap the Home button again to summon your iPad's Home screen.

You can rearrange icons on your iPad in three steps:

1. **Press and hold any icon until all the icons begin to "wiggle."**

2. **Drag the icons around until you're happy with their positions.**

3. **Press the Home button to save your arrangement and stop the "wiggling."**

If you haven't rearranged your icons, you see the following applications on your Home screen, starting at the top left:

- **Calendar:** No matter what calendar program you prefer on your Mac or PC (as long as it's iCal, Microsoft Entourage, or Microsoft Outlook), you can synchronize events and alerts between your computer and your iPad. Create an event on one device, and the event is automatically synchronized with the other device the next time the two devices are connected. Neat stuff.

- **Contacts:** This handy little app contains information about the people you know. Like the Calendar app, it synchronizes with the Contacts app on your Mac or PC (as long as it's Address Book, Microsoft Entourage, or Microsoft Outlook), and you can synchronize contacts between your computer and your iPad. If you create a contact on one device, the contact is automatically synchronized with the other device the next time your devices are connected. Chapter 12 explains how to start using the Calendar and Contacts apps.

- **Notes:** This program enables you to type notes while you're out and about. You can send the notes to yourself or to anyone else through e-mail, or just save them on your iPad until you need them. For help as you start using Notes, flip to Chapter 12.

- ✓ **Maps:** This application is among our favorites. View street maps or satellite imagery of locations around the globe, or ask for directions, traffic conditions, or even the location of a nearby pizza joint. You can find your way around the Maps app with the handy tips in Chapter 6.

- ✓ **Videos:** This handy app is the repository for your movies, TV shows, and music videos. You add videos via iTunes on your Mac or PC, or by purchasing them from the iTunes Store using the iTunes app on your iPad. Check out Chapter 9 to read more.

- ✓ **YouTube:** This application lets you watch videos from the popular YouTube web site. You can search for a particular video or browse through thousands of offerings. It's a great way to waste a lot of time. Chapter 6 also explains the joys of YouTube.

- ✓ **iTunes:** Tap this puppy to purchase music, movies, TV shows, audiobooks, and more, and also download free podcasts and courses from iTunes U. There's more info about iTunes (and the iPod app) in Chapter 8.

- ✓ **App Store:** This icon enables you to connect to and search the iTunes App Store for iPad applications that you can purchase or download for free over a Wi-Fi or cellular data network connection. Chapter 7 is your guide to buying and using apps from the App Store.

- ✓ **Game Center:** Apple's social networking app for game enthusiasts. Compare achievements, boast of your conquests and high scores, or challenge your friends to battle. You hear more about social networking and Game Center near the end of Chapter 6.

  If you have an iPad 2, you see the following three icons between your Game Center and Settings icons.

  - • *FaceTime:* Use this app to participate in FaceTime video chats, as you'll discover in Chapter 9.

  - • *Camera:* This app's for shooting pictures or videos with the iPad 2's front- or rear-facing camera.

  - • *Photo Booth:* This one's a lot like those old-time photo booths but you don't have to feed it money.

    If you just can't wait, flip to the details on FaceTime in Chapter 9 and Camera and Photo Booth in Chapter 10.

- ✓ **Settings:** This is where you change settings for your iPad and its apps. D'oh. With so many different settings in the Settings app, you'll be happy to hear that Chapter 13 is dedicated exclusively to Settings.

- ✓ **Safari:** Safari is your web browser. If you're a Mac user, you know that already. If you're a Windows user who hasn't already discovered the wonderful Safari for Windows, think Internet Explorer on steroids. Chapter 4 shows you how to start using Safari on your iPad.

✔ **Mail:** This application lets you send and receive e-mail with most POP3 and IMAP e-mail systems and, if you work for a company that grants permission, Microsoft Exchange, too. Chapter 5 helps you start e-mailing everyone you know from your iPad.

✔ **Photos:** This application is the iPad's terrific photo manager. It lets you view pictures from a camera or SD card (using the optional Camera Connection Kit), synced from your computer, saved from an e-mail or Safari, or saved from one of the myriad of third-party apps that save their handiwork in the Photos app. You can zoom in or out, create slide shows, e-mail photos to friends, and much more. To get started, see Chapter 10.

✔ **iPod:** Last but not least, this icon unleashes all the power of an iPod right on your iPad, so you can listen to music or podcasts. You discover how it works in Chapter 8.

2

iPad Basic Training

*B*y now you know that the original iPad and the iPad 2 are very different from other computers. You also know that these slate-style machines are rewriting the rulebook for mainstream computing. How so? For starters, iPads don't have a mouse or any other kind of pointing device. They lack traditional computing ports or connectors, such as USB. And they have no physical or built-in keyboard.

iPads even differ from other so-called tablet PCs, some of which feature a pen or stylus and let you write in digital ink. As we point out (pun intended) in Chapter 1, the iPad relies on an input device that you always have with you: your finger.

Tablet computers of one form or another have actually been around since the last century. They just never captured the fancy of Main Street. Apple's very own *Newton,* an ill-fated 1990s personal digital assistant, was among the machines that barely made a dent in the market.

What's past is past, of course, and technology, not to mention Apple itself, has come a long way since Newton. And suffice it to say that tablets moving forward, led by the iPad brigade of course, promise to enjoy a much rosier outlook. Indeed, just since the iPad burst onto the scene, numerous tech titans (as well as smaller companies) have introduced their own touch-enabled tablets, many that rely on Google's Android mobile operating system. Some solid machines are among them, but the iPad remains the market leader and a true pioneer in the space.

If you got caught up in the initial mania surrounding the iPad, you probably plotted for weeks about how to land one. After all, the iPad, like its close cousin the iPhone, rapidly emerged as the hippest computer you could find. (We consider you hip just because you're reading this book.)

Speaking of the iPhone, if you own one or its close relative, Apple's iPod touch, you already have a gigantic start in figuring out how to master the iPad multitouch method of navigating the interface with your fingers. You have our permission to skim over the rest of this chapter, but we urge you to stick around anyway because some things on the iPad work in subtly different ways than on the iPhone or iPod touch. If you're a total novice, don't fret. Nothing about multitouch is painful.

Getting Started on Getting Started

To enjoy the iPad, you need the following four things, and there's a darn good chance you already have them:

✔ **Another computer:** This can be either a Macintosh running Mac OS X Version 10.5.8 or later, or a PC running Windows 7, Windows Vista, or Windows XP Home or Professional with Service Pack 3 or later. That's the official word from Apple anyway; we got the original iPad to make nice with a Dell laptop that had XP Pro and SP2 and we've known XP Home systems that play nice.

✔ **iTunes software:** More specifically, you need version 10.2.1 or later of iTunes — emphasis on the *later* because by the time you read this, it probably will be later. That is, unless you're a fan of the popular TV show *Lost* and no longer have any sense of what's now, what was, and what's next. All kidding aside, Apple constantly tweaks iTunes to make it better. Because Apple doesn't supply iTunes software in the box, head to www.itunes.com/download to fetch a copy. Or, launch your current version of iTunes and then choose iTunes (Help on Windows)⇨Check for Updates.

For the uninitiated, *iTunes* is the nifty Apple jukebox software that owners of iPods and iPhones, not to mention others, use to manage music, videos, applications, and more. iTunes is at the core of the iPad as well because an iPod is built into the iPad. You use iTunes to synchronize a bunch of stuff from your Mac or PC to and from an iPad, including (but not limited to) applications, photos, movies, TV shows, podcasts, iTunes U lectures, and of course, music.

Syncing is such a vital part of this process that we devote an entire chapter (see Chapter 3) to the topic.

✔ **An iTunes Store account:** Read Chapter 8 for details on how to set one up, but like most things Apple, the process isn't difficult.

✔ **Internet access:** Your iPad can connect to the Internet in either of two ways: Wi-Fi or 3G (if you bought an iPad with 3G capabilities and connect to a 3G service). You can connect your iPad to cyberspace via Wi-Fi in your home, office, school, favorite coffeehouse, bookstore, or numerous other spots.

A *3G* (third generation) wireless data connection at press time was available only in the United States through AT&T or Verizon Wireless. Unlike with the cellphone contract you may have with AT&T or Verizon (or most every other cellular carrier), no long-term service commitment is required to connect your iPad to the network. That means you can come and go as you please without penalty. Instead, you prepay 30 days worth of 3G connectivity through your credit card. The charge doesn't show up in your iTunes account, or AT&T or Verizon statement (if you have one).

As this book goes to press, data rates are quite reasonably priced, too:

- *AT&T:* $25 a month for 2 gigabytes (GB) or $14.99 a month for 250 megabytes (MB). Overages are $10 per additional GB.

- *Verizon:* $20 a month for 1GB, $35 for 3GB, $50 for 5GB, and $80 for 10GB. As with AT&T, overages are $10 per GB.

Turning the iPad On and Off

Apple has taken the time to partially charge your iPad, so you get some measure of instant gratification. After taking your iPad out of the box, press and hold the Sleep/Wake button on the top-right edge. (See Chapter 1 for the location of all the buttons.) The first thing you likely see is an image of a cable with a dock connector, signifying that you connect the iPad to iTunes to set it up. If the iPad was instead set up on your behalf at the Apple Store, you see the famous Apple logo, followed less than a minute or so later by an image of what looks to be a gray glass scene doused in raindrops. (You can replace this scene with one of your own pictures, as we describe in Chapter 10.)

To turn the device completely off, press and hold the Sleep/Wake button again until a red arrow appears at the top of the screen. Then drag the arrow from the left to the right with your finger. Tap Cancel at the bottom of the screen if you change your mind.

Locking the iPad

Carrying a naked cellphone in your pocket is begging for trouble. Unless the phone has a locking mechanism, you may inadvertently dial a phone number at odd hours.

You don't have to worry about dialing your boss at 4 a.m. on an iPad — it's not a phone after all (though such apps as Line2 or Skype can turn it into one). But you still have sound reasons for locking an iPad:

- You can't inadvertently turn it on.
- You keep prying eyes at bay.
- You spare the battery some juice.

Apple makes locking the iPad a cinch.

In fact, you don't need to do anything to lock the iPad; it happens automatically as long as you don't touch the screen for a minute or two. As you find out in Chapter 13, you can also set the amount of time your iPad must be idle before it automatically locks.

Can't wait? To lock the iPad immediately, press the Sleep/Wake button.

Unlocking the iPad is easy, too; here's how:

1. **Press the Sleep/Wake button. Or, press the Home button on the front of the screen.**

   Either way, the onscreen slider appears.

2. **Drag the slider to the right with your finger.**

3. **In some cases, you also need to enter a passcode.**

   See Chapter 13 to find out how to password-protect your iPad.

Mastering the Multitouch Interface

With very few exceptions, until the iPad came along, most every computer known to mankind has had a physical mouse and a typewriter-style QWERTY keyboard to help you accomplish most of the things you can do on a computer. (The term *QWERTY* is derived from the first six letters on any standard typewriter or computer keyboard.)

The iPad, like the iPhone, dispenses with a physical mouse and keyboard. Apple (as is its wont) is once again living up to an old company advertising slogan to "Think Different."

Indeed, the iPad (and iPhone and iPod touch) remove the usual physical buttons in favor of a *multitouch display*. And this beautiful and responsive finger-controlled screen is at the heart of the many things you do on the iPad.

In the following sections, you discover how to move around the multitouch interface with ease.

Training your digits

Rice Krispies have *Snap! Crackle! Pop!* Apple's response for the iPad is *Tap! Flick! Pinch!* (Yikes, another ad comparison!) Oh yeah, and *Drag!*

Fortunately, tapping, flicking, pinching, and dragging are not challenging gestures, so you can master many of the iPad's features in no time:

- **Tap:** Tapping serves multiple purposes. Tap an icon to open an application from the Home screen. Tap to start playing a song or to choose the photo album you want to look through. Sometimes, you *double-tap* (tapping twice in rapid succession), which has the effect of zooming in (or out) of web pages, maps, and e-mails.

- **Flick:** Flicking is just what it sounds like. A flick of the finger on the screen itself lets you quickly scroll through lists of songs, e-mails, and picture thumbnails. Tap the screen to stop scrolling, or merely wait for the scrolling list to stop.

- **Pinch/spread:** Place two fingers on the edges of a web page, map, or picture and then spread your fingers apart to enlarge the images. Or, pinch your fingers together to make the map or picture smaller. Pinching and spreading (or what we call *unpinching*) are cool gestures that are easy to master and sure to wow an audience.

- **Drag:** Here's where you slowly press your finger against the touchscreen without lifting it. You might drag to move around a web page or map that's too large for the iPad's display area.

Navigating beyond the Home screen

The Home screen we discuss in Chapter 1 is not the only screen of icons on your tablet. After you start adding apps from the iTunes App Store (which you discover in Chapter 7), you may see two or more tiny dots among the Safari, Mail, Photos, and iPod icons and the row of icons directly above them, plus a tiny Spotlight search magnifying glass to the left of the dots. Those dots denote additional screens, each containing up to 20 additional icons, not counting the 4 to 6 separate icons that are docked at the bottom of each of these Home screens. (You can actually have fewer than 4 docked icons at the bottom, but we can't think of a decent reason why you'd want to ditch any of them. In any case, more on these in a moment.)

To navigate between screens, flick your finger from right to left or left to right across the middle of the screen, or tap directly on the dots. You can also drag your finger in either horizontal direction to get to a different screen.

Unlike flicking — you may prefer the term *swiping* — dragging your finger means keeping it pressed against the screen until you reach your desired page.

You must be very precise, or you'll open one of the application icons instead of switching screens.

The number of dots you see represents the current number of screens on your iPad. The dot that's all white denotes the screen that you're currently viewing. Finally, the four icons in the bottom row — Safari, Mail, Photos, and iPod — are in a special part of the screen known as the *Dock*. When you switch from screen to screen as we describe earlier in this chapter, these icons remain on the screen. In other words, only the first 20 icons on the screen change when you move from one screen to another. You can add one or two more icons to the Dock if you so choose. Or move one of the four default icons into the main area of the Home screen to make space available for additional app icons you may use more often.

Press the Home button to jump back to the Home screen.

The incredible, intelligent, and virtual iPad keyboard

Instead of a physical keyboard, several "soft" or "virtual" English-language keyboard layouts slide up from the bottom of the iPad screen, all variations on the alphabetical keyboard, the numeric and punctuation keyboard, and the more punctuation and symbols keyboard. Figure 2-1 shows six examples of different iPad keyboards.

Indeed, the beauty of a software keyboard is that you see only the keys that are pertinent to the task at hand. The layout you see depends on the application. The keyboards in Safari differ from the keyboards in Notes. For example, while having a dedicated .com key in the Safari keyboard makes perfect sense, having such a key in the Notes keyboard isn't essential.

Keyboards in Notes

Keyboards in Safari

Figure 2-1: Six faces of the iPad keyboard.

Before you consider how to actually *use* the keyboard, we want to share a bit of the philosophy behind its so-called *intelligence*. Knowing what makes this keyboard smart can help you make it even smarter when you use it:

✔ It has a built-in English dictionary that even includes words from today's popular culture. It has dictionaries in other languages too, automatically activated when you use a given international keyboard as described in the sidebar "A keyboard for all borders," elsewhere in this chapter.

- ✔ It adds your contacts to its dictionary automatically.

- ✔ It uses complex analysis algorithms to predict the word you're trying to type.

- ✔ It suggests corrections as you type. It then offers you the suggested word just below the misspelled word. When you decline a suggestion and the word you typed is *not* in the iPad dictionary, the iPad adds that word to its dictionary and offers it as a suggestion if you mistype a similar word in the future.

Remember to decline suggestions (by tapping the characters you typed as opposed to the suggested words that appear beneath what you've typed) because doing so helps your intelligent keyboard become even smarter.

- ✔ It reduces the number of mistakes you make as you type by intelligently and dynamically resizing the touch zones for certain keys. You can't see it, but it is increasing the zones for keys it predicts might come next and decreasing the zones for keys that are unlikely or impossible to come next.

A keyboard for all borders

Apple is expanding the iPad's reach globally with international keyboard layouts on the iPad for more than four-dozen languages. To access a keyboard that isn't customized for Americanized English, tap Settings⇨General⇨Keyboard⇨International Keyboards⇨Add New Keyboard. Then flick through the list to select any keyboard you want to use. (Alternatively, tap Settings⇨General⇨International⇨Keyboards.) Up pops the list shown in the figure included here, with custom keyboards for German, Japanese, Portuguese, and so on. Apple even supplies two versions of French (including a keyboard geared to Canadian customers) and several keyboards for Chinese. Heck, there's even a U.K. version of English.

Have a multilingual household? You can select as many of these international keyboards as you might need by tapping the language in the list. Of course, you can call upon only one language at a time. So when you're inside an application that summons a keyboard, tap the little International Keyboard button sandwiched between the Toggle and spacebar (refer to Figure 2-1) or Toggle and : keys until the keyboard you want to call on for the occasion shows up. Tap again to pick the next keyboard on the corresponding list of international keyboards that you turned on in Settings. If you keep tapping, you come back to your original English keyboard.

To remove a keyboard that you've already added to your list, tap the Edit button in the upper-right corner of the screen and then tap the red circle with the white horizontal line that appears next to the language to which you want to say *adios.*

One more note about the Chinese keyboards: You can use handwriting character recognition for simplified and traditional Chinese, as shown here. Just drag your finger in the box provided.

We make apologies in advance for not knowing what the displayed characters here mean (we neither speak nor read Chinese).

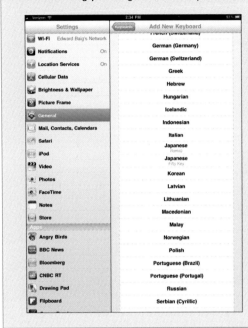

Discovering the special-use keys

The iPad keyboard contains several keys that don't actually type a character. Here's the scoop on each of these keys:

- **Shift:** If you're using the alphabetical keyboard, the Shift key (arrow pointing up) switches between uppercase and lowercase letters. You can tap the key to change the case, or hold down Shift and slide to the letter you want to be capitalized.

- **#+= or 123:** If you're using keyboards that just show numbers and symbols, the traditional Shift key is replaced by a key labeled #+= or 123 (sometimes shown as .?123). Pressing that key toggles between keyboards that just have symbols and numbers.

- **Caps Lock:** To turn on Caps Lock and type in all caps, you first need to enable Caps Lock (if not already enabled). You do that by tapping the Settings icon (usually found on the first Home screen), tapping General➪Keyboard. Tap the Enable Caps Lock item to turn it on. After the Caps Lock setting is enabled, double-tap the Shift key to turn on Caps Lock. (The Shift key turns blue whenever Caps Lock is on.) Tap the Shift key again to turn off Caps Lock. To disable Caps Lock completely, just reverse the process by turning off the Enable Caps Lock setting (tap Settings➪General➪Keyboard).

- **Toggle:** Switches between the different keyboard layouts.

- **International Keyboards:** Only shows up if you've turned on an international keyboard, as explained in the sidebar "A keyboard for all borders."

- **Delete:** Otherwise known as Backspace, tapping this key erases the character immediately to the left of the cursor.

- **Return:** Moves the cursor to the beginning of the next line.

- **Hide Keyboard:** Tap to hide the keyboard. Tap the screen in the appropriate app to bring back the keyboard.

If you have an iPhone or iPad touch, it's worth noting that keyboards on the iPad more closely resemble the keyboard layout of a traditional computer rather than those smaller model devices. That is, the Backspace key is on the upper right, the Return key is just below it, and Shift keys are on either side. This similarity to traditional keyboard layouts certainly improves the odds of successful touch-typing.

Finger-typing on the virtual keyboards

The virtual keyboards in Apple's multitouch interface just might be considered a stroke of genius. And they just might as equally drive you nuts, at least initially.

If you're patient and trusting, in a week or so, you'll get the hang of finger-typing — which is vital to moving forward, of course, because you rely on a virtual keyboard to tap a text field, enter notes, type the names of new contacts, and so on.

As we already note, Apple has built intelligence into its virtual keyboard, so it can correct typing mistakes on the fly and take a stab at predicting what you're about to type next. The keyboard isn't exactly Nostradamus, but it does an excellent job in coming up with the words you have in mind.

As you start typing on the virtual keyboard, we think you'll find the following tips extremely helpful:

- ⊭ **See what letter you're typing.** As you press your finger against a letter or number on the screen, the individual key you press darkens until you lift your finger, as shown in Figure 2-2. That way, you know that you struck the correct letter or number.

- ⊭ **Slide to the correct letter if you tap the wrong one.** No need to worry if you touched the wrong key. You can slide your finger to the correct key because the letter isn't recorded until you release your finger.

- ⊭ **Tap and hold to access special accent marks, alternate punctuation, or URL endings.** Sending a message to an overseas pal? Keep your finger pressed against a letter, and a row of keys showing variations on the character for foreign alphabets pops up, as shown in Figure 2-3. This lets you add the appropriate accent mark. Just slide your finger until the key with the relevant accent mark is pressed.

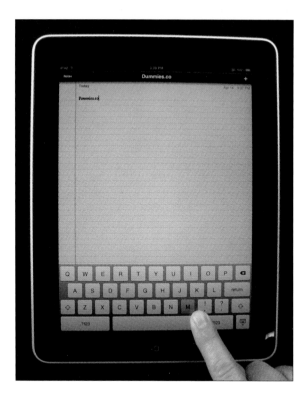

Figure 2-2: The ABCs of virtual typing.

Figure 2-3: Accenting your letters.

Meanwhile, if you press and hold the .com key in Safari, it offers you the choice of .com, .net, .edu, or .org, with additional options if you also use international keyboards. Pretty slick stuff.

🖙 **Tap the spacebar to accept a suggested word, or tap the suggested word to decline the suggestion.** Alas, mistakes are common at first. Say that you meant to type a sentence in the Notes application that reads, "I am typing an important . . ." But because of the way your fingers struck the virtual keys, you actually entered "I am typing an *importsnt* . . ." Fortunately, Apple knows that the *a* you meant to press is next to the *s* that showed up on the keyboard, just as *t* and *y* and *e* and *r* are side by side. So the software determines that *important* was indeed the word you had in mind and places it in red under the suspect word. To accept the suggested word, merely tap the Space key. And if for some reason you actually did mean to type *importsnt* instead, tap the suggested word (*important* in this example) to decline it.

If you don't appreciate this feature, you can turn off Auto-Correction in Settings. See Chapter 13 for details.

Because Apple knows what you're up to, the virtual keyboard is fine-tuned for the task at hand. This is especially true when you need to enter numbers, punctuation, or symbols. The following tips help you find common special characters or special keys that we know you'll want to use:

- ✒ **Finding keys for web addresses:** If you're entering a web address, the keyboard inside the Safari web browser (see Chapter 4) includes dedicated period, forward slash, and .com keys but no spacebar.

  If you're using the Notes application (see Chapter 12), the keyboard does have a spacebar.

- ✒ **Putting the @ in an e-mail address:** And if you're composing an e-mail message (see Chapter 5), a dedicated @ key pops up on the keyboard.

- ✒ **Switching from letters to numbers:** When you're typing notes or sending e-mail and want to type a number, symbol, or punctuation mark, tap the 123 key to bring up an alternative virtual keyboard. Tap the ABC key to return to the first keyboard. This toggle isn't hard to get used to, but some may find it irritating.

- ✒ **Adding apostrophes:** If you press and hold the Exclamation Mark/Comma key on the iPad, it changes to an apostrophe.

Editing mistakes

We think typing with abandon, without getting hung up over mistyped characters, is a good idea. The self-correcting keyboard can fix many errors. That said, plenty of typos are likely to turn up, especially in the beginning, and you have to correct them manually.

A neat trick for doing so is to hold your finger against the screen to bring up the magnifying glass, as shown in Figure 2-4. Use the magnifying glass to position the pointer on the spot where you need to make the correction. Then use the Backspace key (also called the Delete key) to delete the error, and press whatever keys you need to type the correct text.

Select, cut, copy, and paste

Being able to select and then copy and paste from one place on a computer to another has seemingly been a divine right since Moses, and that's the case on the Apple tablet as well. You can copy and paste (and cut) with pizzazz.

On the iPad, you might copy text or images from the web and paste them into an e-mail or a note. Or, you might copy a bunch of pictures or video into an e-mail.

Say you're jotting down ideas in the Notes application that you'll eventually copy into an e-mail. Here's how to exploit the copy-and-paste feature, using this scenario as an example:

Figure 2-4: Magnifying errors while typing in Notes.

1. **Double-tap a word to select it.**

2. **Tap Select to select the adjacent word or tap Select All to grab everything.**

   You can also drag the blue grab points or handles to select a larger block of text or to contract the text you've already selected, as shown in Figure 2-5. This too may take a little practice.

3. **After you select the text, tap Copy. If you want to delete the text block, tap Cut instead.**

4. **Open the Mail program (see Chapter 5) and start composing a message.**

5. **When you decide where to insert the text you just copied, tap the cursor.**

   Up pops commands to Select, Select All, and Paste, as shown in Figure 2-6.

6. **Tap Paste to paste the text into the message.**

   Here's the pizzazz part. If you made a mistake when you were cutting, pasting, or typing, shake the iPad. Doing so undoes the last edit (provided you tap the Undo Typing option when it appears).

If you happen to Select a word with a typo, you'll have the option, in addition to Cut, Copy and Paste, to Replace it. Tap Replace and the iPad may show you possible replacement words. For example, replacement words for *test* might be *fest, rest* or *text.* Tap the word to sub for the word you originally typed.

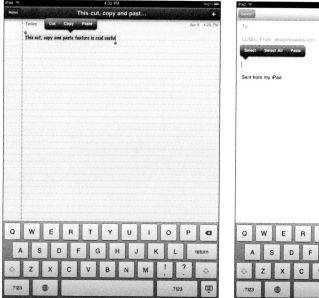

Figure 2-5: Drag the grab points to select text.

Figure 2-6: Tap Paste to make text appear from nowhere.

Multitasking

When iOS 4 first appeared, it added a bevy of important features, of which multitasking was arguably the most significant. (Apple had moved to iOS 4.3 by the time this book went to press.) *Multitasking* simply lets you run numerous apps in the background simultaneously or easily switch from one app to another. For example, a third-party app, such as Slacker Personal Radio, continues to play music while you surf the web, peek at pictures, or check e-mail. Without multitasking, Slacker would shut down the moment you opened another app. (Previously, Apple did let you multitask by, for example, playing audio in the background with its own iTunes app. But multitasking was limited to Apple's own apps, not those produced by outside developers.)

Among other tricks, the multitasking feature lets a navigation app update your position while you're listening, say, to Pandora Internet radio. From time to time, the navigation app will pipe in with turn-by-turn directions, lowering the volume of the music so you can hear the instructions.

And if you're uploading images to a photo web site and the process is taking longer than you want, you can switch to another app, confident that the images will continue to upload behind the scenes. We've also been able to leave voice notes in the Evernote app while checking out a web page.

Multitasking couldn't be simpler. Double-press the Home button, and a tray appears, as shown in Figure 2-7. The tray holds icons for applications running in the background or "suspended." Swipe from right to left on the tray to see more apps. Tap the app you want to switch to; the app remembers where you left off.

Figure 2-7: A tray for recently used apps.

Or swipe the tray from left to right for instant access to convenient controls for iPod audio (Volume, Play/Pause, Next/Previous Track), Brightness, and Screen Rotation Lock.

To remove an app from the tray holding icons of apps running in the background or suspended — and thus remove the app from those in the multitasking rotation — press and hold your finger against any app until they all start to wiggle. Then tap the red circle with the white line that appears inside the app you want to remove. Poof, it's gone.

Multitasking on the iPad differs from multitasking on a Mac or PC. You can't display more than one screen at a time. Moreover, there's some philosophical debate about whether this feature is multitasking, fast task switching, or a combination. Rather than getting bogged down in the semantics, we're just glad that multitasking, or whatever you want to call it, has arrived.

Organizing icons into folders

Finding the single app you want to use among apps spread out over 11 pages may seem like a daunting task. But Apple felt your pain and added a handy organizational tool — Folders. The Folders feature lets you create folder icons, each with up to 20 icons for apps.

To create a folder, follow these steps:

1. **Press your finger against an icon until all the icons on the screen jiggle.**

2. **Decide which apps you want to move to a folder, and drag the icon for the first app on top of the second app.**

   The two apps now share living quarters inside a newly created folder. Apple names the folder according to the category of apps inside the folder.

3. **(Optional) Change the folder name by tapping the X in the bar where the folder name appears and substituting a new name.**

To launch an app that's inside a folder, tap that folder's icon and then tap the icon for the app that you want to open.

You can drag apps into and out of any folder as long as there's room for them.

When you drag all the apps from a folder, the folder disappears automatically.

Printing

Apple didn't include built-in printer functionality with the first generation iPad. A variety of third-party apps helped fill the bill to some degree, but still the faithful waited for Apple to come up with a solution. The AirPrint feature, that subsequently arrived, provided just such a remedy — to a point. You can print wirelessly from the iPad to an AirPrint-capable printer. The first of these compatible printers emerged on more than a dozen HP models. The expectation is other printer manufacturers will unveil AirPrint printers of their own perhaps by the time you read this. We sure hope so. For that matter we hope that Apple will support Bluetooth wireless printing, but that's not happened as of this writing either. AirPrint works with Mail, Photos, Safari, and iBooks (PDFs). You can also print from apps in Apple's optional iWork software suite, as well as third-party apps with built-in printing.

Although AirPrint printers don't need any special software, they do have to be connected to the same Wi-Fi network as the iPad.

To print, follow these steps:

1. **Tap the Print command, which appears in different places depending on the app you're using.**

2. **Tap Select Printer to select a printer, which the iPad locates in short order.**

3. **Depending on the printer, specify the number of copies you want to print, the number of double-sided copies, and a range of pages to print.**

4. **When you're happy with your settings, tap Print.**

If you happen to double-click the Home button while a print job is underway, the Print Center app icon appears on the multitasking tray along with all your other recently used apps. A red badge indicates how many documents are in the print queue, along with the currently printing document.

Searching for content on your iPad

Using the Safari browser (see Chapter 4), you can search the web via the Google or Yahoo! search engines.

But you can also search people and programs across your iPad and within specific applications. We show you how to search within apps in the various chapters dedicated to Mail, Contacts, Calendar, and the iPod.

Searching across the iPad, meanwhile, is based on the powerful Spotlight feature familiar to Mac owners. Here's how it works:

1. **To access Spotlight, flick to the left of the main Home screen (or, as we mention earlier in this chapter, press the Home button from the main Home screen).**

2. **Tap the bar at the top of the screen that slides into view and enter your search query using the virtual keyboard.**

   The iPad spits out results the moment you type a single character, and the list narrows as you type additional characters.

   The results are pretty darn thorough. Say you entered **Ring** as your search term, as shown in Figure 2-8. Contacts whose last names have Ring in them show up, along with friends who might do a trapeze act in the Ringling Bros. circus. All the songs on your iPad by Ringo Starr show up too, as do such song titles as Tony Bennett's "When Do The Bells Ring For Me," if that happens to be in your library. Same goes for apps, videos, audiobooks, events, and notes with the word *Ring*.

3. **Tap any listing to jump to the contact, ditty, or application you seek.**

Figure 2-8: Putting the Spotlight on search.

In Settings (see Chapter 13), you can specify the order of search results so that apps come first, contacts second, songs third, and so on.

The Kitchen Sync: Getting Stuff to and from Your iPad

In This Chapter

▶ Starting your first sync

▶ Disconnecting during a sync

▶ Synchronizing contacts, calendars, e-mail accounts, and bookmarks

▶ Synchronizing music, podcasts, video, photos, books, and applications

*W*e have good news and . . . more good news. The good news is that you can easily copy any or all of your contacts, appointments, events, mail settings, bookmarks, books, music, movies, TV shows, podcasts, photos, and applications from your computer to your iPad. And the more good news is that after you do that, you can choose to synchronize your contacts, appointments, and events so that they're kept up to date automatically in both places — on your computer and your iPad — whenever you make a change in one place or the other. So when you add or change an appointment, an event, or a contact on your iPad, that information automatically appears on your computer the next time your iPad and computer communicate.

This communication between your iPad and computer is *syncing* (short for *synchronizing*). Don't worry: It's easy, and we walk you through the entire process in this chapter.

But wait. There's even more good news. Items you manage on your computer, such as movies, TV shows, podcasts, and e-mail account settings, are synchronized only one way: from your computer to your iPad, which is the way it should be.

The information in this chapter is based on iTunes version 10.2.1 and iPhone OS version 4.3, which were the latest and greatest when these words were written. If your screens don't look exactly like ours, you probably need to upgrade to iTunes 10.2.1 or higher (choose iTunes⇨Check for Updates) and iPhone OS 4.3 or higher (click the Check for Updates button on the Summary tab shown in the upcoming Figure 3-2 and follow the instructions for updating your iPad). By the way, both upgrades are free, and both offer significant advantages over their predecessors.

Starting to Sync

Synchronizing your iPad with your computer is a lot like syncing an iPod or iPhone with your computer. If you're an iPod or iPhone user, the process will be a piece of cake. But it's not too difficult even for those who've never used an iPod, an iPhone, or iTunes. Follow these steps:

1. **Start by connecting your iPad to your computer with the USB cable that came with your iPad.**

   When you connect your iPad to your computer, iTunes should launch automatically. If it doesn't, chances are that you plugged the cable into a USB port on your keyboard, monitor, or hub. Try plugging it into one of the USB ports on your computer instead. Why? Because USB ports on your computer supply more power to a connected device than USB ports on a keyboard, monitor, or most hubs and the iPad requires a lot of that power — even more than an iPod or an iPhone.

   If iTunes still doesn't launch automatically, try launching it manually.

2. **Select your iPad in the iTunes sidebar.**

   You see the Set Up Your iPad pane, as shown in Figure 3-1. If you've already set up and named your iPad, you can skip Steps 3 and 4a, and continue with Step 4b.

   If you don't see an iPad in the sidebar, and you're sure that it's connected to a USB port on your computer (not the keyboard, monitor, or hub), restart your computer.

3. **Name your iPad by typing a name in the Name text box.**

   We've named this one *BobLiPad*.

4a. **Decide whether you want iTunes to automatically synchronize the items shown in Figure 3-1 with your iPad every time you connect it to your computer.**

Figure 3-1: This is the first thing you see in iTunes.

- *If you do want iTunes to do any of these things automatically,* select the check box next to the appropriate option so that it displays a check mark, click the Done button, and continue with the "Synchronizing Your Media" section, later in this chapter.

- *If you want to synchronize manually,* make sure that all three check boxes are deselected, as shown in Figure 3-1, and click Done. The "Synchronizing Your Data" section, later in this chapter, tells you all about how to configure your contacts, calendars, bookmarks, notes, e-mail accounts, and applications manually; the "Synchronizing Your Media" section shows you how to sync apps, music, and so on.

You don't have to decide now. If you're not sure, just leave all three check boxes deselected for now. It's easy to enable one or all three at any time.

We've chosen to not select any of the three check boxes so that we can show you how to manually set up each type of sync in the upcoming sections.

After you click the Done button (applies only to those who just performed Steps 3 and 4a), the Summary pane appears.

4b. If the Summary pane doesn't appear, make sure that your iPad is still selected in the sidebar on the left side of the iTunes window and then click the Summary tab near the top of the window, as shown in Figure 3-2.

5. (Optional) If you want iTunes to launch automatically whenever you connect your iPad to your computer, select the Open iTunes When This iPad Is Connected check box (in the Options area).

Why might you choose not to enable this option? If you intend to connect your iPad to your computer to charge it, for example, you might not want iTunes to launch every time you connect it.

If you do choose to enable it, iTunes launches and synchronizes automatically every time you connect your iPad.

Don't worry about this too much right now. If you change your mind, you can always come back to the Summary tab and deselect the Open iTunes When This iPad Is Connected check box.

Figure 3-2: The Summary pane is pretty painless.

If you do select the Open iTunes When This iPad Is Connected check box but don't want your iPad to sync automatically every time it's connected, launch iTunes and choose iTunes⇨Preferences (Mac) or Edit⇨ Preferences (PC). Click the Devices tab at the top of the window and select the Prevent iPods, iPhones, and iPads from Syncing Automatically check box. This method prevents your iPad from syncing automatically even if the Open iTunes When This iPad Is Connected option is enabled. If you choose this option, you can sync your iPad by clicking the Sync or Apply button that appears in the lower-right corner of the iTunes window when your iPad is selected in the sidebar (it says "Apply" in Figure 3-2).

6. **(Optional) If you want to sync only items that have check marks to the left of their names in your iTunes library, select the Sync Only Checked Songs and Videos check box.**

7. **(Optional) If you want high-definition videos you import to be automatically converted into smaller standard-definition video files when you transfer them to your iPad, select the Prefer Standard Definition Videos check box.**

Standard-definition video files are significantly smaller than high-definition video files. You'll hardly notice the difference when you watch the video on your iPad but you can have more video files on your iPad because they take up less space.

The conversion from HD to standard definition takes a *long* time, so be prepared for very long sync times when you sync new HD video and have this option enabled.

If you plan to use Apple's $39 Digital AV Adapter to display movies on an HDTV, you might want to consider going with high definition. Although the files will be bigger and your iPad will hold fewer videos, the HD versions look spectacular on a big screen TV.

8. **(Optional) If you want songs with bit rates higher than 128 kbps converted into smaller 128-kbps AAC files when you transfer them to your iPad, select the Convert Higher Bit Rate Songs to 128 kbps AAC check box.**

A *higher* bit rate means that the song will have better sound quality but use a lot of storage space. Songs that you buy at the iTunes Store or on Amazon, for example, have bit rates of around 256 kbps. So, a 4-minute song with a 256-kbps bit rate is around 8MB; convert it to 128-kbps AAC and it's roughly half that size (that is, around 4MB), while sounding almost as good.

Bob tested bit rates and ears extensively when he was writing *The Little iTunes Book* (published by Peachpit Press) many years ago and concluded that most people don't notice much (if any) difference in audio quality when listening to music on most consumer audio gear. So unless you have your iPad hooked up to a great amplifier and superb speakers or headphones, you probably won't hear much difference, but your iPad can hold roughly twice as much music if you enable this option. Put another way, we're very picky about our audio and we both enable this option to allow us to carry more music around with us on our iPads. And neither of us has noticed much impact on sound quality with the headphones or speakers we use with our iPads.

9. **(Optional) To turn off automatic syncing in the Music and Video panes, select the Manually Manage Music and Videos check box.**

10. **(Optional) To password-protect your iPad backups (your iPad creates a backup of its contents automatically every time you sync), select the Encrypt iPad Backup check box.**

And, of course, if you decide to select the Prevent iPods, iPhones, and iPads from Syncing Automatically check box on the iTunes Preferences (that's iTunes⇨Preferences on a Mac and Edit⇨Preferences on a PC), in the Devices tab, you can still synchronize manually by clicking the Sync or Apply button in the lower-right corner of the window.

Why the Sync *or* Apply button? Glad you asked. If you've changed *any* sync settings since the last time you synchronized, the Sync button instead says Apply. When you click that button — regardless of its name — your iPad will start to sync.

Disconnecting the iPad

When the iPad is syncing with your computer, its screen says Sync in Progress, and iTunes displays a message that says that it's syncing with your iPad. After the sync is finished, iTunes displays a message that the iPad sync is complete and that it's okay to disconnect your iPad.

If you disconnect your iPad before a sync is completed, all or part of the sync may fail.

To cancel a sync so that you can *safely* disconnect your iPad, drag the Slide to Cancel slider on the iPad during the sync.

Synchronizing Your Data

Did you choose to set up data synchronization manually by not selecting any of the three check boxes in the Set Up Your iPad pane, as shown in Figure 3-1? If so, your next order of business is to tell iTunes what data you want to synchronize between your iPad and your computer. You do this by selecting your iPad in the sidebar on the left side of the iTunes screen. Then click the Info tab, which is to the right of the Summary tab.

The Info pane has five sections: Contacts, Calendars, Mail Accounts, Other, and Advanced.

TIP

Unless your Mac or PC has an absolutely humongous display you see only one or two sections at any time and have to scroll to see the others.

The following sections take a look at the Info pane sections one by one, but first you may want to check out the brief interlude . . . er, sidebar, "MobileMe."

Contacts

The Contacts section of the Info pane determines how iTunes handles synchronization for your contacts. One method is to synchronize all your contacts, as shown in Figure 3-3. Or, you can synchronize any or all groups of contacts you've created in your computer's address book program. Just select the appropriate check boxes in the Selected Groups list, and only those groups will be synchronized.

MobileMe

MobileMe is Apple's $99-a-year service for keeping your iPad, iPod touch, Macs, and PCs synchronized. MobileMe is the latest iteration of what Apple used to call .Mac (pronounced *dot Mac*) and, before that, iTools. The big allure of MobileMe is that it can "push" information such as e-mail, calendars, contacts, and bookmarks from your computer to and from your iPad, and keep those items synchronized on your iPad and computer(s) wirelessly and without human intervention. It also includes non-synchronizing options including beautiful, easy-to-create online photo galleries as well as e-mail, web space, 20GB of online storage, and more.

If you want to have your e-mail, calendars, contacts, and bookmarks synchronized automatically and wirelessly, click the Set Up Now button. Your web browser launches, and instructions appear for subscribing to MobileMe if you're not already a subscriber or for setting up each of your devices for MobileMe if you are already a subscriber.

If you're going to use MobileMe to sync your e-mail, calendars, contacts, and bookmarks, you can safely ignore the information in three of the next five sections: "Contacts," "Calendars," and "Advanced." Those three sections deal with using iTunes for synchronization, and you don't need them if you're using MobileMe. The other two sections, "Mail Accounts" and "Other," both contain information even MobileMe users may find useful.

And here's a final MobileMe tip: Although the suggested retail price of a year's subscription to MobileMe is $99, Amazon is currently offering it for $72.18, and we've seen it offered for even less by other vendors. The point is that when it comes to MobileMe, it might pay to shop around.

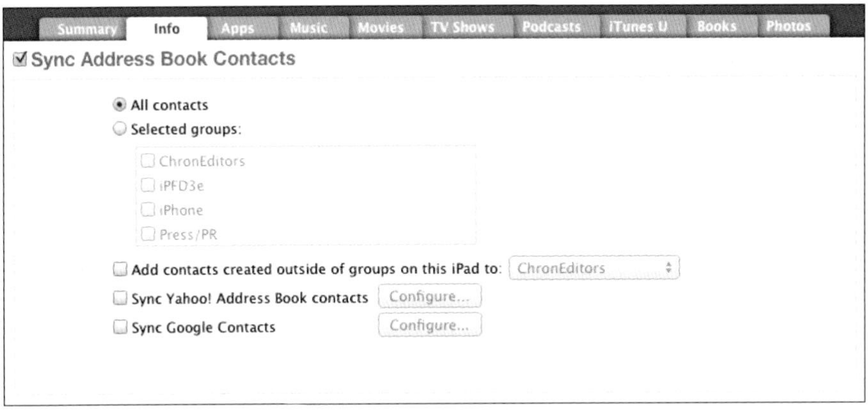

Figure 3-3: Want to synchronize your contacts? This is where you set up things.

Note that the section is named Sync Address Book Contacts because Figure 3-3 was captured in iTunes on a Mac and Address Book is what it syncs with. If you use a PC, you see a drop-down list that gives you the choices of Outlook, Google Contacts, Windows Address Book, or Yahoo! Address Book. Don't worry — the process works the same on either platform.

The iPad syncs with the following address book programs:

- **Mac:** Address Book
- **PC:** Outlook or Windows Address Book
- **Mac and PC:** Yahoo! Address Book and Google Contacts

On a Mac, you can sync contacts with multiple applications. On a PC, you can sync contacts with only one application at a time.

If you use Yahoo! Address Book, select the Sync Yahoo! Address Book Contacts check box and then click the Configure button to enter your Yahoo! ID and password. If you use Google Contacts, select the Sync Google Contacts check box and then click the Configure button to enter your Google ID and password.

Syncing doesn't delete a contact from your Yahoo! Address Book if it has a Yahoo! Messenger ID, even if you delete that contact on the iPad or on your computer.

To delete a contact that has a Yahoo! Messenger ID, log on to your Yahoo! account with a web browser and delete the contact in your Yahoo! Address Book.

If you sync with your employer's Microsoft Exchange calendar and contacts, any personal contacts or calendars already on your iPad will be wiped out.

Calendars

The Calendars section of the Info pane determines how synchronization is handled for your appointments and events. You can synchronize all your calendars, as shown in Figure 3-4. Or, you can synchronize any or all individual calendars you've created in your computer's calendar program. Just select the appropriate check boxes.

Figure 3-4: Set up sync for your calendar events here.

The Calendars section is named Sync iCal Calendars because Figure 3-4 was captured in iTunes for the Mac. If you use a PC, this section is named Sync Calendars with Outlook. As before, don't worry — regardless of its name, it works the same on either platform.

The iPad syncs with the following calendar programs:

- **Mac:** iCal
- **PC:** Microsoft Outlook 2003, 2007, 2010

On a Mac, you can sync calendars with multiple applications. On a PC, you can sync calendars with only one application at a time.

Mail Accounts

You can sync account settings for your e-mail accounts in the Mail Accounts section of the Info pane. You can synchronize all your e-mail accounts (if you have more than one), or you can synchronize individual accounts, as shown in Figure 3-5. Just select the appropriate check boxes.

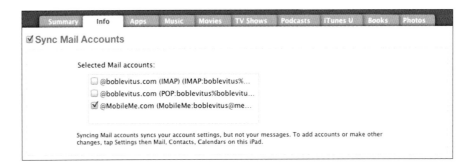

Figure 3-5: Transfer e-mail account settings to your iPad here.

The iPad syncs with the following mail programs:

- **Mac:** Mail
- **PC:** Microsoft Outlook 2003, 2007, 2010

E-mail account settings are synchronized only one way: from your computer to your iPad. If you make changes to any e-mail account settings on your iPad, the changes aren't synchronized back to the e-mail account on your computer. Trust us, this is a very good feature and we're glad Apple did it this way.

By the way, the password for your e-mail account may or may not be saved on your computer. If you sync an e-mail account and the iPad asks for a password when you send or receive mail, do this: Tap Settings on the Home screen, tap Mail, tap your e-mail account's name, and then type your password in the appropriate field.

Other

The Other section has a mere two items: Sync Safari Bookmarks and Sync Notes.

Select the check box for Sync Safari Bookmarks if you want to sync your Safari bookmarks; don't select it if you don't.

Just so you know, the iPad syncs bookmarks with the following web browsers:

- **Mac:** Safari
- **PC:** Microsoft Internet Explorer and Safari

Select the check box for Sync Notes to sync notes in the Notes application on your iPad with notes in Apple Mail (Mac) or Microsoft Outlook (PC).

Note that on a Mac, you must have Mac OS X 10.5.8 or later installed to sync notes.

Advanced

Every so often the contacts, calendars, mail accounts, or bookmarks on your iPad get so screwed up that the easiest way to fix things is to erase that information on your iPad and replace it with information from your computer.

If that's the case, just click to select the appropriate check boxes, as shown in Figure 3-6. Then, the next time you sync, that information on your iPad will be replaced with information from your computer.

Figure 3-6: Replace the information on your iPad with the information on your computer.

Because the Advanced section is at the bottom of the Info pane and you have to scroll down to see it, you can easily forget that the Advanced section is there. Although you probably won't need to use this feature very often (if ever), you'll be happy you remembered that it's there if you do need it.

Synchronizing Your Media

If you chose to let iTunes manage synchronizing your data automatically, welcome. This section looks at how you get your media — your music, podcasts, video, and photos — from your computer to your iPad.

Podcasts and video (but not photos) are synced only one way: from your computer to your iPad. Deleting any of these items from your iPad does not delete them from your computer when you sync. The exceptions are songs, podcasts, videos, iBooks, and apps that you purchase or download on your iPad, and playlists you create on your iPad. Such items are, as you'd expect, copied back to your computer automatically when you sync. And if you save pictures from e-mail messages, the iPad 2 camera, web pages (by pressing and holding on an image and then tapping the Save Image button), or screen shots (which can be created by pressing the Home and Sleep/Wake buttons simultaneously), these too can be synced.

Taking a screen shot creates a photo of what's on your screen. It's a handy tool and it's what we used to generate almost every figure in this book.

You use the Apps, Music, Podcasts, Movies, TV Shows, Podcasts, iTunes U, Books, and Photos panes to specify the media that you want to copy from your computer to your iPad. The following sections explain the options you find on each pane.

To view any of these panes, make sure that your iPad is still selected in the sidebar and then click the appropriate tab near the top of the window.

The following sections focus only on syncing. If you need help acquiring apps, music, movies, podcasts, or anything else for your iPad, this book contains chapters dedicated to each of these topics. Just flip to the most applicable chapter for help.

The last step in each section is "Click the Sync or Apply button in the lower-right corner of the window." You have to do this only when enabling that item for the first time and if you make any changes to the item after that.

Apps

If you've downloaded or purchased any iPad apps from the iTunes App Store, set your automatic syncing options as follows:

1. **Click the Apps tab, and then select the Sync Apps check box.**

2. **Choose the individual apps you want to transfer to your iPad by selecting their check boxes.**

   For your convenience, you can sort your applications by name, category, or date acquired. Or, you can type a word or phrase into the Search field (the oval with the magnifying glass in the upper right corner of the iTunes window) to search for a specific app.

3. **(Optional) Rearrange app icons in iTunes by dragging them where you want them to appear on your iPad (see Figure 3-7).**

   If you have a lot of apps, you're sure to love this feature (which was introduced in iTunes 9) as much as we do.

4. **Click the Sync or Apply button in the lower-right corner of the window.**

   Your apps are synced, and your icons are rearranged on your iPad just the way you arranged them in iTunes.

Drag Dictation icon from here (A) to here (B)

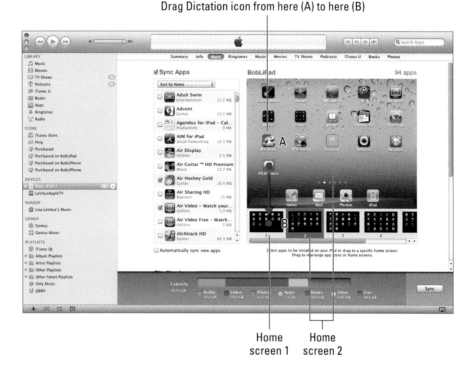

Home   Home
screen 1   screen 2

Figure 3-7: We're dragging the Dictation icon from Home screen 2 to Home screen 1 to make it easier to get to.

Note that apps are so darn cool we've given them an entire chapter of their very own, namely Chapter 7. There you discover how to find, rearrange, review, and delete apps, and much, much more.

Music, music videos, and voice memos

To transfer music to your iPad, follow these steps:

1. **Click the Music tab, and then select the Sync Music check box in the Music pane.**

2. **Select the button for Entire Music Library or Selected Playlists, Artists, and Genres.**

   If you choose the latter, select the check boxes next to particular playlists, artists, and genres you want to transfer. You can also choose to include music videos, voice memos, or both by selecting the appropriate check boxes at the top of the pane (see Figure 3-8).

If you select the Automatically Fill Free Space with Songs check box, iTunes fills any free space on your iPad with music.

3. **Click the Sync or Apply button in the lower-right corner of the window.**

Your music, music videos, and voice memos are synced.

Music, podcasts, and video are notorious for chewing up massive amounts of storage space on your iPad. If you try to sync too much media, you see error messages that warn you there's not enough room on your iPad for everything you tried to sync. Forewarned is forearmed. To avoid these errors, select playlists, artists, and/or genres that total less than the free space on your iPad.

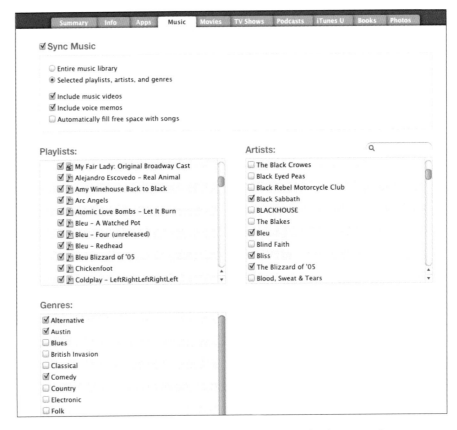

Figure 3-8: Use the Music pane to copy music, music videos, and voice memos from your computer to your iPad.

How much free space does your iPad have? Glad you asked. Look near the bottom of the iTunes window while your iPad is selected. You see a chart that shows the contents of your iPad, color-coded for your convenience. See Chapter 18 for a tip on working with this graph.

Movies

To transfer movies to your iPad, follow these steps:

1. **Click the Movies tab and select the Sync Movies check box.**

2. **Choose an option for movies that you want to include automatically from the pop-up menu, as shown in Figure 3-9, or select the check box for each movie you want to sync.**

   Regardless of the choices you make in the pop-up menu, you can always select individual movies by selecting their check boxes.

3. **Click the Sync or Apply button in the lower-right corner of the window.**

   Your movies are synced.

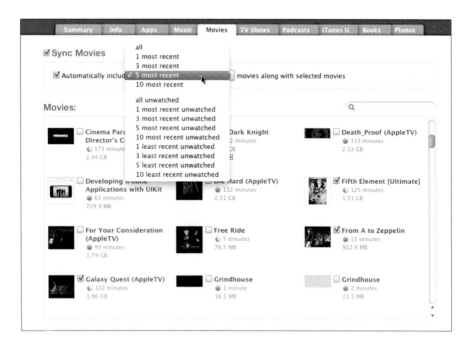

Figure 3-9: Your choices in the Movies pane determine which movies are copied to your iPad.

TV shows

The procedure for syncing TV shows is slightly different from the procedure for syncing movies. Here's how it works:

1. **Click the TV Shows tab and select the Sync TV Shows check box to enable TV show syncing.**

2. **Choose how many episodes to include from the pop-up menu in the upper-left corner, as shown in Figure 3-10.**

3. **In the upper-right corner, choose whether you want all shows or only selected shows from the pop-up menu (again, see Figure 3-10).**

4. **If you want to also include individual episodes or episodes on playlists, select the appropriate check boxes in the Episodes (which is labeled Family Guy Episodes in Figure 3-10) and the Include Episodes from Playlists sections (lower left in Figure 3-10) of the TV Shows pane.**

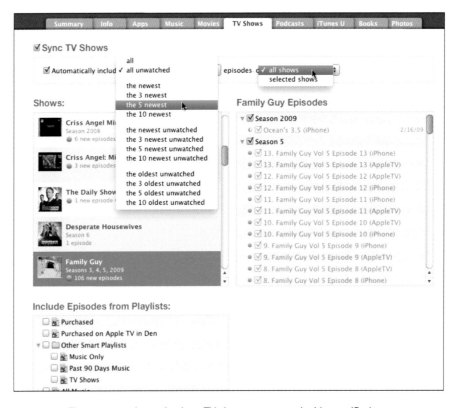

Figure 3-10: These menus determine how TV shows are synced with your iPad.

5. **Click the Sync or Apply button in the lower-right corner of the window.**

Your TV shows are synced.

Regardless of the choices you make in the pop-up menus, you can always select individual episodes by selecting their check boxes.

Podcasts

To transfer podcasts to your iPad, follow these steps:

1. **Click the Podcasts tab and select the Sync Podcasts check box in the Podcasts pane.**

   Two pop-up menus allow you to specify which episodes and which podcasts you want to sync, as shown in Figure 3-11.

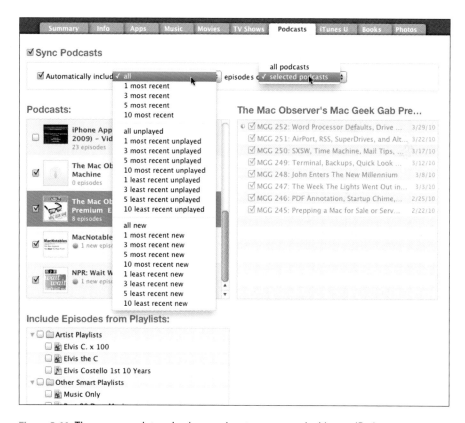

Figure 3-11: These menus determine how podcasts are synced with your iPad.

2. **Select how many episodes of a podcast you want to sync in the pop-up menu on the left.**

3. **Choose whether to sync all podcasts or just selected podcasts from the pop-up menu in the upper-right corner.**

4. **If you have podcast episodes on playlists, you can include them by selecting the appropriate check boxes under Include Episodes from Playlists.**

5. **Click the Sync or Apply button in the lower-right corner of the window.**

   Your podcasts are synced.

Regardless of the choices you make in the pop-up menus, you can always select individual episodes by selecting their check boxes.

iTunes U

To sync educational content from iTunes U, follow these steps:

1. **Click the iTunes U tab and select the Sync iTunes U check box to enable iTunes U syncing.**

2. **Choose how many items to include using the first pop-up menu.**

3. **Choose whether you want all collections or only selected collections from the second pop-up menu.**

4. **If you want to also include individual items on playlists, select the appropriate check boxes in the iTunes U Collections and Items sections of the iTunes U pane.**

5. **Click the Sync or Apply button in the lower-right corner of the window.**

   Your iTunes U episodes are synced.

Regardless of the choices you make in the pop-up menus, you can always select individual items by selecting their check boxes.

Books

To sync e-books and audiobooks, follow these steps:

1. **Click the Books tab and select the Sync Books check box to enable book syncing.**

Two pop-up menus at the top of the Books section may make it easier to manage your book collection. The first pop-up lets you see Only Books, Only PDF files, or both. The second lets you sort your books by either Title or Author.

2. **Choose All Books or Selected Books by clicking the appropriate radio button.**

3. **If you chose Selected Books, select the check boxes of the books you wish to sync.**

4. **Scroll down the page a little and select the Sync Audiobooks check box to enable audiobook syncing.**

5. **Choose All Audiobooks or Selected Audiobooks.**

6. **If you chose Selected Audiobooks, select the check boxes of the audiobooks you wish to sync.**

   If the book is divided into parts, you can select check boxes for the individual parts if you wish.

7. **Click the Sync or Apply button in the lower-right corner of the window.**

   Your books and audiobooks are synced.

Photos

The iPad syncs photos with the following programs:

- **Mac:** iPhoto or Aperture
- **PC:** Adobe Photoshop Elements or Adobe Photoshop Album

You can also sync photos with any folder on your computer that contains images. To sync photos, follow these steps:

1. **Click the Photos tab and select the Sync Photos From check box.**

2. **Choose an application or folder from the pop-up menu (which says iPhoto in Figure 3-12).**

3. **To further refine what photos are synced, you may have any of the following options:**

   - *Select albums, events, and more:* If you choose an application that supports photo albums, events, and/or facial recognition, as we have in Figure 3-12, by choosing iPhoto, you can automatically include events by making a selection from the pop-up menu or select specific albums, events, and/or faces to sync by selecting them in the areas below.

   - *Search for photos to sync:* If you're using iPhoto, you can also type a word or phrase into the Search field (the oval with the magnifying glass) to search for a specific event(s).

• *Select a folder of images:* If you choose a folder full of images, you can create subfolders inside it that appear as albums on your iPad.

But if you choose an application that doesn't support albums or events, or a single folder full of images with no subfolders, you have to transfer all or nothing.

Because we selected iPhoto in the Sync Photos From menu, and iPhoto '09 and '11 — the two most recent releases — support events and faces in addition to albums, we also have the option of syncing events, albums, faces, or all three.

4. Click the Sync or Apply button in the lower-right corner of the window.

Your photos are synced.

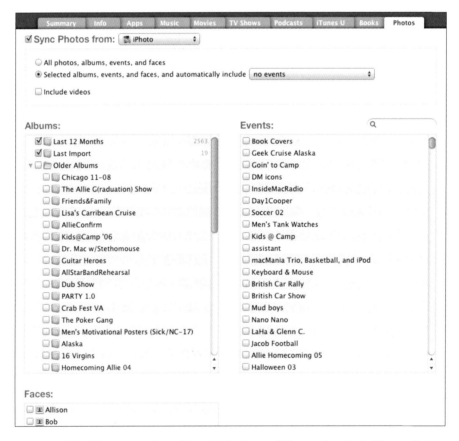

Figure 3-12: The Photos pane determines which photos will be synchronized with your iPad.

Part II
The Internet iPad

The 5th Wave — By Rich Tennant

iPad

"In fact it does come with a compass."

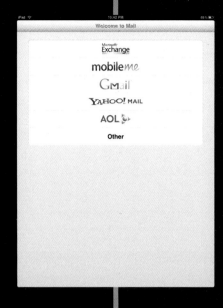

In this part . . .

The first thing most people want to do with their iPad is surf the Internet with the delight-fully large and colorful touchscreen. Safari, the iPad's Web browser, is the place to start, and that's where this part begins as well — with an introduction to navigating the Web with Safari.

Then we visit the Mail program and see how easy it is to set up e-mail accounts and to send and receive real honest-to-goodness e-mail messages and attachments.

In Chapter 6, we examine a few superb Web-enabled applications. In Maps, you determine the businesses and restaurants you'd like to visit, get driving directions and the traffic en route, and take advantage of the iPad's capability to find you. And because everyone loves social media, find out the best ways to use Facebook, Twitter, and YouTube from your iPad, too.

We love going on a shopping spree as much as the next guy. Chapter 7 is all about finding out how to shop in the App Store, an emporium replete with a gaggle of neat little programs and applications. Best of all, unlike most of the stores you shop in, a good number of the items can be had for free.

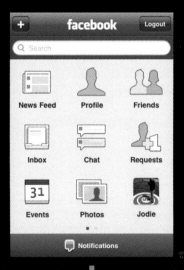

Going on a Mobile Safari

"*Y*ou feel like you're actually holding the web right in the palm of your hand."

Marketers use lines like that because, well, that's what marketers do. Only when an Apple marketer says such a thing to describe surfing the web on the iPad, a lot of truth is behind it. The iPad 2's glorious display, in combination with the snappy new Apple-designed dual-core A5 chip inside the machine, makes browsing on Apple's tablet an absolute delight. Not that the robust single-core A4 predecessor chip in the original iPad was any slouch.

In this chapter, you discover the pleasures — and the few roadblocks — in navigating cyberspace on your iPad.

Living on the EDGE

Wi-Fi is the chief way to prowl the virtual corridors of cyberspace (or send e-mail, access the App Store or iTunes Store, or check out YouTube) on the iPad. But for all the places you can find an Internet *hotspot* nowadays — airports, colleges, coffeehouses, offices, schools, and yes, homes — Wi-Fi still isn't available everywhere.

If you buy the Wi-Fi + 3G iPad model, you often have a viable alternative when Wi-Fi isn't available. In the United States, such models from AT&T work with Wi-Fi, AT&T EDGE, and AT&T 3G. Verizon's iPad 3G version works with Verizon Wireless' so-called CDMA EV-DO Rev network. You can safely avoid the jargon. (They also work with another wireless technology, *Bluetooth,* but that serves a different purpose and is addressed in Chapter 13.)

Cellular customers prepay for 3G access using a credit card, and monthly data is relatively inexpensive ($14.99 for 250MB of data or $25 for 2 gigabytes on AT&T; $20 for 1GB on up to $80 for 10GB on Verizon). Moreover, no one- or two-year contract commitment is required, as is most likely the case with the cellphone in your pocket. That means if you're hiking in the Swiss Alps for a month, or otherwise indisposed, you don't have to pay AT&T or Verizon for Internet access you'll never use.

The iPad automatically hops onto the fastest available network, which is almost always Wi-Fi, the friendly moniker applied to the far geekier 802.11 designation. And *eight-oh-two-dot-eleven* (as it's pronounced) is followed by a letter — typically (but not always) *b, g,* or *n.* You see it written as 802.11b, 802.11g, and so on. The letters relate to differing technical standards that have to do with the speed and range you can expect from the Wi-Fi configuration. But we certainly wouldn't have you lose any sleep over this issue if you haven't boned up on this geeky alphabet.

For the record, because the iPad adheres to 802.11a, b, g, and n standards, you're good to go pretty much anywhere you can find Wi-Fi. If you have to present a password to take advantage of a for-fee hotspot, you can enter it by using the iPad's virtual keyboard.

As we pointed out, the problem with Wi-Fi is that it's far from ubiquitous, which leads us right back to the cellular data network, typically 3G or when not available the pokier EDGE on AT&T or EV-DO on Verizon, which is their faster 3G network.

If you're ever on a million-dollar game show and have to answer the question, *EDGE* is shorthand for Enhanced Datarate for GSM Evolution. It's based on the global GSM phone standard. You may also see an indicator for *GPRS,* shorthand for General Packet Radio Service, another poky data service.

3G, which stands for third generation, is your best bet among available cellular options for the iPad as of this writing. Even faster nascent 4G networks being developed by AT&T, Verizon, and every other major network provider are incompatible with the iPad; 3G websites typically download two times faster than EDGE, in our experience, and sometimes faster than that. But again, Wi-Fi downloads are even zippier.

The bottom line is this: Depending on where you live, work, or travel, you may feel like you're teetering on the EDGE in terms of acceptable Internet coverage, especially if Wi-Fi or true 3G is beyond your reach. We've used the iPad's cousin, the iPhone, in areas where web pages load extremely slowly, not-so-vaguely reminiscent of dialup telephone modems for your computer.

But the picture is brightening. 3G is in more places than ever. And the same can be said of Wi-Fi.

Surfin' Dude

A version of the Apple Safari web browser is a major reason that the 'Net on the iPad is very much like the 'Net you've come to expect on a more traditional computer. Come to think of it, the 'Net often looks a lot better on the iPad thanks to its beautiful screen. Safari for the Mac and for Windows is one of the very best web browsers in the business. In our view, Safari on the iPhone has no rival as a cellphone browser. As you might imagine, Safari on the iPad is equally appealing.

Moreover, with the iOS 4.3 software upgrade, Apple revved-up Safari's performance with what the company refers to as a Nitro JavaScript engine. Even a consumer-friendly company like Apple can't help but rely on geeky terms every now and then.

Exploring the browser

We start our cyber expedition with a quick tour of the Safari browser. Take a gander at Figure 4-1: Not all browser controls found on a Mac or PC are present. Still, Safari on the iPad has a familiar look and feel. We describe these controls and others throughout this chapter.

Before plunging in, we recommend a little detour. Read the "Living on the EDGE" sidebar, earlier in this chapter, to find out more about the wireless networks that enable you to surf the web on the iPad in the first place.

Blasting off into cyberspace

Surfing the web begins with a web address, of course. When you start by tapping the address field in iPad's Safari, the virtual keyboard appears. Here are a few tips for using the keyboard in Safari (and see Chapter 2 for more help with using the virtual keyboard):

- Because so many web addresses end with the suffix `.com` (pronounced *dot com*), the virtual keyboard has a dedicated .com key. For other common web suffixes — `.edu, .net, .org, .us, .ro, .eu` — press and hold the .com key and choose the relevant domain type.

- Of equal importance, both the period (.) and the slash (/) are on the virtual keyboard because you frequently use them when you enter web addresses.

- The moment you tap a letter, you see a list of web addresses that match those letters. For example, if you tap the letter *E* (as we did in the example shown in Figure 4-2), you see web listings for ESPN, eBay, and others. Tapping *U* or *H* instead may display listings for *USA TODAY* or the *Houston Chronicle* (shameless plugs for the newspapers where we're columnists).

Previous

Next Page

New Page

Address field

Bookmarks

Search Google,
Bing, or Yahoo!

Go To...

Reload Web Page

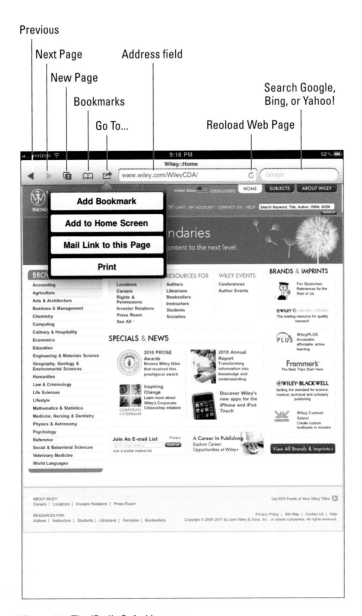

Figure 4-1: The iPad's Safari browser.

Figure 4-2: Web pages that match your search letter.

The iPad has two ways to determine websites to suggest when you tap certain letters:

- **Bookmarks:** One method is the websites you already bookmarked from the Safari or Internet Explorer browsers on your computer (and synchronized, as we describe in Chapter 3). More on bookmarks later in this chapter.

- **History:** The second method iPad uses when suggesting websites when you tap a particular letter is to suggest sites from the History list — those cyber destinations where you recently hung your hat. Because history repeats itself, we also tackle that topic later in this chapter.

You might as well open your first web page now — and it's a full *HTML* page, to borrow from techie lingo:

1. **Tap the Safari icon docked at the bottom of the Home screen.**

   It's another member of the Fantastic Four (along with Mail, Photos, and iPod). Chapter 1 introduces the Home screen.

    2. **Tap the address field (refer to Figure 4-1).**

    3. **Begin typing the web address, or** *URL,* **on the virtual keyboard that slides up from the bottom of the screen.**

    4. **Do one of the following:**

        a. To accept one of the bookmarked (or other) sites that show up on the list, merely tap the name.

        Safari automatically fills in the URL in the address field and takes you where you want to go.

        b. Keep tapping the proper keyboard characters until you enter the complete web address for the site you have in mind and then tap the Go key on the right side of the keyboard.

        You don't need to type **www** at the beginning of a URL. So, if you want to visit www.theonion.com (for example), typing **theonion. com** is sufficient to transport you to the humor site. For that matter, Safari can take you this site even if you type **theonion** without the .com.

Because Safari on the iPad runs a variation of the iPhone mobile operating system, every so often you may run into a site that serves up the light, or mobile, version of a website, sometimes known as a WAP site. Graphics may be stripped down on these sites. Alas, the producers of these sites may be unwittingly discriminating against you for dropping in on them by using an iPad. In fact, you may be provided a choice of which site you want — the light or the full version. Bravo! If not, you have our permission to berate these site producers with letters, e-mails, and phone calls until they get with the program.

I Can See Clearly Now

If you know how to open a web page (if you don't, read the preceding section in this chapter), we can show you how radically simple it is to zoom in on pages so that you can read what you want to read and see what you want to see, without enlisting a magnifying glass.

Try these neat tricks:

   ✓ **Double-tap the screen so that portion of the text fills the entire screen.** It takes just a second before the screen comes into focus. By way of example, check out Figure 4-3, which shows two views of the same *Sports Illustrated* web page. In the first view, you see what the page looks like when you first open it. In the second one, you see how the picture takes over much more of the screen after you double-tap it. The area of the screen you double-tapped is the area that swells up. To return to the first view, double-tap the screen again.

Figure 4-3: Doing a double-tap dance zooms in and out.

- **Pinch the page.** Sliding your thumb and index finger together and then spreading them apart (or as we like to say, *unpinching*) also zooms in and out of a page. Again, wait just a moment for the screen to come into focus.

- **Press down on a page and drag it in all directions, or flick through a page from top to bottom.** You're panning and scrolling, baby.

- **Rotate the iPad to its side.** Watch what happens to the White House website, as shown in Figure 4-4; it reorients from portrait to a wide-screen landscape view. The keyboard (not shown in the image) is also wider, making it a little easier to enter a new URL. This little magic won't happen if you set the Rotate Lock described in Chapter 1.

Opening multiple web pages at a time

When we surf the web on a Mac or PC, we rarely go to a single web page and call it a day. In fact, we often have multiple web pages open at the same time. Sometimes, we choose to hop around the web without closing the pages we visit. Sometimes, a link (see the next section) automatically opens a new page without shuttering the old one. (If these additional pages are advertisements, this isn't always welcome.)

Figure 4-4: Going wide.

Safari on the iPad lets you open up to nine pages simultaneously. After you have one page open, here's how to open additional web pages in Safari:

1. **Tap the New Page icon (refer to Figure 4-1) on the left side of the navigation bar at the top of the screen.**

   You see a tic-tac-toe grid with thumbnails of recently opened sites or pages, similar to Figure 4-5.

2. **Tap the page you want to view or tap New Page to open a fresh page.**

   If you tap New Page, you need to tap the address field and type a URL for your new page.

To close one of your open web pages, tap the white X inside the black circle, which appears in the upper-left corner of each web page thumbnail.

Looking at lovable links

Surfing the web would be a real drag if you had to enter a URL every time you want to navigate from one page to another. That's why bookmarks are so useful, and, it's why handy links are welcome, too. Because Safari functions on the iPad the same way browsers work on your Mac or PC, links on the device behave much the same way, too.

Figure 4-5: All open for business.

Text links that transport you from one site to another are typically underlined or shown in blue or bold type, or merely as items in a list. Tap the link to go directly to that site or page.

Tapping other links leads to different outcomes:

- **Open a map:** Tapping a map launches the Google Maps application that is, um, addressed in Chapter 6.

- **Prepare an e-mail:** Tap an e-mail address, and the iPad opens the Mail program (see Chapter 5) and prepopulates the To field with that address. The virtual keyboard is also summoned so that you can add other e-mail addresses and compose a subject line and message. This shortcut doesn't always work when an e-mail address appears on a web page.

To see the URL for a link, press your finger against the link and keep it there. Use this method also to determine whether a picture has a link.

Not every web link cooperates with the iPad. As this book goes to press, the iPad doesn't support some common web standards — most notably, Adobe Flash video. It's a void that we hope is addressed in the future because Flash is the backbone for video and animations across cyberspace. We're not holding our breath. But all is not lost, even with the absence of Flash. Apple does support an emerging standard for audio and video — *HTML5*, among others. In the meantime, if you see an incompatible link, nothing may happen — or a message may appear, asking you to install a plug-in.

News flash about Flash: You may be able to open Flash videos on the iPad through a couple of workarounds. Skyfire Labs sells a $4.99 iPad app that can support Flash on many sites. But Skyfire's alternative browser is limited to videos; it does not support Flash games or animations. Meanwhile, the free-to-try iSwifter app from YouWeb promises to address this shortcoming. So along with video, iSwifter's browser can deliver Flash games. You'll be encouraged to pay 99 cents for the iSwifter browser.

Book (mark) 'em, Dano

You already know how useful bookmarks are and how you can synchronize bookmarks from the browsers on your computer. It's equally simple to book-mark a web page directly on the iPad:

1. **Make sure that the page you want to bookmark is open and then tap the Add Bookmark icon at the top of the screen.**

   The Add Bookmark icon looks like an arrow trying to escape a rectangle and is labeled in Figure 4-1.

   You have the opportunity to tap Add Bookmark, Add to Home Screen, or Mail Link to This Page or Print.

2. **Tap Add Bookmark, among the options mentioned in the previous step.**

   A new window opens with a default name for the bookmark, its web address, and its folder location.

3. **To accept the default bookmark name and default bookmark folder, tap Save.**

4. **To change the default bookmark name, tap the X in the circle next to the name, enter the new title (using the virtual keyboard), and then tap Save.**

5. **To change the location where the bookmark is saved, tap the > symbol in the Bookmarks field, tap the folder where you want the bookmark to be kept, tap the Add Bookmark button in the upper-left corner of the screen, and then tap Save.**

To open a bookmarked page after you set it up, tap the Bookmarks icon in the upper-left portion of the screen (refer to Figure 4-1) and then tap the appropriate bookmark.

If the bookmark you have in mind is buried inside a folder, tap the folder name first and then tap the bookmark you want.

If you tapped Add to Home Screen rather than Add Bookmark in Step 1 of the preceding set of steps, your iPad adds an icon to your Home screen to let you quickly access the site, a topic we discuss in detail in the section "Clipping a web page," later in this chapter. If you tapped Mail Link to This Page instead, the Mail program opens, with a link for the page in the message and the name of the site in the subject line.

Altering bookmarks

If a bookmarked site is no longer meaningful, you can change it or get rid of it:

- ✓ **To remove a bookmark (or folder),** tap the Bookmarks icon and then tap Edit. Tap the red circle next to the bookmark you want to toss off the list, and then tap Delete.

- ✓ **To change a bookmark name or location,** tap Edit and then tap the bookmark. The Edit Bookmark screen appears, showing the name, URL, and location of the bookmark already filled in. Tap the fields you want to change. In the Name field, tap the X in the gray circle and then use the keyboard to enter a new title. In the Location field, tap the > symbol and scroll up or down the list until you find a new home for your bookmark.

- ✓ **To create a new folder for your bookmarks,** tap Edit and then tap the New Folder button. Enter the name of the new folder and choose where to put it.

- ✓ **To move a bookmark up or down in a list,** tap Edit and then drag the three bars to the right of the bookmark's name to its new resting place.

You can constantly display a Bookmarks bar in Safari by turning on the Always Show Bookmarks Bar setting in Settings. Tap Safari in Settings to display this option. As with many other settings, make sure that the blue On setting is shown rather than the gray Off setting. For more on Settings, head to Chapter 13.

Printing a web page

If you come to a web page that you want to print, tap the icon at the top of the screen that looks like an arrow trying to escape a rectangle. Tap Print from the menu that appears. You need a compatible AirPrint printer, as we touch upon in Chapter 2.

Clipping a web page

You frequent lots of websites, but some way more than others. You're constantly online to consult your daily train schedule, for example. In their infinite wisdom, the folks at Apple let you bestow special privileges on frequently visited sites, not just by bookmarking pages but by affording them their unique Home screen icons. Apple calls these *Web Clips,* and creating one is dead simple:

1. **Open the web page in question and tap the Add Bookmarks icon.**

2. **Tap Add to Home Screen.**

   Apple creates an icon out of the area of the page that was displayed when you saved the clip, unless the page has its own custom icon.

3. **Type a new name for your Web Clip or leave the one that Apple suggests.**

4. **Tap Add.**

   The icon appears on your Home screen.

As with any icon, you can remove a Web Clip by pressing and holding its icon until it starts to wiggle. Then tap the X in the corner of the icon and tap Delete. The operation is completed when you press the Home button.

Letting history repeat itself

Sometimes, you want to revisit a site that you failed to bookmark, but you can't remember the darn destination or what led you there in the first place. Good thing you can study the history books.

Safari records the pages you visit and keeps the logs on hand for several days. Here's how to access your history:

1. **Tap the Bookmarks icon and then tap History.**

   The History option is at the top of the Bookmarks list.

2. **Tap the day you think you hung out at the site.**

3. **When you find it, tap the listing.**

   You're about to make your triumphant return.

To clear your history so that nobody else can trace your steps — and just what is it you're hiding? — tap Clear History at the upper-right corner of the History list. Alternatively, tap Settings on the Home screen, tap Safari, and then tap Clear History. In both instances, per usual, you have a chance to back out without wiping the slate clean.

Launching a mobile search mission

Most people spend a lot of time using search engines on the Internet. And, the search engines we summon most often are Google, Yahoo!, or Microsoft's Bing. So it goes on the iPad.

Although you can certainly use the virtual keyboard to type **google.com**, **yahoo.com**, or **bing.com** in the Safari address field, Apple doesn't require that tedious effort. Instead, you tap into Google, Yahoo!, or Bing by using the dedicated search box shown in Figure 4-6. The default search engine on the iPad is Google.

Figure 4-6: Conducting a Google search about iPads on the iPad.

To conduct a web search on the topic of the iPad, follow these steps:

1. **Tap the search field shown earlier, in Figure 4-1.**

   A funny thing happens. The search field expands (as if Google, Yahoo!, or Bing expected you to enter more text than could fit in the field initially). At the same time, the address bar gets smaller and your ever-obedient virtual keyboard slides up from the bottom. In Chapter 2, we explain how the keyboard adapts to what you're doing. The one that shows up now has a Search key.

2. **Enter your search term or phrase, and then tap the Search key to generate pages of results.**

3. **Tap any search result that looks promising.**

An iOS upgrade brought the ability to find a search word or phrase on the very web page you have opened onscreen. Just enter a search term in the search field as before. At the bottom of the search results list, tap On This Page (refer to Figure 4-6). You may have to scroll down the list to see On This Page. The first occurrence of your search term is highlighted. Tap the Next button at the bottom-left corner of the screen to find the next match. Tap Next again for the match after that, and so on.

To switch the search box from Google to Yahoo! to Bing or whatever is your preference, tap Settings on the Home screen, scroll down and tap Safari, tap Search Engine, and then tap to prioritize one search behemoth over the other.

Saving web pictures

You can capture most pictures you come across on a website — but be mindful of any potential copyright violations, depending on what you plan to do with the images. To copy an image from a website, follow these steps:

1. **Press your finger against the image.**

2. **Tap the Save Image button that appears, as shown in Figure 4-7 (or tap Copy, depending on what you want to do with the image):**

   • Saved images end up in your Photos library, from which they can be synced back to a computer.

   • If you tap Copy instead, you can paste the image into an e-mail or as a link in a program, such as Notes.

In some cases, typically advertisements, you also see an Open button or an Open in New Page button, which takes you to the ad image.

Figure 4-7: Hold your finger against a picture in Safari to save it to the iPad.

Smart Safari Settings

Along with the riches galore found on the Internet are places in cyberspace where you're hassled. You might want to take pains to protect your privacy and maintain your security.

To get started, tap the Settings icon on the Home screen and then tap Safari.

The following settings enable you to tell your iPad what you want to be private and how you want to set your security options:

- **Fill out forms with AutoFill:** When AutoFill is turned on, Safari can automatically fill out web forms by using your personal contact information, usernames and passwords, or information from other contacts in your address book. But turning on AutoFill could also compromise your security if someone gets hold of your computer.

- **Fraud Warning:** Safari can warn you when you land on a site whose producers have sinister intentions. The protection is better than nothing but don't give up your guard. The Fraud Warning isn't foolproof. The setting is on by default.

✔ **Turn JavaScript on or off:** Programmers use JavaScript to add various kinds of functionality to web pages, from displaying the date and time to changing images when you mouse over them. However, some security risks have also been associated with JavaScript. If you do turn it off, though, some things might not work as you expect.

✔ **Block pop-ups:** *Pop-ups* are those web pages that appear whether you want them to or not. Often, they're annoying advertisements. But at some sites, you welcome the appearance of pop-ups, so remember to turn off blocking under such circumstances.

✔ **Accept cookies:** We're not talking about crumbs you may have accidentally dropped on the iPad. *Cookies* are tiny bits of information that a website places on the iPad when you visit so that the site recognizes you when you return. You need not assume the worst; most cookies are benign.

If this concept wigs you out, you can take action: Tap Accept Cookies and then tap Never. Theoretically, you will never again receive cookies on the iPad. A good middle ground is to accept cookies only from the sites you visit. To do so, tap From Visited. You can also tap Always to accept cookies from all sites.

If you set the iPad so that it doesn't accept cookies, certain web pages won't load properly.

Tap Safari to return to the main Safari Settings page.

✔ **Clear the cache:** The cache stores content from some web pages so that they load faster the next time you stop by. Tap Clear Cache and then tap Clear Cache again on the next screen to (you guessed it) clear the cache.

✔ **Developer tool:** Unless you happen to be a developer, we don't ask you to pay much attention to this setting. It lets you turn a debug console (showing errors, warnings, tips, logs, and similar details that developers find useful) on or off.

5

The E-Mail Must Get Through

*O*n any computing device, e-mails come and go with a variety of emotions. Messages may be amusing or sad, frivolous or serious. Electronic missives on the iPad are almost always touching.

The reason, of course, is that you're touching the display to compose and read messages. Okay, so we're having a little fun with the language. But the truth is, the built-in Mail application on the iPad is a modern program designed not only to send and receive text e-mail messages, but also to handle rich HTML e-mail messages — formatted with font and type styles and embedded graphics. If someone sends you mail with a picture, it's quite likely (depending on the sender's e-mail capabilities) that the picture is visible right in the body of the message.

Furthermore, your iPad can read several types of file attachments, including (but not limited to) PDFs, JPG images, Microsoft Word documents, PowerPoint slides, and Excel spreadsheets, as well as stuff produced through Apple's own iWork software. Better still, all this sending and receiving of text, graphics, and documents can happen in the background so that you can surf the web or play a game while your iPad quietly and efficiently handles your e-mail behind the scenes.

Prep Work: Setting Up Your Accounts

First things first. To use Mail, you need an e-mail address. If you have broad-band Internet access (that is, a cable modem, FIOS, or DSL), you probably received one or more e-mail addresses when you signed up. If you're one of the handful of readers who doesn't already have an e-mail account, you can get one for free from Yahoo! (`http://mail.yahoo.com`), Google (`http://mail.google.com`), AOL (`http://www.aol.com`), or numerous other service providers.

Many (if not all) free e-mail providers add a small bit of advertising at the end of your outgoing messages. If you'd rather not be a billboard for your e-mail provider, either use the address(es) that came with your broadband Internet access (*yourname*@comcast.net or *yourname*@att.net, for example) or pay a few dollars a month for a premium e-mail account that doesn't tack advertising (or anything else) onto your messages. You can get a me.com e-mail account as part of Apple's $99-a-year MobileMe service.

Set up your account the easy way

Chapter 3 explains the option of automatically syncing the e-mail accounts on your Mac or Windows PC with your iPad. If you chose that option, your e-mail accounts should be configured on your iPad already. You may proceed directly to the later section "Darling, You Send Me (E-Mail)."

If you haven't yet chosen that option but want to set up your account the easy way now, go to Chapter 3 and read that section, sync your iPad, and then you, too, can proceed directly to the section "Darling, You Send Me (E-Mail)," later in this chapter.

Set up your account the less easy way

If you don't want to sync the e-mail accounts on your Mac or PC, you can set up an e-mail account on your iPad manually. It's not quite as easy as clicking a box and syncing your iPad, but it's not rocket science either. Here's how you get started:

- ✔ **If you have no e-mail accounts on your iPad,** the first time you launch Mail, you see the Welcome to Mail screen, as shown in Figure 5-1. Your choices are Microsoft Exchange (business e-mail), MobileMe, Gmail, Yahoo! Mail, AOL, and Other.

  Merely tap the account type you want to add to the iPad and follow the steps in the section "Setting up an e-mail account with Yahoo!, Google, AOL, or MobileMe," "Setting up an account with another provider," or "Setting up corporate e-mail," later in this chapter.

✔ **If you have one or more e-mail accounts on your iPad already and want to add a new account manually,** tap Settings on the Home screen and then tap Mail, Contacts, Calendars⇨Add Account.

You see an Add Account screen with the same account options that are shown on the Welcome to Mail screen. Proceed to one of the next three sections, depending on the type of e-mail account you selected.

Figure 5-1: Tap a button to set up an account.

Setting up an e-mail account with Yahoo!, Google, AOL, or MobileMe

If your account is with Yahoo!, Google (Gmail), AOL, or Apple's MobileMe service, follow these steps:

1. **Tap the appropriate button on the Add Account screen. (Refer to Figure 5-1.)**

2. **Enter your name, e-mail address, and password, as shown in Figure 5-2.**

   You can describe this account (such as Work or Personal), but the field tends to fill in automatically with the same contents in the Address field unless you tell it differently.

3. **Tap the Next button in the upper-right corner of the screen.**

   You're finished. That's all there is to setting up your account.

Setting up an account with another provider

If your e-mail account is with a provider other than Yahoo!, Google, AOL, or MobileMe, you have a bit more work ahead of you. You're going to need a bunch of information about your e-mail account that you may not know or have handy.

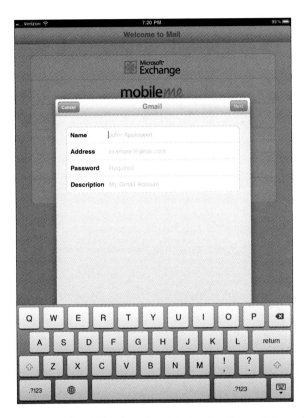

Figure 5-2: Just fill 'em in and tap Next and you're ready to rock.

We suggest that you scan the following instructions, note the items you don't know, and go find the answers before you continue. To find the answers, look at the documentation you received when you signed up for your e-mail account or visit the account provider's website and search there.

Here's how you set up an account:

1. **Starting at the Home screen, tap Settings⇨Mail, Contacts, Calendars⇨ Add Account⇨Other.**

2. **Under Mail, tap Add Mail Account.**

3. **Fill in the name, address, password, and description in the appropriate fields, and then tap Next.**

   With any luck, that's all you'll have to do. The iPad will look up and hopefully be able to retrieve your account credentials. If not, continue with Step 4.

4. **Tap the button at the top of the screen that denotes the type of e-mail server this account uses: IMAP or POP, as shown in Figure 5-3.**

Figure 5-3: If you're not a Yahoo!, Google, AOL, or MobileMe user, you may have a few more fields to fill in before you can rock.

5. **Fill in the Internet hostname for your incoming mail server, which looks something like mail.*providername*.com.**

6. **Fill in your username and password.**

7. **Enter the Internet hostname for your outgoing mail server, which looks something like smtp.*providername*.com.**

8. **Enter your username and password in the appropriate fields.**

9. **Tap the Next button in the upper-right corner to create the account.**

Some outgoing mail servers don't need your username and password. The fields for these items on your iPad note that they're optional. Still, we suggest that you fill them in anyway. It saves you from having to add them later if your outgoing mail server does require an account name and password, which many do these days.

Setting up corporate e-mail

The iPad makes nice with the Microsoft Exchange servers that are a staple in large enterprises, as well as many smaller businesses.

What's more, if your company supports Microsoft Exchange ActiveSync, you can exploit push e-mail so that messages arrive pronto on the iPad, just as they do on your other computers. (To keep everything up to date, the iPad also supports push calendars and push contacts.) For push to work with an Exchange Server — at press time anyway — your company must be simpatico with Microsoft Exchange ActiveSync 2003 (Service Pack 2) or 2007 (Service Pack 1). Ask your company's IT or tech department if you run into an issue.

Setting up Exchange e-mail isn't particularly taxing, and the iPad connects to Exchange right out of the box. You still might have to consult your employer's techie-types for certain settings.

Start setting up your corporate e-mail on your iPad by following these steps:

1. **Tap the Microsoft Exchange icon on the Add Account screen. (Refer to Figure 5-1.)**

2. **Fill in what you can: your e-mail address, domain, username (sometimes *domain\user*), and password. Or, call on your IT staff for assistance. Tap Next when you're done.**

3. **On the next screen, as shown in Figure 5-4, enter the Server address, assuming that the Microsoft Autodiscover service didn't already find it. Tap Next when you're done.**

   That server address may begin with *exchange.company.com.*

Figure 5-4: You're on your way to a corporate e-mail account.

4. **Choose which information you want to synchronize through Exchange by tapping each item you want.**

   You can choose Mail, Contacts, and Calendars. After you choose an item, you see the blue On button next to it, as shown in Figure 5-5.

5. **Tap Save.**

Figure 5-5: Keeping your mail, contacts, and calendars in sync.

The company you work for doesn't want just anybody having access to your e-mail — heaven forbid if your iPad is lost or stolen. So your bosses may insist that you change the passcode lock inside Settings on your iPad. (This is different from the password for your e-mail account.) Skip over to Chapter 13 to find instructions for adding or changing a passcode. (We'll wait for you.) And, if your iPad ends up in the wrong hands, your company can remotely wipe the contents clean.

By default, the iPad keeps e-mail synchronized for three days. To sync for a longer period, head to Settings and tap Mail, Contacts, Calendars and then tap the Mail account using ActiveSync. Tap Mail Days to Sync and tap No Limit or pick another time frame (1 day, 1 week, 2 weeks, or 1 month).

If you're moonlighting at a second job, you can now configure more than one Exchange ActiveSync account on your iPad; there used to be a limit of just one such account per device.

See Me, Read Me, File Me, Delete Me: Working with Messages

Now that your e-mail accounts are all set up, it's time to figure out how to receive and read the stuff. Fortunately, you've already done most of the heavy lifting when you set up your e-mail accounts. Getting and reading your mail is a piece of cake.

Your first clue that there's *unread* mail comes when you look at the Mail icon at the bottom of the Home screen. The cumulative number of unread messages appears in a little red circle in the upper-right area of the icon.

In the following sections, you find out how to read messages and attached files and send messages to the Trash or maybe a folder when you're done reading them. Or, if you can't a find a message, check out the section on searching your e-mail messages. You can read your e-mail just like you can on a desktop or notebook computer; the way you do so just works a little differently on the iPad's touchscreen.

Reading messages

To read your mail, tap the Mail icon on the Home screen. Remember that what appears on the screen depends on whether you're holding the iPad in landscape or portrait mode, and what was on the screen the last time you opened the Mail application.

- ✔ **Landscape:** Held in landscape mode, you see All Inboxes at the top of the Inboxes section (see Figure 5-6), which as its name suggests, is a repository for all the messages across all your accounts. The number to the right of All Inboxes matches the number on the Mail icon on your Home page. Again, it's the cumulative tally of unread messages across all your accounts.

 Depending on the last time the Mail application was open, you may alternatively see previews of the actual messages in your inbox in the left panel mentioned previously. Previews show the name of the sender, the subject header, and the first two lines of the message. (In Settings, you can change the number of lines shown in the preview from one line to five. Or, you can show no preview lines.)

- ✔ **Portrait:** When you hold the iPad in portrait mode, the last incoming message fills the entire screen. Figure 5-7 shows this view. You have to tap an Inbox button (in the upper-left corner of the screen) to summon a panel that shows other accounts or message previews. These overlay the message that otherwise fills the screen.

Compose New Message

Reply, Forward, or Print

Trash Message

Move Message

Tap to see All Inboxes
or individual accounts

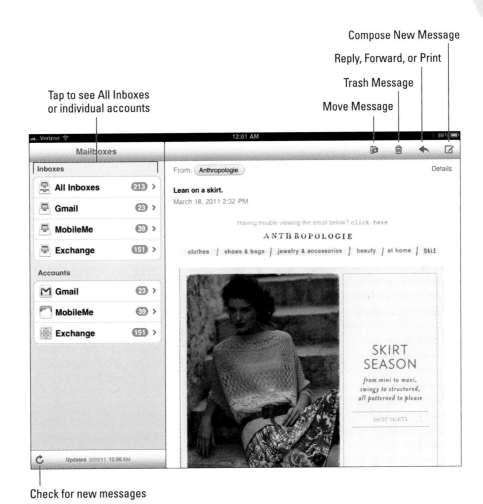

Check for new messages

Figure 5-6: When holding the iPad sideways, Mail looks something like this.

Below the All Inboxes listing are the inboxes for your individual accounts. The tally this time is only for the unread messages in those accounts. If you tap the listings here, you see any subfolders for each individual account (Drafts, Sent Mail, Trash, and so on). Messages display in *threads,* or conversations, making them easy to follow. Of course, you can still view accounts individually. Follow these steps to read your e-mail:

Figure 5-7: When holding the iPad in portrait mode, the message fills the screen.

1. **If the e-mail mailbox you want to see isn't front and center, tap the Mailboxes button in the upper-left corner of the screen to summon the appropriate one.**

   Again, this button may say Inbox or some other folder name, and it may say the name of the e-mail account that is currently open. Within an e-mail account, you can see the number of unread messages in each mailbox.

2. **(Optional) Tap the Check for New Messages icon (refer to Figure 5-6) to summon new messages.**

3. **Tap one of the inboxes or accounts to check for any new messages within those mailboxes. To summon the unified inbox, tap All Inboxes instead.**

If a blue dot appears next to a message, the message hasn't been read. When you open a mailbox by tapping it, the iPad displays the number of "recent" messages that you specify in Settings — 50 by default, though you can display up to 200. To see more than the number you specified, tap Load Additional Messages.

4. **Tap a message to read it.**

   When a message is on the screen, the buttons for managing incoming messages appear at the top, most of which you're already familiar with. If you're holding the iPad in portrait mode, you see up/down arrows that correspond to the next or previous message (see Figure 5-7).

5. **In landscape mode (and from within an account), tap a preview listing to the left of a message to read the next or previous message or any other visible message on the list. Scroll up or down to find other messages you may want to read.**

A number next to one of the previews indicates the number of related messages in a thread.

Under a thread, only the first message of the conversation displays in the inbox. Tap that message to reveal the entire back and forth. You can turn off message threading by choosing Settings⇨Mail, Contacts, Calendars. Then tap Organize by Thread to toggle the setting on or off, depending on your preference.

Managing messages

Managing messages typically involves either moving the messages to a folder or deleting them. To herd your messages into folders, you have the following options:

- **To create a folder to organize messages you want to keep,** manage your mail account on your Mac or PC. You can't create a Mail folder on the iPad.

- **To file a message in another folder,** tap the File Message icon. When the list of folders appears, tap the folder where you want to file the message.

- **To move messages to another folder in bulk,** tap Edit. In both portrait and landscape, Edit appears at the top of your inbox or another mailbox when those mail folders are selected. After tapping Edit, it becomes a Cancel button and Delete (in red) and Move (in blue) buttons appear at the bottom of the screen. Tap the circle to the left of each message you want to move so that a check mark appears. Tap Move (see Figure 5-8) and then tap the new folder in which you want those messages to hang out.

✒ **To read a message that you've filed away,** tap the folder where the message now resides, and then tap the header or preview for the message in question.

✒ **To print a message,** tap the Reply, Forward, Print button (see Figure 5-8) and then tap Print.

Figure 5-8: Wiping out or moving messages, en masse.

Delete a message by tapping the Delete Message icon. You have a chance to cancel in case you tap the Delete Message icon by mistake. You can delete e-mail messages without opening them in two ways:

✒ Swipe left or right across the message in its preview pane, and then tap the red Delete button that appears to the right of the message.

✒ Tap the Edit button and then tap the little circle to the left of each message you want to remove. Tapping that circle puts a check mark in it and brightens the red Delete button at the bottom of the screen. Tap that

Delete button to erase all messages you checked off, as shown in Figure 5-8. Deleted messages are moved to the Trash folder. (On some e-mail accounts — Gmail, for example — you can to turn on an Archive setting in Settings. If you do go with the Archive option, the red Delete button appears as an Archive button instead and messages are not be deposited in the Trash but rather archived.)

Searching e-mails

With Spotlight search, you can easily search through a bunch of messages to find the one you want to read fast — such as that can't-miss stock tip from your broker. You can type **stock** or whichever search term seems relevant in the search box at the top of a mailbox preview pane. All matching e-mails that have already been downloaded appear. When you tap the search box in Mail, tabs appear that let you narrow the search to the From, To, or Subject fields. It's too bad that (at press time, anyway) you can't run a search to find words within the body of an e-mail message.

If you're using Exchange, MobileMe, or certain IMAP-type e-mail accounts, you may even be able to search messages that are stored out on the server. When available, tap Continue Search on Server.

Don't grow too attached to attachments

Your iPad can even receive e-mail messages with attachments in a wide variety of popular file formats. Which file formats (see sidebar) does the iPad support? Glad you asked:

- **Images:** `.jpg`, `.tiff`, `.gif`, `.png`
- **Microsoft Word:** `.doc`, `.docx`
- **Microsoft PowerPoint:** `.ppt`, `.pptx`
- **Microsoft Excel:** `.xls`, `.xlsx`
- **Web pages:** `.htm`, `.html`
- **Apple Keynote:** `.key`
- **Apple Numbers:** `.numbers`
- **Apple Pages:** `.pages`
- **Preview and Adobe Acrobat:** `.pdf`
- **Rich Text:** `.rtf`
- **Text:** `.txt`
- **Contact information:** `.vcf`

Keeping files in order

In very simple terms, computers of any type, including tablets like the iPad, and the software that runs on such machines, have to have some way to recognize and appropriately act upon the files that run on the system. Long ago the bright minds in technology cooked up standard ways to organize the layout of data so that files that serve a particular purpose adhere to a similar structure. You recognize such files by their extensions, the three or four letter suffix that is separated by a dot or period after its name. Needless to say there are many more file formats than most folks will ever need to become familiar with. But you, or more precisely the hardware and software you are working with, will encounter some popular file types over and over, including such formats as .doc for Microsoft Word documents and .jpg for images. If you ever encounter files on any computer you are using that don't seem to open up or respond, it's likely because you don't have the software on the machine to recognize such files. The good news is that the iPad supports most of the common file types it encounters. But not quite everything.

If the attachment is a file format that the iPad doesn't support (for example, a Photoshop .psd file), you see the name of the file but you can't open it on your iPad.

Here's how to read an attachment:

1. **Open the mail message that contains the attachment.**

2. **Tap the attachment (it appears at the bottom of the message, so you probably need to scroll down to see it).**

   The attachment downloads to your iPad and opens automatically.

3. **Read the attachment.**

4. **Tap the document you're reading (in the case of a document) and tap Done to return to the message text.**

   Or, you can (again, for a document) open the Pages word processor if you have purchased that application for your iPad. See Chapter 12 for more on Pages.

You can open an attachment from a different app than may have otherwise been summoned to duty. Just touch and hold the attachment in the e-mail, and then tap the app from the options that present themselves. For example, you might open a Word document with Apple's Pages word processor if that optional app resides on your iPad.

More things you can do with messages

Wait! You can do even more with your incoming e-mail messages:

- ✔ **To see all recipients of a message,** tap Details (displayed in blue) to the right of the sender's name.

  If all recipients are displayed, the word in blue is Hide rather than Details; tap it to hide all names except the sender's.

- ✔ **To add an e-mail recipient or sender to your contacts,** tap the name or e-mail address at the top of the message, and then tap Create New Contact or Add to Existing Contact.

- ✔ **To mark a message as unread,** tap Mark as Unread, which appears in the subject line of an open message. When you do, the message is again included in the unread message count on the Mail icon on your Home screen, and its mailbox again has a blue dot next to it in the message list for that mailbox.

- ✔ **To zoom in and out of a message,** use the pinch and unpinch gestures, at which we suspect you now excel at. See Chapter 2 if you need help with your touchscreen moves.

- ✔ **To follow a link in a message,** tap the link. Links typically display in blue but sometimes other colors and sometimes underlined. If the link is a URL, Safari opens and displays the web page. If the link is a phone number, the iPad gives you the chance to add it to your contacts. If the link is a map, Maps opens and displays the location. And, last but not least, if the link is an e-mail address, a new preaddressed blank e-mail message is created.

  If the link opens Safari, Contacts, or Maps and you want to return to your e-mail, press the Home button on the front of your iPad and then tap the Mail icon. Or double-press Home and select it from the gallery of running apps.

Darling, You Send Me (E-Mail)

Sending e-mail on your iPad is a breeze. You'll encounter several subspecies of messages: pure text, text with a photo, a partially finished message (a *draft*) that you want to save and complete later, or a reply to an incoming message. You can also forward an incoming message to someone else — and in some instances print messages. The following sections examine these message types, one at a time.

Sending an all-text message

To compose a new e-mail message, tap Mail on the Home screen. Once again, what you see next depends on how you're holding your iPad. In landscape mode, your e-mail accounts or e-mail folders are listed in a panel along the left side of screen, with the actual message filling the larger window on the right.

Now, to create a new message, follow these steps:

1. **Tap the Compose New Message button (refer to Figure 5-6).**

   The New Message screen like the one shown in Figure 5-9 appears.

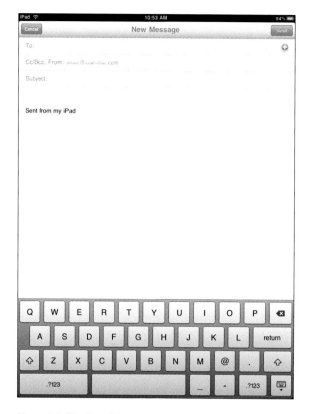

Figure 5-9: The New Message screen appears, ready for you to start typing the recipient's name.

2. **Type the names or e-mail addresses of the recipients in the To field, or tap the + button to the right of the To field to choose a contact(s) from your iPad's contacts list.**

3. **(Optional) Tap the field labeled Cc/Bcc, From.**

   Doing so breaks the field into separate Cc, Bcc, and From fields.

   The Cc/Bcc label stands for *carbon copy/blind carbon copy.* Carbon copy (a throwback term from another era) is kind of an FYI to a recipient. It's like saying, "We figure you'd appreciate knowing this, but you don't need to respond."

   When using Bcc, you can include a recipient on the message but other recipients can't see that this recipient has been included. It's great for those secret agent e-mails! Tap the respective Cc or Bcc field to type names. Or, tap the + symbol that appears in those fields to add a contact.

4. **(Optional) If you tap From, you can choose to send the message from any of your e-mail accounts on the fly, assuming, of course, that you have more than one account set up on the iPad.**

   If you start typing an e-mail address, e-mail addresses that match what you typed appear in a list below the To or Cc field. If the correct one is in the list, tap it to use it.

5. **Type a subject in the Subject field.**

   The subject is optional, but it's considered poor form to send an e-mail message without one.

6. **Type your message in the message area.**

   The message area is immediately below the Subject field. You have ample space to get your message across.

7. **Tap the Send button in the upper-right corner of the screen.**

Your message wings its way to its recipients almost immediately. If you aren't in range of a Wi-Fi network or the AT&T or Verizon Wireless data networks when you tap Send, the message is sent the next time you're in range of one of these networks.

Apple includes a bunch of landscape-orientation keyboards in various applications, including Mail. When you rotate the iPad to its side, you can compose a new message using a wider-format virtual keyboard.

Sending a photo with a text message

Sometimes a picture is worth a thousand words. When that's the case, here's how to send an e-mail message with a photo enclosed:

1. **Tap the Photos icon on the Home screen.**

2. **Find the photo you want to send.**

3. **Tap the button that looks like a little rectangle with a curved arrow springing out of it in the upper-right corner of the screen.**

4. **Tap the Email Photo button.**

   An e-mail message appears onscreen with an icon for the photo already attached. In fact, the image may appear to be embedded in the body of the message, but the recipient receives it as a regular e-mail attachment.

   On the CC/Bcc line of your outgoing message, you see the size of the attached image. If you tap Image Size, a new line appears, giving you the option to choose an alternative size among Small, Medium, Large, or Actual Size. Tap the size you want.

5. **Address the message and type whatever text you like, as you did for an all-text message in the preceding section, and then tap the Send button.**

Saving an e-mail to send later

Sometimes you start an e-mail message but don't have time to finish it. When that happens, you can save it as a draft and finish it some other time. Here's how:

1. **Start an e-mail message, as described in one of the two previous sections.**

2. **When you're ready to save the message as a draft, tap the Cancel button in the upper-left corner of the screen.**

3. **Tap the Save Draft button if you want to save this message as a draft and complete it another time.**

If you tap the Delete Draft button, the message disappears immediately without a second chance. Don't tap Delete Draft unless you mean it.

To work on the message again, tap the Drafts mailbox. A list of all messages you saved as drafts appears. Tap the draft you want to work on, and it reappears on the screen. When you're finished, you can tap Send to send it or tap Cancel to save it as a draft again.

The number of drafts appears to the right of the Drafts folder, the same way that the number of unread messages appears to the right of other mail folders, such as your inbox.

Replying to, forwarding, or printing an e-mail message

When you receive a message and want to reply to it, open the message and then tap the Reply/Reply All/Forward/Print button — or what we like to call the "act on it" button. It looks like a curved arrow at the upper-right corner of the screen, as shown in Figure 5-10. Then tap the Reply, Reply All, Forward, or Print button.

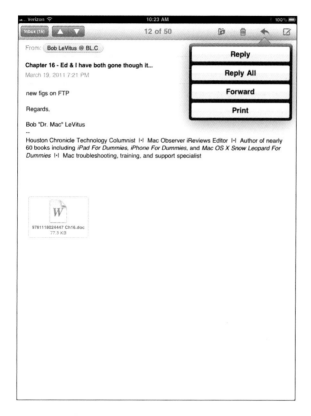

Figure 5-10: Reading and managing an e-mail message.

✔ **Reply and Reply All:** The Reply button creates a blank e-mail message addressed to the sender of the original message. The Reply All button creates a blank e-mail message addressed to the sender and all other recipients of the original message, plus CCs. (The Reply All option appears only if more than one recipient was on the original e-mail.) In both cases, the subject is retained with a *Re:* prefix added. So if the original subject were *iPad Tips,* the reply's subject would be *Re: iPad Tips.*

✔ **Forward:** Tapping the Forward button creates an unaddressed e-mail message that contains the text of the original message. Add the e-mail address(es) of the person or people you want to forward the message to, and then tap Send. In this case, rather than a *Re:* prefix, the subject is preceded by *Fwd:*. So this time, the subject would be *Fwd: iPad Tips.*

✔ **Print:** Of course, you'd tap Print if you wanted to print using an AirPrint capable printer.

You can edit the subject line of a reply or a forwarded message or edit the body text of a forwarded message the same way you'd edit any other text. It's usually considered good form to leave the subject lines alone (with the *Re:* or *Fwd:* prefix intact), but you may want to change them sometimes. Now that you know you can.

To send your reply or forwarded message, tap the Send button as usual.

Settings for sending e-mail

You can customize the mail you send and receive in lots of ways. In this section, we explore settings for sending e-mail. Later in this chapter, we show you settings that impact the way you receive and read messages. In each instance, start by tapping Settings on the Home screen. Then:

✔ **To hear an alert when you successfully send a message:** From the main Settings screen, tap General⇨Sounds. Make sure that the Sent Mail setting is turned on (so that the blue On button is showing rather than the gray Off button). If you want to change other settings, tap the General button at the top of the screen, which is shaped like a left-pointing arrow. If you're finished setting the settings, tap the Home button on the front of your iPad.

The preceding paragraph is similar for all the settings we discuss in this section and later sections, so we don't repeat them again. To summarize, if you want to continue using settings, tap whichever left-pointing button appears at the top of the screen — sometimes it's General, sometimes Mail, sometimes Contacts, or sometimes something else. The point is that the button always returns you to the previous screen so that you can change other settings. The same concept applies to tapping the Home button on the front of your iPad when you're finished setting a setting. That action always saves the change you just made and returns you to the Home screen.

✔ **To add a signature line, phrase, or block of text to every e-mail message you send:** Tap Settings⇨Mail, Contacts, Calendars⇨Signature on the right. The default signature is *Sent from my iPad.* You can add text before or after it, or delete it and type something else. Your signature is affixed to the end of all your outgoing e-mail.

✔ **To have your iPad send you a copy of every message you send:** Tap Settings⇨Mail, Contacts, Calendars and then turn on the Always Bcc Myself setting.

✔ **To set the default e-mail account for sending e-mail from outside the Mail application:** Tap the Settings icon on the Home screen, and then tap Mail, Contacts, Calendars⇨Default Account. Tap the account you want to use as the default. For example, when you want to e-mail a picture directly from the Photos application, this designated e-mail account is the one that's used. Note that this setting applies only if you have more than one e-mail account on your iPad.

Setting Your Message and Account Settings

This final discussion of Mail involves more settings that deal with your various e-mail accounts. (If you're looking for settings that let you apply a signature and other settings related to sending e-mail, read the preceding section "Settings for sending e-mail.")

Checking and viewing e-mail settings

Several settings affect the way you can check and view e-mail. You might want to modify one or more, so we describe what they do and where to find them:

✔ **To specify how often the iPad checks for new messages:** Tap the Settings icon on the Home screen; tap Mail, Contacts, Calendars⇨ Fetch New Data. You're entering the world of *fetching* or *pushing.* Check out Figure 5-11 to glance at your options. If your e-mail program (or more precisely the e-mail server behind it) supports push and you have it turned on (the On button displays), fresh messages are sent to your iPad automatically as soon as they hit the server. If you turned off push or your e-mail program doesn't support it in the first place (Off displays), the iPad fetches data instead. Choices for fetching are Every 15 Minutes, Every 30 Minutes, Hourly, and Manually. Tap the one you prefer.

Figure 5-11: Fetch or push? It's your call.

Tap Advanced to determine these push and fetch settings for each individual account. Tap the account in question. Push is shown as an option only if the e-mail account you tapped supports the feature.

✔ **To hear an alert sound when you receive a new message:** Tap General on the main Settings screen, tap Sounds, and then turn on the New Mail setting.

✔ **To set the number of recent messages that appears in your inbox:** From the main Settings screen, tap Mail, Contacts, Calendars⇨Show. Your choices are 25, 50, 75, 100, and 200 recent messages. Tap the number you prefer.

You can always see more messages in your inbox regardless of this setting by scrolling all the way to the bottom and tapping Load Additional Messages.

- ✔ **To set the number of lines of each message to be displayed in the message list:** From the main Settings screen, tap Mail, Contacts, Calendars⟹ Preview; then choose a number. Your choices are 0, 1, 2, 3, 4, and 5 lines of text. The more lines of text you display in the list, the fewer messages you can see at a time without scrolling. Think before you choose 4 or 5.

- ✔ **To set the font size for messages:** From the main Settings screen, tap Mail, Contacts, Calendars⟹Minimum Font Size. Your options are Small, Medium, Large, Extra Large, and Giant. Use trial and error to find out which size you prefer. Choose one and then read a message. If it's not just right, choose a different size. Repeat until you're happy.

- ✔ **To specify whether the iPad shows the To and Cc labels in message lists:** From the main Settings screen, tap Mail, Contacts, Calendars and turn the Show To/Cc Label setting on or off.

- ✔ **To turn the Ask before Deleting warning on or off:** From the main Settings screen, tap Mail, Contacts, Calendars; then turn the Ask before Deleting setting on or off. If this setting is turned on, you need to tap the Trash icon at the bottom of the screen and then tap the red Delete button to confirm the deletion. When the setting is turned off, tapping the Trash icon deletes the message and you never see a red Delete button.

- ✔ **To specify whether the iPad will automatically load remote images:** Tap Load Remote Images so that the On button displays. If it's off, you can still manually load remote images. Certain security risks have been associated with loading remote images.

- ✔ **To organize your mail by thread:** Tap Organize by Threads so that the setting is toggled On.

Altering account settings

The last group of settings we explore in this chapter deals with your e-mail accounts. You most likely will never need most of these settings, but we'd be remiss if we didn't at least mention them briefly. So here they are, whether you need 'em or not:

- ✔ **To stop using an e-mail account:** Tap the Settings icon on the Home screen; tap Mail, Contacts, Calendars⟹*Account Name*⟹Delete Account⟹ Keep on My iPad to turn off the account.

  This setting doesn't delete the account; it only hides it from view and stops it from sending or checking e-mail until you turn it on again.

- ✔ **To delete an e-mail account:** Tap the Settings icon on the Home screen; tap Mail, Contacts, Calendars⟹*Account Name*⟹Delete Account⟹Delete. Tap Cancel if you change your mind and don't want your account blown away.

You can find still more advanced Mail settings, reached the same way: Tap the Settings icon on the Home screen; tap Mail, Contacts, Calendars; and then tap the name of the account you want to work with.

The settings you see under Advanced and how they appear vary by account. This list describes some of the ones you might see:

- **To specify how long until deleted messages are removed permanently from your iPad:** Tap Advanced⇨Remove. Your choices are Never, After One Day, After One Week, and After One Month. Tap the choice you prefer.

- **To choose whether drafts, sent messages, and deleted messages are stored on your iPad or on your mail server:** Tap Advanced, and then choose the setting under Mailbox Behaviors stored On My iPad or stored On the Server. You can decide for Drafts, Sent Messages, and Trash. If you choose to store any or all of them on the server, you can't see them unless you have an Internet connection (Wi-Fi, or cellular). If you choose to store them on your iPad, they're always available, even if you don't have Internet access.

We strongly recommend that you don't change these next two items unless you know exactly what you're doing and why. If you're having problems with sending or receiving mail, start by contacting your ISP (Internet service provider), e-mail provider, or corporate IT person or tech department. Then change these settings only if they tell you to. Again, these settings and exactly where and how they appear, vary by account.

- **To reconfigure mail server settings:** Tap Host Name, User Name, or Password in the Incoming Mail Server or Outgoing Mail Server section of the account settings screen and make your changes.

- **To adjust Use SSL, Authentication, IMAP Path Settings, or Server Port:** Tap Advanced, and then tap the appropriate item and make the necessary changes.

And that, as they say in baseball, retires the side. You're now fully qualified to set up e-mail accounts and send and receive e-mail on your iPad.

6

Surfin' the Web without a Board (or at Least without Safari)

*1*n this chapter, you look at apps that require Internet access to function but don't rely on your iPad's web browser (Safari). We call them *Internet-enabled* apps because they display information collected over your Internet connection — whether Wi-Fi or cellular data network — in real time. These include apps for maps, YouTube videos, and social networking.

Maps Are Where It's At

In our other book, *iPhone For Dummies*, we said that the Maps feature was one of the sleeper hits of our iPhone experience and an application we both use more than we expected because it's so darn handy. Since we first discovered the Maps app via our iPhones, the app has become better and more capable. With Maps, you can quickly and easily discover exactly where you are, find nearby restaurants and businesses, get turn-by-turn driving instructions from any address to any other address, and see real-time traffic information and a photographic street view of many locations as well.

You can't use the apps in this chapter unless you're connected to the Internet via either Wi-Fi or 3G.

Finding your current location with Maps

We start with something supremely simple yet extremely useful — determining your current location. At the risk of sounding like self-help gurus, here's how to find yourself:

1. **Make sure Location Services is enabled by tapping Settings⇨General⇨ Location Services.**

2. **Tap the Maps icon on your Home screen.**

 3. **Tap the little arrow icon in the middle of the gray bar at the top of the screen.**

   You'll soon see a blue circle (see Figure 6-1), which indicates your approximate location. And if you move around, your iPad can update your location and adjust the map so that the location indicator stays in the middle of the screen.

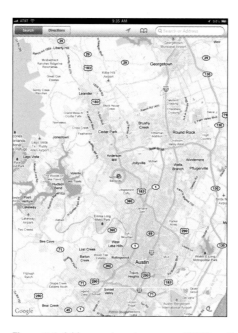

Figure 6-1: A blue marker shows your GPS location.

Just so you know, if you tap, drag the map, or zoom in and/or out, your iPad continues to update your location, but it doesn't continue to center the marker. That's a good thing, but it also means that the location indicator can move off the screen.

Finding a person, place, or thing

To find a person, place, or thing with Maps, follow these steps:

1. **Tap the Search field in the upper-right corner of the screen to make the keyboard appear and then type what you're looking for.**

   You can search for addresses, zip codes, intersections, towns, landmarks, and businesses by category and by name, or combinations, such as *New York, NY 10022; pizza 60645;* or *Auditorium Shores Austin, TX.*

2. **(Optional) If the letters you type match names in your contacts list, the matching contacts appear in a list below the Search field; tap a name to see a map of that contact's location.**

   Maps is smart about it, too; it displays only the names of contacts that have a street address. See the section "Connecting maps and contacts," later in this chapter, for more details.

3. **When you finish typing, tap Search.**

   After a few seconds, a map appears. If you searched for a single location, it's marked with a pushpin. If you searched for a category (*pizza 60645,* for example), you see multiple pushpins, one for each matching location, as shown in Figure 6-2.

You can tap the little circle with three horizontal lines on the right in the Search field, and a drop-down list of matching locations appears, as shown in Figure 6-2.

How does Maps do that?

Maps uses iPad's Location Services to determine your approximate location using available information from your wireless data network. Wi-Fi-only models use local Wi-Fi networks; iPad Wi-Fi + 3G models use assisted GPS plus cellular data. If you're not using Location Services, turning it off conserves your battery. (To turn it off, tap Settings➪General➪Location Services.) Don't worry if Location Services is turned off when you tap the Compass icon — you're prompted to turn it on. Finally, Location Services may not be available in all areas at all times.

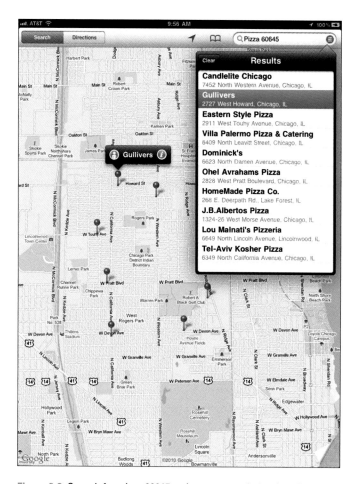

Figure 6-2: Search for *pizza 60645* and you see pushpins for all nearby pizza joints.

Views, zooms, and pans

The preceding section talks about how to find just about anything with Maps. Now here's a look at some ways you can use what you find. First, find out how to work with what you see on the screen. Four views are available at any time: Classic, Satellite, Hybrid, and Terrain. (Figure 6-2 shows the Classic view.) Select one view by tapping the curling page in the lower-right corner of the screen. The map then curls back and reveals several buttons, as shown in Figure 6-3.

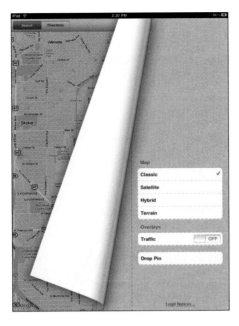

Figure 6-3: The map curls back to reveal these buttons.

In Classic, Satellite, Hybrid, or Terrain view, you can zoom to see either more or less of the map — or scroll (pan) to see what's above, below, or to the left or right of what's on the screen:

- **To zoom out:** Pinch the map or tap using *two* fingers. To zoom out even more, pinch or tap using two fingers again.

  This may be a new concept to you. To tap with two fingers, merely tap with two fingers touching the screen simultaneously (rather than the usual one finger).

- **To zoom in:** Unpinch the map (some people refer to this as a *spread*) or double-tap (the usual way — with just one finger) the spot you want to zoom in on. Unpinch or double-tap with one finger again to zoom in even more.

  An *unpinch* is the opposite of a pinch. Start with your thumb and a finger together and then spread them apart.

  You can also unpinch with two fingers or two thumbs, one from each hand, but you'll probably find that a single-handed pinch and unpinch are handier.

- **To scroll:** Flick or drag up, down, left, or right.

Connecting maps and contacts

Maps and contacts go together like peanut butter and jelly. For example, here are two helpful tasks that illustrate maps and contacts at work.

To see a map of a contact's street address, follow these steps:

1. **Tap the little Bookmarks icon to the left of the Search field.**

2. **Tap the Contacts button at the bottom of the overlay.**

3. **Tap the contact's name whose address you want to see on the map.**

   Alternatively, just type the first few letters of a contact's name in the Search field and then tap the name in the Suggestions list that appears below the Search field whenever what you type matches one or more contact names.

If you find a location by typing an address into the Search field, you can add that location to one of your contacts or create a new contact with a location you've found. To do either one, follow these steps:

1. **Tap the location's pushpin on the map.**

2. **Tap the little *i* in a blue circle to the right of the location's name or description (as shown next to Gullivers Pizzeria in Figure 6-2) to display its Info screen (see Figure 6-4).**

3. **Tap the Add to Contacts button to create a new entry for the location in your contacts list.**

4. **Tap Create New Contact or Add to Existing Contact, whichever is applicable.**

5. **Fill in the new contact information and tap Done. Or, select an existing contact from the list that appears.**

You work with your contacts by tapping the Contacts icon on your Home screen.

You can also get driving, walking, and public transit directions from most locations including a contact's address to any other location including another contact's address. You see how to do that in the "Smart map tricks" section, later in this chapter.

Saving time with Bookmarks, Recents, and Contacts

In Maps, three tools can save you from typing the same locations over and over again. You see these options on the overlay displayed when you tap the little Bookmarks icon to the left of the Search field.

Figure 6-4: The Info screen for Gullivers Pizzeria appears as an overlay when you tap the little *i* in a blue circle on the right side of Gullivers' name.

At the bottom of this overlay, you see three buttons: Bookmarks, Recents, and Contacts. The following sections give you the lowdown on these buttons.

Bookmarks

Bookmarks in the Maps application work like bookmarks in Safari. When you have a location you want to save as a bookmark so that you can reuse it later without typing a single character, follow these steps:

1. **Tap the little *i* in a blue circle to the right of the location's name or description.**

   The Info screen for that location appears (refer to Figure 6-4).

2. **Tap the Add to Bookmarks button.**

   You may have to scroll down the Info screen to see the Add to Bookmarks button.

After you add a bookmark, you can recall it at any time. To do so, tap the Bookmarks icon, tap the Bookmarks button at the bottom of the overlay, and then tap the bookmark name to see it on a map.

The first things you should bookmark are your home and work addresses and your zip codes. These are things you use all the time with Maps, so you might as well bookmark them now to avoid typing them over and over.

Use zip code bookmarks to find nearby businesses. Choose the zip code bookmark, and then type what you're looking for, such as *78729 pizza, 60645 gas station,* or *90201 Starbucks.*

You can also drop a pin anywhere on the map. A *pin* is similar to a bookmark but is often handier than a bookmark because you can drop it by hand. Why? If you don't know the exact address or zip code for a location but can point it out on a map, you can drop a pin (but you couldn't create a bookmark). You drop a pin as follows:

1. **Tap the curling page in the lower-right corner.**

2. **Tap the Drop Pin button (refer to Figure 6-3).**

   A pin drops onscreen, and you see the words `Tap and Hold Anywhere to Drop a Pin` with a little *i* in a blue circle after it.

3. **Tap and hold on the location you want to mark with a pin.**

4. **Tap the little *i.***

   The Dropped Pin overlay appears, where you can fill in some details about the pin and take similar actions to those that appear in the screen shown in Figure 6-4.

To manage your bookmarks, tap the Edit button in the upper-left corner of the Bookmarks overlay. Then:

- **To move a bookmark up or down in the Bookmarks list:** Drag the little icon with three gray bars that appears to the right of the bookmark upward to move the bookmark higher in the list or downward to move the bookmark lower in the list.

- **To delete a bookmark from the Bookmarks list:** Tap the – sign in a red circle to the left of the bookmark's name and then tap the red Delete button.

When you're finished using bookmarks, tap anywhere outside the overlay to return to the map.

Recents

Maps automatically remembers locations you've searched for and directions you've viewed in its Recents list. To see this list, tap the Bookmarks icon and then tap the Recents button at the bottom of the overlay. To see a recent item on the map, tap the item's name.

To clear the Recents list, tap the Clear button in the upper-left corner of the overlay and then tap the big red Clear All Recents button at the bottom of the overlay or tap Cancel if you change your mind.

When you're finished using the Recents list, tap anywhere outside the overlay to return to the map.

Contacts

To see a list of your contacts, tap the Bookmarks icon and then tap the Contacts button at the bottom of the overlay. To see a map of a contact's location, tap the contact's name in the list.

To limit the contacts list to specific groups (assuming that you have some groups in your contacts list), tap the Groups button in the upper-left corner of the overlay and then tap the name of the group. Now only contacts in this group display in the list.

When you're finished using the contacts list, tap the Done button in the upper-right corner of the overlay to return to the map.

Smart map tricks

The Maps application has more tricks up its sleeve. Here are a few nifty features you may find useful.

Get route maps and driving directions

You can get route maps and driving directions to any location from any location as follows:

1. **Tell your iPad to get directions for you.**

   You can do so in a couple of ways:

   - *If a pushpin is already on the screen:* Tap the pushpin and then tap the little *i* in a blue circle to the right of the name or description. This action displays the item's Info screen. Tap the Directions to Here or Directions from Here button to get directions to or from that location, respectively.

   - *When you're looking at a map screen:* Tap the Directions button in the upper-left corner of the screen. The Search field transforms into Start and End fields.

2. **Tap in the Start or End field to designate the starting and ending points of your trip.**

You can either type them or choose them from a list of your bookmarks, recent maps, or contacts.

3. **(Optional) If you need to swap the starting and ending locations, tap the little swirly arrow button between the Start and End fields.**

4. **When the start and end locations are correct, tap the Start button in the blue banner overlay near the lower-right corner of the screen, as shown in Figure 6-5.**

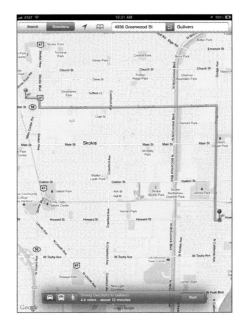

Figure 6-5: The route map from Bob's first house in Skokie to Gullivers Pizza in Chicago.

When you tap the Start button, it changes into left- and right-arrow buttons.

5. **Navigate your directions using the arrows or a list:**

   • *Arrows:* Tap the arrow buttons, as shown in Figure 6-6, to display the next or previous step in your route. Tap the right-arrow button to see the first of your turn-by-turn driving directions. Then, to see the next step in the directions, tap the right arrow again; to see the preceding step, tap the left arrow.

List button

Left arrow
(previous step)

Right arrow
(next step)

Figure 6-6: The blue banner shows you each step of your route.

- *List:* If you prefer to see your driving directions displayed as a list with all the steps at once, tap the List button on the left side of the blue banner; the directions appear in an overlay, as shown in Figure 6-7. Tap any step in the list to see that leg of the trip displayed on the map.

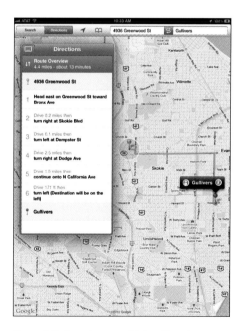

Figure 6-7: Step-by-step driving directions displayed as a list with the final leg of the trip displayed on the map.

If you want to return to the step-by-step directions in the blue banner and use the arrow buttons to navigate again, tap the little rectangle to the left of the word *Directions* in the overlay. The list disappears and the banner reappears.

6. **When you're finished with the step-by-step directions, tap the Search button at the top of the screen to return to the regular map screen and single Search field.**

As well as step-by-step directions work, we wish the iPad offered the type of audible turn-by-turn directions feature found on some dedicated GPS devices. You know — where some friendly male or female voice barks out instructions (such as "turn right on Main Street").

However, several companies, including TomTom (`www.tomtom.com`), NAVIGON (`www.navigon.com`), Magellan (`www.magellangps.com`), and MotionX (`http://drive.motionx.com`), offer iPhone apps that do just that. And although none of them has released an iPad version of their GPS navigation app at the time of this writing, we think it's only a matter of time before some (or all) do. Chapter 7 explains how to determine whether you can use iPhone apps on your iPad and how to find iPad-specific apps.

Get public transportation information and walking directions

After you provide a starting and ending location but before you tap the Start button, the blue banner displays three icons on its left side: a car, a bus, and a person walking (refer to Figure 6-5). In the preceding example, we showed directions by car, which is the default.

For public transportation information, tap the Bus icon. You then have the following options:

✓ **To see the departure and arrival times for the next bus or train,** as shown in Figure 6-8, tap the little clock that appears on the blue banner. Tap the Load More Times button to see additional departures and arrivals.

These schedules are occasionally out of date, so you might want to confirm the schedule with another source.

✓ **To see the route directions,** tap the Start button. Then, to see the next step in the directions, tap the right-arrow button; to see the preceding step, tap the left arrow.

Or, if you prefer to see the public transportation directions displayed as a list with all the steps at once, tap the List button on the left side of the blue banner; the directions appear in an overlay, as shown in Figure 6-9.

Tap any item in the list to see that leg of the trip displayed on the map. If you want to return to the step-by-step directions in the blue banner and use the arrow buttons to navigate again, tap the little rectangle to the left of the word *Directions* in the overlay. The list disappears and the banner reappears.

Figure 6-8: The bus route and schedule.

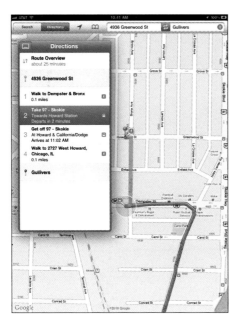

Figure 6-9: Step-by-step directions for public transportation to Gullivers with the second step showing on the map.

For step-by-step directions for walking, tap the Person Walking icon. Walking directions generally look a lot like driving directions except for your travel time. For example, driving time in Figure 6-5 is approximately 10 minutes with traffic; walking time (not shown) is estimated at 1 hour and 25 minutes.

Get traffic info in real time

You can find out the traffic conditions for the map you're viewing by tapping the curling page in the lower-right corner of the screen and then tapping the Traffic switch so that it says On. When you do this, major roadways are color-coded to inform you of the current traffic speed, as shown in Figure 6-10. Here's the key:

- **Green:** 50 or more miles per hour
- **Yellow:** 25 to 50 miles per hour
- **Red:** Under 25 miles per hour
- **Gray:** No data available at this time

Figure 6-10: Lower Manhattan in mid-afternoon has more traffic than most cities at rush hour.

Traffic info doesn't work in every location, but the only way to find out is to give it a try. If no color codes appear, assume that it doesn't work for that particular location.

More about the Info screen

If a location has a little *i* in a blue circle to the right of its name or description (refer to Figure 6-2), you can tap it to see additional information about that location.

As we explain earlier in this chapter, you can get directions to or from that location, add the location to your bookmarks or contacts, or create a new contact from it. You can do two more things with some locations from their Info screen:

- ✔ Tap its e-mail address to launch the Mail application and send an e-mail to it.
- ✔ Tap its URL to launch Safari and view its web site.

Not all locations have any or all of these three options, but we thought you should know anyway.

See a location in Street View

If you see the little icon shown in the margin on an Info screen, tap it to see that location in Street View. Drag your finger left or right to scroll up to 360°. A tiny proxy map in the lower right corner even shows you the direction of what's shown on the screen.

Hey You, It's YouTube

YouTube has come to define video sharing on the Internet. The wildly popular site, now owned by Google, has become so powerful that American presidential hopefuls and even politicians in other countries campaign and hold debates there. As you might imagine, YouTube has also generated controversy. The site has been banned in some foreign countries. And Viacom has sued YouTube for more than $1 billion over alleged copyright infringements. (Let the lawyers fight over such matters.)

All the while, YouTube staked a humongous claim on mainstream culture. That's because YouTube is, well, about you and us, and our pets, and so on. It is the cyber destination, as YouTube boldly proclaims, to "Broadcast Yourself."

Apple has afforded YouTube its own cherished icon on the Home screen. Many millions of videos are available on the iPad, nearly the complete YouTube catalog.

Hunting for YouTube gems

So where exactly do YouTubers find the videos that can offer them a blissful respite from their day? You might want to start by tapping one of the seven buttons along the bottom of the screen.

But before we start down that road, if you know what you're looking for, you can search for it, be it a specific video, topic, videographer's name, or almost anything else you might want to search for, from any of the seven "departments" we're about to describe. You see, all seven of 'em offer a Search field in their upper-right corner. Just tap in it, and the by-now-familiar virtual keyboard appears. Type a search phrase and then tap the Search key on the keyboard to generate results.

In Figure 6-11, we typed (what else?) **iPad**.

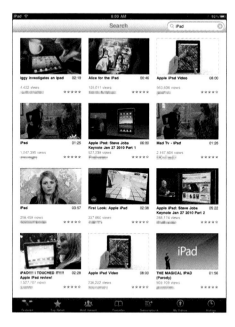

Figure 6-11: Finding iPad videos on YouTube.

Now all you have to do is tap one of 'em to watch it.

Time to go over those seven buttons at the bottom of the screen, namely:

- ✏ **Featured:** Videos recommended by YouTube's staff. Flick upward to scroll down the page and see more videos.

  When you get to the bottom of the page, tap the Load More button to see even more featured videos.

- ✏ **Top Rated:** These are videos that are rated highly by YouTube viewers. Tap the Today, This Week, or All button in the upper-left corner of the screen to filter the videos you see.

  You can rate videos on your iPad as long as you have a YouTube account, but don't waste your time trying to figure out how to create one from within the YouTube app — you can't. You have to launch Safari or another web browser (on your iPad or computer) and surf to www.youtube.com to create your account. We suggest you do that now because several of the features we're about to describe are useful only if you're signed in to your (you guessed it) YouTube account.

- ✏ **Most Viewed:** These are the videos that most YouTube viewers are watching. Tap All to see the most watched YouTube videos of all time. Tap Today or This Week to check out the videos most currently in vogue.

- ✏ **Favorites:** If you're signed in to your YouTube account, you can add videos that you like to your Favorites list. Tap the Favorites button, which looks like an open book at the bottom of the screen and also appears when you're watching a video, We think it's supposed to be an open book, but we could be wrong.

  At the top of the Favorites screen are two tabs: Favorites and Playlists, with Favorites selected by default. Favorites is one big list of videos you like; Playlists are individual lists of your favorite videos categorized however you like. Bob, for example, has a Family Guy playlist, a South Park playlist, a Stupid Mac Tricks playlist, and so on.

  If you tap the Playlists tab, you can see a list of your playlists. Of course, you must be signed in to a YouTube account to use this feature. And, surprisingly, you can't *create* a playlist while using the YouTube app. You have to visit www.youtube.com with a web browser to create one.

  After you create a playlist, you can add videos to it the same way you add them to your Favorites list (which, as we mentioned, you find out how to do very soon).

The Edit button in the upper-left corner of the Favorites and Playlists screens lets you delete videos that are no longer your favorites. Tap the button and then tap the little X in the upper-left corner of each video that you want to remove from your Favorites list or playlists. When you're finished deleting videos, tap the Done button (also found in the upper-left corner).

Your Favorites list and playlists are automatically saved and synced among all your devices — Mac, PC, iPhone, iPod touch, and/or iPad. Add a video to your Favorites list or a playlist on your iPad, and the next time you visit YouTube with your web browser, you see the video in your Favorites list or playlist. Nice touch!

 ✔ **Subscriptions:** These are videos from any YouTube accounts you subscribe to. Say it together now: You can't subscribe to a videographer's YouTube channel with the YouTube app. And you need to be logged on to your YouTube account to use this feature.

 ✔ **My Videos:** These are videos you've uploaded to YouTube. Of course, you must be logged on to your YouTube account to use this feature. What else is new? And, of course, if you've never uploaded a video to YouTube, this screen will be blank even if you are logged on.

 ✔ **History:** This is a list of all the videos you've viewed recently.

Watch this: Watching YouTube videos

To watch a YouTube video regardless of how you got to it — through one of the seven methods we describe in the preceding section or by searching for it — just tap it. The movie begins to load, and after a brief wait — how long a wait is determined by the speed of your Wi-Fi or 3G network — the video begins to play.

You should see the controls described in this section, but if you don't, just tap the video to bring up the video controls if they're hidden. Many of these controls are identical to the video controls we explain in Chapter 9, but YouTube videos also display special controls of their own, including buttons for adding this video to your Favorites list or playlists, sharing this video with friends, rating this video, and several others, as shown in Figure 6-12.

In the gray banner across the top of the screen, you have (from left to right) the Back button (which says Favorites because that's the screen I was on when I tapped this video), the name of this video (Idiot rides bike off picnic table EPIC FAIL!), and the Search field.

Figure 6-12: YouTube video controls.

Below the gray banner are four buttons:

- **Add:** Add this video to your Favorites list or a playlist.

- **Share:** Opens a new e-mail message with the title of the video as its subject and Check out this video on YouTube, and the URL for the video as the message. Just tap the blue plus button to choose an addressee from your contacts list or type an e-mail address and then tap the Send button.

- **Rate:** Lets you rate this video from one to five stars.

- **Flag:** Lets you flag this video as inappropriate.

Beneath the video in another gray banner (from left to right) is the Play/Pause button (a pair of vertical lines in Figure 6-12), the Scrubber bar, the playhead, and a pair of arrows. The first three are self-explanatory; tap the arrows to expand the video to full-screen.

If you don't see the controls and Scrubber bar, tap anywhere on the movie, and they magically reappear.

While viewing a video full-screen, a slightly different set of controls appears. To make them go away, tap the video once. The only button you may not recognize is the one in the upper-right corner, which looks like either a movie screen (top) or TV screen (bottom), as shown in the margin. This button toggles the video between widescreen and normal modes. If you don't know what that means, tap it a few times and you will. Tap the Done button in the upper-left corner of the screen or the little arrows (refer to Figure 6-12) to return to the video's Info screen.

Last but not least, you can see a gray banner below the Scrubber bar with four additional buttons: Info, Related, More From, and Comments. Tap one to see that particular information about this video.

Restricting YouTube (and other) usage

If you've given an iPad to your kid or someone who works for you, you may not want that person spending time watching YouTube videos. You want him to do something more productive, such as homework or the quarterly budget.

That's where parental (or might we say "mean boss") restrictions come in. Please note that the use of this iron-fist tool can make you really unpopular.

To restrict access to YouTube, follow these steps:

1. **Tap Settings⇨General⇨Restrictions⇨Enable Restrictions.**

2. **When prompted, establish or enter a previously established passcode — twice.**

3. **Tap YouTube so that the Off button rather than the On button displays.**

If you made YouTube a no-no, when you return to the Home screen, the YouTube icon is missing in action. Same goes for any other restricted activities. To restore YouTube or other privileges, go back into Restrictions and tap Disable Restrictions or tap the Off switch so that it says On again. Of course, you have to reenter your passcode before you can do so.

 Restrictions can also be applied to iTunes, Safari, the App Store, new app installation, and location settings, as you see when we delve into Settings further (see Chapter 13).

Socializing with Social Media Apps

Your iPad doesn't include any specific social media apps right out of the box, but you can add free client apps for the major social media networks including Facebook, MySpace, Twitter, and the new kid on the block, Apple's Game Center.

That's the good news. The bad news is that as of this writing, only Game Center and Twitter offer client apps that run natively on the iPad. Although we're certain they'll get around to releasing bigger, better, iPad-friendly apps soon, for now all we can show you are the iPhone versions of their apps running at iPhone resolution.

Note: You don't necessarily need an app to participate in social networking. Three of the four networks we mentioned can be fully utilized using Safari on your iPad. And frankly, unlike the iPhone, where the Safari experience was hampered by the tiny screen and keyboard, all three web sites are eminently usable on your iPad. So, if you want to check them out and don't feel like downloading their apps, here are their URLs:

- **Facebook:** www.facebook.com
- **MySpace:** www.myspace.com
- **Twitter:** http://twitter.com

Now we'd be remiss if we didn't at least point out some of the niceties you get when you access one of these social media networks using an app instead of a browser, so the following sections offer a few of our insights.

Note: Both of your authors grew up in an era when telephones had cords and dials, televisions used rabbit-ear antennas, and gas was a mere 30 cents a gallon. In other words, we're both long past the age where social networking is as important to us as breathing. That said, Bob has a couple of kids who *are* of an age (18 and 21) where they'd rather be without food or water than be without Facebook. And although Bob's not exactly a prolific social networker, he does maintain a modest presence on Facebook (Bob LeVitus) and Twitter (@LeVitus). Give him a shout on either service if you're a social networking type. Being a social guy, Ed is a semiregular in all these places, so feel free to say hi. You can find and follow him as @edbaig on Twitter. And if you're the social networking type yourself, kindly spread the word about our book here, assuming of course that you do like it (which we hope very much).

Game Center

Game Center is the odd duck of the bunch. Unlike the others, Game Center has no web site; you have to use the Game Center app that came with your iPad. And unlike the others, which are broad-based and aimed at anyone and everyone, Game Center is designed for a specific segment of the iPad (and iPhone and iPad touch) universe, namely users who have one or more games on their iPads (or other devices).

Game Center acts as a match-up service, letting you challenge your friends or use the Auto-Match Invite Friend button to challenge a stranger who also happens to be looking for someone to play against. Figure 6-13 shows Bob about to initiate a two-player game of *Flight Control HD*.

Of course, to make a social network like Game Center a success, there need to be lots of games that support Game Center. And therein lies the rub. Because Game Center is relatively new (born in late 2010), there are only a few dozen games available with Game Center support, some of which are seen in Figure 6-14.

Figure 6-13: Invite a stranger to play (Auto-Match) or click the Invite Friend button to challenge a friend.

Figure 6-14: Some of the games with Game Center support.

Although not many games are Game Center-aware yet, the ones that are available already include such top sellers as *Angry Birds, Real Racing HD, Pinball HD,* and the *World Series of Poker.*

Facebook

The Facebook iPhone app, as shown in Figure 6-15, makes it easy to access the most popular Facebook features with a single finger tap.

That said, we hope the Facebook iPad app is something more than just a higher-resolution version of the iPhone app. Why? Well, the iPad, unlike the iPhone, has a thoroughly usable web browser, and quite frankly, we'd rather look at our Facebook News Feed in Safari, as shown on the left in Figure 6-16, than in the current version of the Facebook iPhone app, as shown on the right in Figure 6-16.

Figure 6-15: The Facebook iPhone app sports a clean interface with quick access to many popular Facebook features.

Figure 6-16: Bob's Facebook News Feed as seen in Safari (left) and in the Facebook iPhone app (right).

On the other hand, Safari can't provide push notifications for Facebook events such as messages, Wall posts, friend requests and confirmations, photo tags, events, and comments, whereas the iPhone app does all that and more.

The bottom line is that there's nothing to prevent having the best of both worlds. So if you're a heavy Facebook user, consider using the Facebook iPhone app for some things (such as push notifications and status updates) and Safari for others (such as reading your Wall or News Feeds).

Disclaimer: We reserve the right to take back everything we just said if an iPad version of the Facebook app becomes available and if it's more appropriate for the iPad than the iPhone app.

MySpace

The MySpace app provides us with the same dilemma as the Facebook app (and the official Twitter app, which we get to in a minute): As of this moment, an iPad version isn't available. And as far as we can see, you don't have any reason to use the iPhone app 'cause it doesn't even offer push notifications (as the Facebook app does).

Take a look at the MySpace app and MySpace viewed with Safari in Figure 6-17 and then decide.

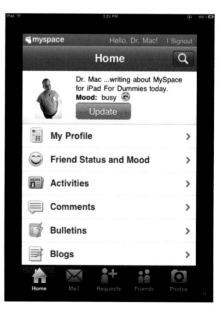

Figure 6-17: Bob's MySpace home page as seen in Safari (left) and in the MySpace iPhone app (right).

Again, we reserve the right to say something nice about the MySpace iPad app if they introduce one. But for now, we think you'll enjoy interacting with MySpace more if you use Safari.

Twitter

Twitter puts a slightly different spin on social networking. Unlike Facebook or MySpace, it doesn't try to be encompassing or offer dozens of features, hoping that some of them will appeal to you. Instead, Twitter does one thing and does it well. That thing is letting its users post short messages, or *tweets,* quickly and easily from a variety of platforms including web browsers, mobile phones, smartphones, and other devices.

Twitter users then have the option of following any other Twitter user's tweets. The result is a stream of short messages like the ones shown in Figure 6-18.

Figure 6-18: The official Twitter iPad app through the eyes of Bob (@LeVitus).

Just how short are tweets? Glad you asked. You're limited to a mere 140 characters. That's barely longer than this Tip. So be as concise as possible.

Apply Here (to Find Out about iPad Apps)

*O*ne of the best things about the iPad is that you can download and install apps created by third parties, which is to say apps not created by Apple (the first party) or you (the second party). At the time of this writing, more than 300,000 apps are available in the iTunes App Store. Furthermore, iPhone, iPod touch, and iPad owners have downloaded over 10,000,000,000 (yes, ten billion) apps. Many apps are free, but others cost money; some apps are useful, but others are lame; and some apps are perfectly well-behaved, but others quit unexpectedly (or worse). The point is that among the many apps, some are better than others.

In this chapter, we take a broad look at apps you can use with your iPad. You discover how to find apps on your computer or your iPad, and you find some basics for managing your apps. Don't worry: We have plenty to say about specific third-party apps in Chapters 16 and 17.

Tapping the Magic of Apps

Apps enable you to use your iPad as a game console, a streaming Netflix player, a recipe finder, a sketchbook, and much, much more. You can run three categories of apps on your iPad:

- **Apps made exclusively for the iPad:** This is the newest kind, so you find fewer of these than the other two types. These apps won't run on an iPhone or iPod touch, so don't bother to try them on either device.

- **Apps made to work properly on an iPad, iPhone, or iPod touch:** This type of app can run on any of the three devices at full resolution. What is the full-screen resolution for each device? Glad you asked. For most iPhones and iPod touch, it's 320 x 480 pixels; for the iPhone 4 it's 960 x 640; for the iPad and iPad 2, it's 1024 x 768 pixels.

- **Apps made for the iPhone and iPod touch:** These apps run on your iPad but only at iPhone/iPod touch resolution (320 x 480) rather than the full resolution of your iPad (1024 x 768).

  You can double the size of an iPhone/iPod touch app by tapping the little 2x button in the lower-right corner of the screen; to return it to its native size, tap the 1x button.

  Frankly, most iPhone/iPod apps look pretty good at 2x size, but we've seen a few that have jagged graphics and don't look as nice. Still, with 300,000 or more to choose from, we're sure that you can find a few that make you happy.

  Figure 7-1 shows you what this looks like.

You can obtain and install apps for your iPad in two ways:

- On your computer
- On your iPad

To use the App Store on your iPad, it must be connected to the Internet. And, if you obtain an app on your computer, it isn't available on your iPad until you sync it with your computer.

But before you can use the App Store on your iPad or your computer, you first need an iTunes Store account. If you don't already have one, we suggest that you launch iTunes on your computer, click Sign In near the upper-right corner of the iTunes window, click Create New Account, and follow the onscreen instructions.

If you don't have an iTunes Store account, you can't download a single cool app or iBook for your iPad. 'Nuff said.

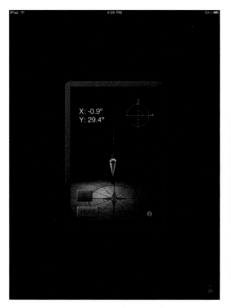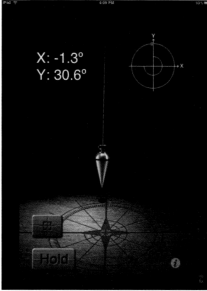

Figure 7-1: iPhone/iPod touch apps run at a smaller size (left), but can be "blown up" to double size (right).

Using Your Computer to Find Apps

Okay, start by finding cool iPad apps using iTunes on your computer. Follow these steps:

1. **Launch iTunes.**

2. **Click the iTunes Store link in the sidebar on the left.**

 3. **Click the App Store link.**

   The iTunes App Store appears, as shown in Figure 7-2.

4. **(Optional) If you want to look only for apps designed to run at the full resolution of your iPad, click the iPad tab at the top of the window.**

Browsing the App Store from your computer

After you have the iTunes App Store on your screen, you have a couple of options for exploring its virtual aisles. Allow us to introduce you to the various "departments" available from the main screen.

Scroll bar   iPad tab

iTunes Store (in sidebar)   App Store link   Search iTunes Store

Figure 7-2: The iTunes App Store in all its glory (with the iPad tab selected).

The main departments are featured in the middle of the screen, and ancillary departments appear on either side of them. We start with the ones in the middle:

- The **New and Noteworthy** department has 12 visible icons in Figure 7-2. These represent apps that are — what else? — new and noteworthy.

Only 12 icons are visible, but the New and Noteworthy department actually has more than that. Look to the right of the words *New and Noteworthy.* See the See All link? Click it to see *all* apps in this department on a single screen. Or, you can click and drag the scroll bar to the right to see more icons.

✔ The **What's Hot** department actually displays 12 icons, as shown in Figure 7-2, representing apps that are popular with other iPad users.

✔ The **Staff Favorites** department appears below the What's Hot department and is not visible in Figure 7-2.

Apple has a habit of redecorating the iTunes Stores every so often, so allow us to apologize in advance if things aren't exactly as described here when you visit.

You also see display ads for four featured apps between the New and Noteworthy department and the What's Hot department (Games, GarageBand, Elle, and AirPlay-enabled apps in Figure 7-2).

Three other departments appear to the right, under the Top Charts heading: Paid Apps; one of our favorite departments, Free Apps; and Top Grossing Apps (which is not visible in Figure 7-2). The number-one app in each department displays both its icon and its name; the next nine apps show text links only.

The App Store link near the top of the screen is also a drop-down list (as are most of the other department links to its left and right). If you click and hold most of these department links, a menu with a list of the department's categories appears. For example, if you click and hold the App Store link, you can choose specific categories such as Great Free Apps, Books, Entertainment, Apps Starter Kit, and others from the drop-down list, allowing you to bypass the App Store home page and go directly to that category.

One last thing: The little triangle to the right of each item's price is another drop-down list, as shown for the Flashlight 3D app in Figure 7-3. This drop-down list lets you give this app to someone as a gift, add it to your wish list (selected in Figure 7-3), send an e-mail to a friend with a link to it, copy the link to this product to the Clipboard so that you can paste it elsewhere, or share this item on Facebook or Twitter.

Using the Search field

Browsing the screen is helpful, but if you know exactly what you're looking for, we have good news and bad news. The good news is that there's a faster way: Just type a word or phrase into the Search field in the upper-right corner of the main iTunes window, refer to Figure 7-3, and then press Return or Enter to initiate the search.

Figure 7-3: I want to use my iPad as a flashlight, so I searched for *flashlight*.

The bad news is that you have to search the entire iTunes Store, which includes music, television shows, movies, and other stuff in addition to iPad apps.

Ah, but we have more good news: Your search results are segregated into categories — one of which is iPad Apps (refer to Figure 7-3). And, here's even more good news: If you click the See All link to the right of the words *iPad Apps* in Figure 7-3, all the iPad apps that match your search word or phrase appear on a single screen.

If you search for a common word, such as *Twilight* or *Rat,* the screen displays choices from Albums, Songs, Movies, TV Shows, Music Videos, and more, so you might have to scroll down to see the iPad Apps section.

Fortunately, it's easy to filter by media type. Just tap *Apps* in the Filter by Media Type list near the upper-left corner of the screen, and everything but iPhone and iPad apps disappears from the screen. Sweet!

Getting more information about an app

Now that you know how to find apps in the App Store, this section delves a little deeper and shows you how to find out more about an application that interests you.

To find out more about an application icon, a featured app, or a text link on any of the iTunes App Store screens, just click it. A detail screen like the one shown in Figure 7-4 appears.

This screen tells you most of what you need to know about the application, such as basic product information and a narrative description, what's new in this version, the language it's presented in, and the system requirements to run it. In the following sections, you take a closer look at the various areas on the screen.

Finding the full app description

Notice the blue More link in the lower-right corner of the Description section; click it to see a much longer description of the app.

Figure 7-4: The detail screen for SketchBook Pro, a nifty drawing and painting app for your iPad.

Bear in mind that the application description on this screen was written by the application's developer and may be somewhat biased. Never fear, gentle reader: In an upcoming section, we show you how to find reviews of the application — written by people who have used it (and, unfortunately, sometimes people who haven't).

Understanding the app rating

Notice that the SketchBook Pro app is rated 4+, as you can see below the Buy App button, near the top of the screen shown in Figure 7-4. The rating means that this app contains no objectionable material. Here are the other possible ratings:

- **9+:** May contain mild or infrequent occurrences of cartoon, fantasy, or realistic violence; or infrequent or mild mature, suggestive, or horror-themed content that may not be suitable for children younger than the age of 9.

- **12+:** May contain infrequent mild language; frequent or intense cartoon, fantasy, or realistic violence; mild or infrequent mature or suggestive themes; or simulated gambling that may not be suitable for children younger than the age of 12.

- **17+:** May contain frequent and intense offensive language; frequent and intense cartoon, fantasy, or realistic violence; mature, frequent, and intense mature, suggestive, or horror-themed content; sexual content; nudity; or depictions of alcohol, tobacco, or drugs that may not be suitable for children younger than the age of 17. You must be at least 17 years old to purchase games with this rating.

Following related links

Just below the application description, notice the collection of useful links, such as Autodesk Inc. Web Site and SketchBook Pro Support. We urge you to explore these links at your leisure.

Checking requirements and device support for the app

Last but not least, remember the three categories of apps we mention earlier in the chapter, in the section "Tapping the Magic of Apps?" If you look between the rating (Rated 4+) and Customer Ratings (4.5 stars), you can see the requirements for this particular app. Because it says `Compatible with iPad. Requires iPhone OS 3.2 or later` and doesn't mention the iPhone or iPod touch, this app falls into the first category — apps made exclusively for the iPad. Another clue that it falls into the first category is that it says `iPad Screenshots` above the two and a half pictures shown in Figure 7-4.

If the app belonged to the second or third categories — apps made to work properly on an iPad, iPhone, or iPod touch, or apps made for the iPhone or iPod touch — it would say `Compatible with iPhone, iPod touch, and iPad` rather than `Compatible with iPad`.

Now you're probably wondering how you can tell whether an app falls into the second or third category. The first clue is the little gray plus sign under the price. Apps with this symbol are "Universal," and run at full resolution on iPhones and iPads. Another clue is to look at the screen shots. If you see *two* tabs — iPhone and iPad — after *Screenshots,* the app will work at the full resolution of an iPad, iPhone, or iPod touch. Conversely, if you only see one tab that says `iPhone Screenshots`, the app will run at iPhone/iPod touch resolution on your iPad.

One way to ensure that you look only for apps that take advantage of your iPad's big screen is to click the iPad tab on the front page of the App Store (shown in Figure 7-2). All the apps displayed under the iPad tab are of the first or second type and can run at the full resolution of your iPad.

Reading reviews

If you scroll down the detail screen, near the bottom you find a series of customer reviews written by users of this app. You can see the first of these in Figure 7-4. Each review includes a star rating, from zero to five. If an app is rated four or higher, as SketchBook Pro is, the app is well-liked by people who use it.

In Figure 7-4, you can see that this application has an average rating of 4½ stars based on 1,832 user ratings for all versions. That means it's probably a pretty good app.

You see a few more reviews with star ratings below the review shown in Figure 7-4. If you care to read even more reviews than are shown on the detail page, click the small buttons on the right side of the Customer Reviews section — Back, 1, 2, and Next — to navigate to the second page of comments for this app.

Finally, just above these icons is a pop-up Sort By menu that says `Most Helpful` in Figure 7-4. This menu lets you sort the customer reviews by your choice of Most Helpful, Most Favorable, Most Critical, or Most Recent.

Don't believe everything you read in reviews. Some people buy an app without reading its description or try to use it without following the included instructions. Then, when the app doesn't do what they expected, they give it a low rating. The point is, take the ratings and reviews with a grain of salt.

Downloading an app

This part is simple. When you find an application you want to try, while browsing the App Store on your computer, just click the app's Free App or Buy App button. When you do so, you have to log on to your iTunes Store account, even if the app is free.

After you log on, the app begins downloading. When it's finished, it appears in the Apps section of your iTunes library, as shown in Figure 7-5.

Downloading an app to your iTunes library is only the first half of getting it onto your iPad. After you download an app, you have to sync your iPad before the application will be available on it. Chapter 3 covers syncing in detail.

Figure 7-5: Apps that you download appear in the Apps section of your iTunes library.

By the way, if your iTunes App library doesn't look like ours (with big icons in a grid pattern), try clicking the third icon from the left in the quartet of icons to the right of the Search field, near the top of the iTunes window. Just so you know, the leftmost icon displays your apps in a list; the next one shows them in a list with icons; the third one displays them as a grid; and the rightmost icon displays your apps in the Cover Flow view.

Updating an app

Every so often, the developer of an iPad application releases an update. Sometimes these updates add new features to the application, sometimes they squash bugs, and sometimes they do both. In any event, updates are usually a good thing for you and your iPad, so it makes sense to check for them every so often.

To do this in iTunes, try any of the following methods:

- Click the Check for Updates link near the lower-right corner of the Apps screen. Note that if any updates are available, this link tells you how many updates are available (three updates are available in Figure 7-5) instead of Check for Updates.

- Look at the little number in a circle next to the Apps item in the iTunes sidebar (which is 3 in Figure 7-5).

- Check the App Store icon on your iPad — it sprouts a little number in a circle in its upper-right corner when updates are waiting.

To grab any available updates, either click the Download All Free Updates button or click the Get Update button next to each individual app. After you download an update this way, it replaces the older version on your iPad automatically the next time you sync.

If you click the Get More Apps link next to the Check for Updates link, you find yourself back at the main screen of the iTunes App Store (refer to Figure 7-2).

Using Your iPad to Find Apps

Finding apps with your iPad is almost as easy as finding them by using iTunes. The only requirement is that you have an Internet connection of some sort — Wi-Fi or wireless data network — so that you can access the iTunes App Store and browse, search, download, and install apps.

Browsing the App Store on your iPad

To get started, tap the App Store icon on your iPad's Home screen. After you launch the App Store, you see five icons at the bottom of the screen, representing five ways to interact with the store, as shown in Figure 7-6. The first four icons at the bottom of the screen — Featured, Genius, Top Charts, and Categories — offer four different ways to browse the virtual shelves of the App Store. (The fifth icon we cover a little later, in the section "Updating an app.")

Figure 7-6: The icons across the bottom represent the five sections of the App Store.

These icons are described as follows:

- ✓ **The Featured section** has three tabs at the top of the screen: New (see Figure 7-6), What's Hot, and Release Date. Tap one to see the apps for that category.

- ✓ **The Genius section** has two tabs at the top: The iPad Apps tab displays the Genius's app recommendations based on the apps you already own. The iPad Upgrades tab has upgrades to the iPad version of your iPhone apps.

✔ **The Top Charts section** offers lists of the Top Paid iPad apps and the Top Free iPad apps. These are, of course, the most popular apps that either cost money or don't.

In the upper-left corner of the Top Charts screen is a Categories button. Tap it and you see a list of categories such as Books, Education, Games, Music, News, and Productivity, to name a few. Tap one of these categories to see the Top Paid and Top Free iPad apps for that category.

✔ **The Categories section** works a little differently: It has no tabs, and its main page contains no apps. Instead, it offers a list of categories such as Games, Entertainment, Utilities, Music, and Lifestyle, to name a few. Tap a category to see a page full of apps of that type.

Most pages in the App Store display more apps than can fit on the screen at once. For example, the New and Noteworthy section in Figure 7-6 contains more than six apps. A few tools help you navigate the multiple pages of apps:

✔ **The little triangles** at the top and bottom of the New and Noteworthy section are actually buttons you click to see the next or previous page of apps in that section. Tap them to see the next or previous page of apps.

✔ **The little dots** in the middle of the gray area above and below most sections (four dots appear in Figure 7-6) tell you how many pages the section contains; the white dot indicates which page you're currently viewing (the first one in Figure 7-6).

✔ Finally, tap **the See All link** at the top of most sections to (what else?) see all the apps in the section on the same screen.

Using the Search field

If you know exactly what you're looking for, rather than simply browsing, you can tap the Search field in the upper-right corner of the iPad screen and type a word or phrase; then tap the Search key on the keyboard to initiate the search.

Finding details about an app

Now that you know how to find apps in the App Store, the following sections show you how to find out more about a particular application. After tapping an app icon as you browse the store or in a search result, your iPad displays a detail screen like the one shown in Figure 7-7.

Remember that the application description on this screen was written by the developer and may be somewhat biased.

Figure 7-7: *Pocket Legends* is an awesome free
3D Massively-Multiplayer Online Role-Playing
Game (MMORPG) for the iPad.

The information you find on the detail screen on your iPad is similar to that
in the iTunes screen on your computer. The links, rating, and requirements
simply appear in slightly different places on your iPad screen. (See the section
"Getting more information about an app," earlier in this chapter, for
explanations of the main onscreen items.)

The Reviews section differs most from the computer version. To read reviews
from your iPad, scroll down to the bottom of any detail screen and you find a
star rating for that application. It's also the link to that application's reviews;
tap it to see a page full of them. At the bottom of that page is another link:
More Reviews. Tap it to see (what else?) more reviews.

Downloading an app

To download an app to your iPad (while using your iPad), follow these steps:

1. **Tap the price button near the top of its detail screen.**

   In Figure 7-7, it's the gray Free button. The button is replaced by a green
   Install App button.

2. **Tap the Install App button.**

3. When prompted, type your iTunes Store account password.

After you do, the App Store closes and you see the Home screen where the new application's icon will reside. The new app's icon is slightly dimmed and has the word *Loading* beneath it, with a blue progress bar near its bottom to indicate how much of the app remains to be downloaded, as shown in Figure 7-8.

Progress bar

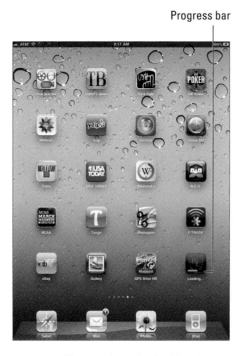

Figure 7-8: The app above the iPod icon is downloading; the blue progress bar indicates that it's half done.

4. If necessary, if the app is rated 17+, click OK in the warning screen that appears after you type your password to confirm that you're older than 17 before the app downloads.

The application is now on your iPad, but it isn't copied to your iTunes library on your Mac or PC until your next sync. If your iPad suddenly loses its memory (unlikely) or if you delete the application from your iPad before you sync (as we describe later in this chapter, in the section "Deleting an app"), that application is gone forever. That's the bad news.

The good news is that after you pay for an app, you can download it again if you need to — from iTunes on your computer or the App Store app on your iPad — and you don't have to pay for it again.

After you download an app to your iPad, the next time you sync your iPad, the application is transferred to your iTunes Apps library.

Updating an app

As we mention earlier in this chapter, every so often the developer of an iPad application releases an update. If an update awaits you, a little number in a circle appears on the Updates icon at the bottom of the iPad screen. (That number happens to be 1 in Figures 7-6 and 7-7.) Follow these steps to update your apps from your iPad:

1. **Tap the Updates icon if any of your apps needs updating.**

   If you tap the Updates button and see (in the middle of the screen) a message that says All Apps are Up-to-Date, none of the apps on your iPad requires an update at this time. If apps need updating, they appear with Update buttons next to them.

2. **Tap the Update button that appears next to any app to update it.**

   If more than one application needs updating, you can update them all at once by tapping the Update All button in the upper-right corner of the screen.

If you try to update an application purchased from any iTunes Store account except your own, you're prompted for that account's ID and password. If you can't provide them, you can't download the update.

Working with Apps

Most of what you need to know about apps involves simply installing third-party apps on your iPad. However, you might find it helpful to know how to delete, review, or report a problem with an app.

Deleting an app

You can delete an application in two ways: in iTunes on your computer, or directly from your iPad.

To delete an application in iTunes (that is, from your computer), click Apps in the sidebar and then do one of the following:

✔ Click the app to select it and press the Delete or Backspace key on the keyboard.

✔ Click the app to select it and then choose Edit➪Delete.

✔ Right-click the app and choose Delete.

After taking any of the actions in this list, you see a dialog that asks whether you're sure that you want to remove the selected application. If you click the Remove button, the application is removed from your iTunes library, as well as from any iPad that syncs with your iTunes library.

Here's how to delete an application on your iPad:

1. **Press and hold any icon until all the icons begin to "wiggle."**

2. **Tap the little *x* in the upper-left corner of the app that you want to delete, as shown in Figure 7-9.**

   A dialog appears, informing you that deleting this app also deletes all its data.

3. **Tap the Delete button.**

Little X

Figure 7-9: Tap an app's little x, and then tap Delete to remove the app from your iPad.

To stop the icons from wiggling, just press the Home or Sleep/Wake button.

Deleting an app from your iPad this way doesn't get rid of it permanently. The app remains in your iTunes library until you delete it from iTunes, as we describe earlier in this section. Put another way: Even though you deleted the app from your iPad, it's still in your iTunes library. If you want to get rid of an app for good after you delete it on your iPad, you must also delete it from your iTunes library.

You also make icons wiggle to move them around on the screen or move them from page to page (as we describe in Chapter 3). To rearrange wiggling icons, press and drag them one at a time. If you drag an icon to the left or right edge of the screen, it moves to the next or previous Home screen. You can also drag two additional icons to the Dock (where Safari, Mail, Photos, and iPod live) and have a total of six apps available from every Home screen.

Writing an app review

Sometimes you love or hate an application so much that you want to tell the world about it. In that case, you should write a review. You can do this in two ways: in iTunes on your computer or directly from your iPad.

To write a review using iTunes on your computer, follow these steps:

1. **Navigate to the detail page for the application in the iTunes App Store.**

2. **Scroll down the page to the Reviews section and click the Write a Review link.**

   You may or may not have to type your iTunes Store password.

3. **Click the button for the star rating (1 to 5) you want to give the app.**

4. **In the Title field, type a title for your review; and in the Review field, type your review.**

5. **Click the Submit button when you're finished.**

   The Preview screen appears. If the review looks good to you, you're done. If you want to change something, click the Edit button.

To write a review from your iPad, follow these steps:

1. **Tap the App Store icon to launch the App Store.**

2. **Navigate to the detail screen for the app.**

3. **Scroll down the page and tap the Write a Review link.**

   You probably have to type your iTunes Store password.

4. **Tap one to five of the stars at the top of the Write a Review screen to rate the app.**

5. **In the Title field, type a title for your review; and in the Review field, type your review.**

6. **Tap the Submit button in the upper-right corner of the screen.**

Whichever way you submit your review, Apple reviews your submission. As long as the review doesn't violate the (unpublished) rules of conduct for app reviews, it appears in a day or two in the App Store, in the Reviews section for the particular app.

Reporting a problem

Every so often, you find an app that's recalcitrant — a dud that doesn't work properly or else crashes, freezes, or otherwise messes up your iPad. When this happens, you should definitely report the problem so that Apple and the developer know about it and (hopefully) can fix it.

If you try to report a problem using iTunes on your computer, you click a number of times, only to end up at a web page that says, If you are having issues with your application, report the issue directly to the developer of the app by visiting the developer's website. Don't bother.

You can, however, report a problem from your iPad. Here's how:

1. **Tap the App Store icon to launch the App Store.**

2. **Navigate to the detail screen for the app.**

3. **Tap the Report a Problem button near the upper-right corner of the detail screen.**

   You probably have to type your iTunes Store password.

4. **Tap one of the three buttons to identify the type of problem you're reporting: This Application Has a Bug, This Application Is Offensive, or My Concern Is Not Listed Here.**

5. **Type your report in the Comments field.**

6. **Tap the Report button in the upper-right corner of the screen to submit the report.**

Part III
The iPad at Work and Play

The 5th Wave — By Rich Tennant

"You ever notice how much more streaming media there is than there used to be?"

In this part . . .

Your iPad is arguably the best iPod ever invented. So in this part we look at the multimedia side of your tablet — audio, video, pictures, and books. Never before has a tablet been this much fun to use; in this part, we show you how to wring the most out of every multimedia bit of it.

First we explore how to enjoy listening to music, podcasts, and audiobooks on your iPad. Then we look at some video, both literally and figuratively. You find out how to use the iPad 2 video camera, how to find good video for your iPad, and instructions for watching video on your iPad.

In Chapter 10, you find everything you always wanted to know about taking, managing, and displaying photos: how take still photos with iPad 2, how to find photos on your iPad, how to use the iPad's unique Picture Frame feature, how to create and display slideshows, and how to do other interesting things with them.

In Chapter 11, you visit the iBook Store, Apple's newest shopping destination — a nifty digital bookstore. You'll be amazed at how many books you can carry without breaking your back.

Chapter 12 is all about getting down to business with your iPad. As journalists, we especially appreciate Notes, the the bundled app that enables to become a champion note-taker. Chapter 12 also helps you to stay on top of your appointments and messages with Calendar and Contacts. And check out the sections on Pages, Keynote, and Numbers — iWork apps for creating documents, presentations, and spreadsheets on the go.

8

Get in Tune(s): Audio on Your iPad

*Y*our iPad is perhaps the best iPod ever — especially for working with audio and video. In this chapter, we show you how to use your iPad for audio; in Chapter 9, we cover video.

We start with a quick tour of the iPad's iPod application. Then we look at how to use your iPad as an audio player. After you're nice and comfy with using it this way, we show you how to customize the listening experience so that it's just the way you like it. Then we offer a few tips to help you get the most out of using your iPad as an audio player. Finally, we show you how to use the iTunes application to buy music, audiobooks, videos, and more and how to download free content, such as podcasts.

We assume that you already synced your iPad with your computer and that your iPad contains audio content — songs, podcasts, or audiobooks. If you don't have any audio on your iPad yet, we humbly suggest that you get some (flip to Chapter 3 and follow the instructions) before you read the rest of this chapter — or Chapter 9, for that matter.

Okay, now that you have some audio content on your iPad to play with, are you ready to rock?

Introducing the iPod inside Your iPad

To use your iPad as an iPod, just tap the iPod icon on the right side of the Dock at the bottom of the screen (unless you've moved it elsewhere).

Here's a quick overview of what you see when the iPod app starts:

- **Audio library:** Along the left side of the screen you see your iPad audio library, which contains all the music, podcasts, audiobooks, and playlists you've synced with or purchased on your iPad. For the sake of this demonstration, we're going to ask you to tap on the first item in the library — the one labeled Music — now.

  Along the right side of the screen, running from top to bottom, you see the letters of the alphabet from A to Z (unless you're looking at the Genres tab, which doesn't need them). Tap one to jump to that letter instantly when you're browsing Songs, Artists, Albums, or Composers.

  If you don't see the alphabet on the right side of the screen, you either didn't tap Music in the library when we asked you to or you've selected the Genres tab. So tap Music in the library and then tap any tab at the bottom of the screen except Genres, and we're on the same page as you again.

- **Player controls:** At the top of the screen, from left to right, you can see the volume control, the Rewind/Previous Track button, the Play/Pause button, the Fast Forward/Next Track button, and the Search field.

- **Playlist and tab navigation:** At the bottom of the screen, from left to right, you can see a plus sign for adding new playlists, the Genius symbol for creating Genius playlists, and five tabs: Songs, Artists, Albums, Genres, and Composers.

  If you don't see five tabs at the bottom of the screen, chances are you didn't tap Music in the library when we asked you to a few paragraphs back.

We take a closer look at all these features, but for now, Figure 8-1 shows them all for your enjoyment and edification.

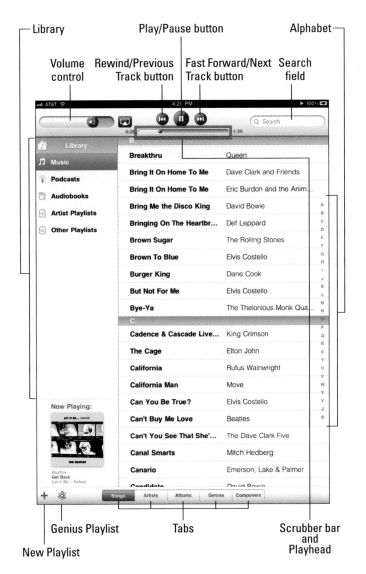

Figure 8-1: These components are what you find on the iPod app's main screen.

Checking Out Your Library

The Music item in your library displays every single song on your iPad. So while the Music item is selected, you can always see every song, artist, album, genre, or composer, depending on the tab you've selected at the bottom of the screen — Songs, Artists, Albums, Genres, or Composers.

If you don't see every song in your library, chances are you've typed something into the Search field.

You can find a particular song, artist, album, genre, or composer using the Search box or the tabs. The following sections show you how.

Finding music with the Search field

With the iPod app open, the easiest way to find music is to type a song, artist, album, or composer name into the Search field in the upper-right corner of the screen.

You can also find songs (or artists, for that matter) without opening the iPod app by typing their names in a Spotlight search, as we mention in Chapter 2.

Browsing among the tabs

If you'd rather browse your music library, tap the appropriate tab at the bottom of the screen — Songs, Artists, Albums, Genres, or Composers — and the items of that type appear.

Now you can find a song, artist, album, genre, or composer by

- ✔ **Flicking upward or downward** to scroll up and down the list until you find what you're looking for

  or

- ✔ **Tapping one of the little letters on the right side of the screen** to jump to that letter in the list (all tabs except Genres)

Then, when you find what you're looking for, here's what happens based on which tab is selected:

- ✔ **Songs:** The song plays.

  If you're not sure which song you want to listen to, try this: Tap the Shuffle button at the top of the list (just above the first song). Your iPad then plays songs from your music library at random.

✓ **Artists:** A list of artists' names appears. Tap an artist, and all the albums and songs by that artist appear; tap a song, and it plays; tap an album cover, and the whole album plays; or tap the Play All Songs button just below the Search field to play all songs from all the albums by that artist. To see the list of artists, you can either tap the Artists button to the right of the word *Library* at the top of the screen or tap the Artists tab at the bottom of the screen.

Figure 8-2 is what you see after you tap an artist's name (in this case, that artist is Bleu, one of Bob's favorite singer/songwriters).

Figure 8-2: Bob tapped Bleu in the list of artists, and this is appeared.

✓ **Albums:** Albums works pretty much the same way as Artists, except you see a grid of album covers instead of a list of artists. Tap an album, and its contents appear in an overlay, as shown in Figure 8-3.

To play one of the songs on the album, tap it. To return to the grid of album covers, tap anywhere outside the overlay.

✓ **Genres:** When you tap the Genres tab, a grid of genres — Comedy, Rock, Pop, Hip Hop/Rap, and so on — appears. Tap a genre, and a list of the songs in that genre appears in an overlay.

Figure 8-3: We tapped the Todd Rundgren Anthology album cover, and this appeared.

TIP

If the list of songs in an overlay is longer than the one in Figure 8-3, you may have to flick upward to see the rest of the songs.

✓ **Composers:** A list of composers appears. Tap a composer, and all the albums and songs by that composer appear. Tap a song, and it plays; tap an album cover, and all the songs from that album play; or tap the Play All Songs button just below the Search field to play all songs from all the albums by that composer. Tap the Composers button near the top of the screen and just to the right of the word *Library,* or tap the Composers tab at the bottom of the screen to return to the list of composers.

One last thing: You don't see any tabs at the bottom of the screen if you select Podcasts, Audiobooks, or iTunes U in the sidebar. These libraries work pretty much the same as we've just described except instead of songs, artists, albums, genres, or composers, you see podcasts, audiobooks, and iTunes U courses.

What's the difference between artists and composers?

If you're wondering about the difference between an artist and a composer, imagine this if you will: You have a recording in your iTunes Library of a track entitled "Symphony No. 5 in C Minor." The composer will always be Ludwig van Beethoven, but the artist could be the London Symphony Orchestra, the Los Angeles Philharmonic, the Austin Klezmer Ensemble, or many other performers. Here's another example: The ballad "Yesterday" was composed by John Lennon and Paul McCartney but has been performed by artists that include the Beatles, Ray Charles, Boyz II Men, Dave Grusin, Marianne Faithful, and many others.

Now you may be wondering where your iPad gets this kind of info because you know you didn't supply it. Check this out: Click a track in iTunes on your computer, choose File↪Get Info, and then click the Info tab at the top of the window.

That's just some of the information that can be "embedded" in an audio track. This embedded information, sometimes referred to as the track's *tags,* is what your iPad uses to distinguish between artists and composers. If a track doesn't have a composer tag, you won't find it in the Composers tab on your iPad.

Taking Control of Your Tunes

If you've read along so far, you have down the basics and can find and play songs (and podcasts, audiobooks, and iTunes U courses), here we take a look at some of the things you can do with your iPad when it's in iPod mode.

Playing with the audio controls

First things first: We look at the controls you use after you tap a song, podcast, audiobook, or iTunes U course. We refer to these things — songs, podcasts, audiobooks, and iTunes U courses — as *tracks* to avoid confusion (and unnecessary typing).

Take a peek at Figure 8-1 and you see exactly where all these controls are located on the screen:

- ✐ **Volume control:** Drag the little dot left or right to reduce or increase the volume level.

- ✐ **Previous Track/Rewind button:** When a track is playing, tap once to go to the beginning of the track or tap twice to go to the start of the preceding track in the list. Touch and hold this button to rewind the track at double speed.

- ✐ **Play/Pause button:** Tap to play or pause the track.

✔ **Next Track/Fast Forward button:** Tap to skip to the next track in the list. Touch and hold this button to fast-forward at double speed.

You can display playback controls anytime a track is playing. Better still, this trick works even when you're using another app or your Home screen(s): Just double-tap the Home button and swipe the icon tray from left to right, and the controls appear at the bottom of the screen, as shown in Figure 8-4.

Figure 8-4: These controls appear — even if you're using another app — when you double-click the Home button and swipe the tray while a track plays.

The playback controls *don't* appear if you're using an app that has its own audio, such as many games, any app that records audio, and VoIP (Voice over Internet Protocol) apps like Skype.

A similar set of controls appears at the *top* of the screen when you double-tap the Home button while your iPad is locked.

✔ **Scrubber bar and Playhead:** Drag the little dot (the *Playhead*) along the Scrubber bar to skip to any point within the track.

You can adjust the scrub rate by sliding your finger downward on the screen as you drag the Playhead along the Scrubber bar. Check out the section "The Way-Cool Hidden iTunes Scrub Speed Tip" in Chapter 18 for additional details. By the way, this slick trick also works in many other apps that use a Scrubber, most notably You Tube.

But wait, there's more. You see additional controls after you tap the album art in the Now Playing area near the lower-left corner of the screen. Now, tap anywhere on the artwork that fills the screen and several additional controls appear, as shown in Figure 8-5.

Earlier in this section, we explain how to use the volume control, Rewind/ Previous Track button, Play/Pause button, Fast Forward/Next Track button, and Scrubber bar/Playhead. They may look slightly different on this screen, but they work in exactly the same way.

Repeat   Shuffle

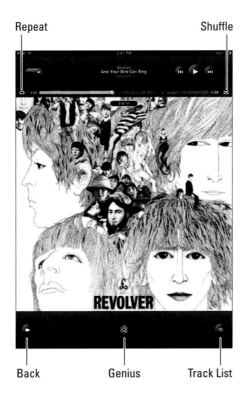

Back   Genius   Track List

Figure 8-5: You see these additional controls after you tap the album art in the Now Playing area.

The new controls you see are as follows:

✔ **Repeat:** Tap once to repeat all songs in the current *list* (that is, playlist, album, artist, composer, or genre) and play them all over and over. Tap again to repeat the current *song* again and again. Tap again to turn off repeat.

The button appears in blue after one tap, in blue with a little 1 inside after two taps, and in black and white when repeat is turned off.

✔ **Shuffle:** Tap this button to play songs at random; tap again to play songs in the order they appear onscreen.

✔ **Track List:** Tap this button to see all the tracks on the album that contains the song currently playing, as shown in Figure 8-6.

Tap any song on this list to play it. Or, swipe your finger across the dots just beneath the Scrubber bar to rate the song from one to five stars. In Figure 8-6, we've rated the song four stars.

Why would you want to assign star ratings to songs? One reason is that you can use star ratings to filter songs in iTunes on your Mac or PC. Another is that you can use them when you create Smart Playlists in iTunes. And last but not least, they look cool.

✔ **Genius:** This feature is so cool, we devote an entire section to it. See the section "It doesn't take a Genius," later in this chapter.

✔ **Back:** Tap this button to return to the previous screen.

Figure 8-6: We've given this tune a four (out of five) star rating.

A brief AirPlay interlude

There's one more icon that you may or may not see in your iPad's iPod app, and it's the AirPlay Selector icon, which appears in Figures 8-1 and 8-4.

But before we get into why you may or may not see it, we talk for a moment about *AirPlay*, which is a wicked-cool technology baked into every copy of iOS (version 4.2 or higher). AirPlay lets you wirelessly stream music, photos, and video to AirPlay-enabled devices such as Apple's AirPort Extreme, AirPort Express Wi-Fi base stations, and Apple TV, as well as third-party AirPlay-enabled devices including (but not limited to) speakers and HDTVs.

AirPlay Selector is a shy little icon that appears only if it detects an AirPlay-enabled device on the same Wi-Fi network. As it happens, Bob has an Apple TV in his den, so he sees the options in the following figure when he taps the AirPlay Selector icon.

Tapping Family Room Apple TV sends whatever is playing on the iPod app (Elton John's "All the

Girls Love Alice" in the figure) to the Apple TV in his den. The Apple TV is, in turn, connected to his home theatre audio system and HDTV via HDMI and/or optical audio cable.

But wait — there's more! If you use an Apple TV as your AirPlay-enabled device, you can also stream music, video, and photos from your Mac or PC or even from your iPhone (to your HDTV).

If you have an HDMI-equipped TV and/or a decent sound system and have decent Wi-Fi bandwidth, you'll love Apple TV.

Twiddling with podcast and audiobook controls

When what's playing is a podcast or audiobook, you see a somewhat different set of controls when you tap the cover art in the Now Playing area. (If you don't see the controls, tap the cover art to make them reappear.)

We explain the basic controls in the preceding section. The controls that are unique to podcasts and audiobooks, as shown in Figure 8-7, are as follows:

   ✔ **E-Mail (podcasts only):** Tap this button to send someone an e-mail link to this podcast.

✔ **Playback Speed:** Tap this button to toggle between normal speed (1X), double speed (2X), or half speed (½x).

✔ **30-Second Repeat:** Tap this button to hear the last 30 seconds of the podcast or audiobook.

E-mail   Playback speed

30-Second Repeat

Figure 8-7: These controls appear only when you listen to a podcast or audiobook.

It doesn't take a Genius

Genius selects songs from your music library that go great together. To use it, tap the Genius button, and your iPad generates a Genius playlist of 25 songs that it picked because it thinks they go well with the song that's playing.

To use the Genius feature on your iPad, you need to turn on Genius in iTunes on your computer and then sync your iPad at least once.

If you tap the Genius button on the main screen (see Figure 8-1) and no song is currently playing, an alphabetical list of songs appears, and you need to select a song before the Genius playlist can be generated.

When you create a Genius playlist, you find an item called Genius in your library list; tap it and you see the 25 songs that Genius selected. You see three buttons in the upper-right corner of the list:

   ✏ **New:** Select a different song to use as the basis for a Genius playlist.

   ✏ **Refresh:** See a list of 25 songs that "go great with" the song you're listening to (or the song you selected).

   ✏ **Save:** Save this Genius playlist so that you can listen to it whenever you like.

When you save a Genius playlist, it inherits the name of the song it's based upon and appears in your library with a Genius icon that looks like the Genius button. And the next time you sync your iPad, the Genius playlist magically appears in iTunes.

The less popular the song, artist, or genre, the more likely Genius will choke on it. When that happens, you see an alert that asks you to try again because this song doesn't have enough related songs to create a Genius playlist.

If you like the Genius feature, you can also create a new Genius playlist in iTunes and then sync it with your iPad.

Creating playlists

Playlists let you organize songs around a particular theme or mood: operatic arias, romantic ballads, British invasion — whatever. Younger folks sometimes call them *mixes.*

Your playlists appear in alphabetical order on the left side of the screen, below your music, podcasts, audiobooks, and iTunes U courses. If you don't see podcasts, audiobooks, and/or iTunes U in your library, don't worry. That merely means you don't have any podcasts, audiobooks, or iTunes U courses in your iPad's library. And don't worry if you don't have any playlists. Just know that if you had some, you'd see them here.

Although it may be easier to create playlists in iTunes on your computer, your iPad makes it relatively easy to create (and listen to) playlists:

   ✏ **To create a playlist on your iPad,** click the New Playlist (+) button (refer to Figure 8-1 for its location). You're asked to name your playlist. Do so and then tap Save. After you do this, you see a list of the songs on your iPad in alphabetical order. Tap the ones you want to have in this playlist, and they turn gray, as shown in Figure 8-8. When you've tapped every song you want in the list, tap the Done button just below the Search field.

✏ **To listen to a playlist,** tap its name in your library and you see a list of the songs it contains. If the list is longer than one screen, flick upward to scroll down. Tap a song in the list, and the song plays. When that song is over or you tap the Next Song button, the next song in the playlist plays. This continues until the last song in the playlist has played, at which point your iPad shuts up.

When you use any playlist — Smart, Genius, or Plain — you can tap the word *Shuffle* at the top of the playlist to hear a song from that playlist (and all subsequent songs) at random. When all songs in the playlist have been played, your iPad shuts up.

Although you can't create Smart Playlists on your iPad, they totally rock. What is a Smart Playlist? Glad you asked. A *Smart Playlist* is a special playlist that selects tracks based on criteria you specify, such as Artist Name, Date Added, Rating, Genre, Year, and many others. Fire up iTunes on your computer and choose File➪New Smart Playlist to get started.

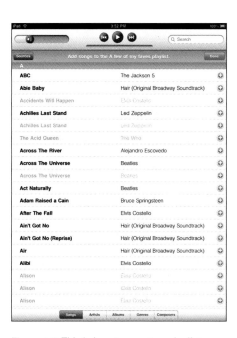

Figure 8-8: This is how to create a playlist on your iPad.

And that's all there is to selecting, creating, and playing songs in a playlist.

Customizing Volume and Equalizer Settings

You can tweak volume and equalizer settings to customize your iPad-as-an-iPod experience. If you've noticed and been bothered that the volume of some songs is higher than others, check out the iTunes Sound Check feature. If you want to adjust certain frequencies, the equalizer enables you to do so. And if you want to set a maximum volume limit, tell your iPad to make it so. The following sections explain how.

Play all songs at the same volume level

The iTunes Sound Check option automatically adjusts the level of songs so that they play at the same volume relative to each other. That way, one song never blasts out your ears even if the recording level is much louder than that of the song before or after it. To tell the iPad to use these volume settings, you first have to turn on the feature in iTunes on your computer. Here's how to do that:

1. **Choose iTunes⇨Preferences (Mac) or Edit⇨Preferences (PC).**

2. **Click the Playback tab.**

3. **Select the Sound Check check box to enable it.**

Now you need to tell the iPad to use the Sound Check settings from iTunes. Here's how to do *that:*

1. **Tap the Settings icon on the iPad's Home screen.**

2. **Tap iPod in the list of settings.**

3. **Tap the Sound Check On/Off switch so that it says On.**

Choose an equalizer setting

An *equalizer* increases or decreases the relative levels of specific frequencies to enhance the sound you hear. Some equalizer settings emphasize the bass (low end) notes in a song; other equalizer settings make the higher frequencies more apparent. The iPad has more than a dozen equalizer presets, with names such as Acoustic, Bass Booster, Bass Reducer, Dance, Electronic, Pop, and Rock. Each one is ostensibly tailored to a specific type of music.

The way to find out whether you prefer using equalization is to listen to music while trying different settings. To do that, first start listening to a song you like. Then, while the song is playing, follow these steps:

1. **Tap the Home button on the front of your iPad.**

2. **Tap the Settings icon on the Home screen.**

3. **Tap iPod in the list of settings.**

4. **Tap EQ in the list of iPod settings.**

5. **Tap different EQ presets (Pop, Rock, R&B, or Dance, for example), and listen carefully to the way they change how the song sounds.**

6. **When you find an equalizer preset that you think sounds good, tap the Home button and you're finished.**

If you don't like any of the presets, tap Off at the top of the EQ list to turn off the equalizer.

At the risk of giving away one of the tips in Chapter 18, we feel obliged to mention that you may get somewhat longer battery life if you keep EQ turned off.

Set a volume limit for music (and videos)

You can instruct your iPad to limit the loudest listening level for audio or video. To do so, here's the drill:

1. **Tap the Settings icon on the Home screen.**

2. **Tap iPod in the list of settings.**

3. **Tap Volume Limit in the list of iPod settings.**

4. **Drag the slider to adjust the maximum volume level to your liking.**

5. **(Optional) Tap Lock Volume Limit to assign a four-digit passcode to this setting so that others can't easily change it.**

The Volume Limit setting limits the volume of only music and videos; it doesn't apply to podcasts or audiobooks. And, although the setting works with any headset, headphones, or speakers plugged into the headset jack on your iPad, it doesn't affect sound played on your iPad's internal speaker.

By the way, speaking of that lone internal iPad speaker, it's not in stereo although it sounds pretty good just the same. Of course, when you plug in headphones, you hear rich stereo output.

Shopping with the iTunes App

Last but certainly not least, the iTunes application lets you use your iPad to download, buy, or rent just about anything you can download, buy, or rent with the iTunes application on your Mac or PC, including music, audiobooks, iTunes U classes, podcasts, and videos. And, if you're fortunate enough to have an iTunes gift card or gift certificate in hand, you can redeem it directly from your iPad.

If you want to do any of that, however, you must first sign in to your iTunes Store account:

1. **Tap the Settings icon on the Home screen.**
2. **Tap Store in the list of settings.**
3. **Tap Sign In.**
4. **Type your username and password.**

Or, in the unlikely event that you don't have an iTunes Store account already:

1. **Tap the Settings icon on the Home screen.**
2. **Tap Store in the list of settings.**
3. **Tap Create New Account.**
4. **Follow the onscreen instructions.**

After the iTunes Store knows who you are (and, more importantly, knows your credit card number), tap the iTunes icon on your Home screen and shop until you drop. It works almost exactly the same as the iTunes App Store, which you read about in Chapter 7.

iPad Video: Seeing Is Believing

*P*icture this scene: The smell of popcorn permeates the room as you and your family congregate to watch the latest Hollywood blockbuster. A motion picture soundtrack swells up. The images on the screen are stunning. And all eyes are fixed on the iPad.

Okay, here comes the reality check. The iPad is not going to replace a wall-sized high-definition television as the centerpiece of your home theater (though as you discover, you can watch material that originates on the iPad on the bigger screen). But we do want to emphasize that with its gorgeous, nearly 10-inch, high-definition display — one of the best we've seen on a handheld device — watching movies and other videos on the iPad can be a cinematic delight. The screen looks terrific even when you're not viewing it straight on.

What's more if you have the iPad 2, you now have front and rear cameras that can help turn you, under certain circumstances, into a filmmaker — right from the device.

And video on the iPad ventures into another area, video chat. You can keep in touch with friends and loved ones by gazing into each other's pupils. It's all done through a version of *FaceTime,* a clever video chat program built right into your tablet.

We get to FaceTime later in this chapter. For now, and without any further ado, we get on with the show!

Finding Stuff to Watch

You have a few main ways to find and watch videos on your iPad. You can fetch all sorts of fare from the iTunes Store, whose virtual doors you can open directly from the iPad.

Or, you can sync content that already resides on your Mac or PC. (If you haven't done so yet, now is as good a time as any to read Chapter 3 for all the details.)

The videos you can watch on the iPad generally fall into one of the following categories:

- ✔ **Movies, TV shows, and music videos that you purchase or fetch free in the iTunes Store:** You can watch these by tapping the Videos icon on the Home screen.

  The iTunes Store features dedicated sections for purchasing or renting episodes of TV shows (from *Glee* to *Modern Family*), as shown in Figure 9-1, and for buying or renting movies (from *Love and Other Drugs* to *127 Hours*), as shown in Figure 9-2.

Figure 9-1: Buying and watching TV on the iPad is gleeful.

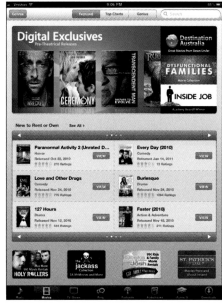

Figure 9-2: You can spend hours watching movies on the iPad.

Pricing varies but it's not atypical as of this writing to fork over $1.99 to pick up an episode of a popular TV show in standard definition or $2.99 for high-def versions. You can rent certain shows commercial-free for 99 cents. And a few shows are free. You can also purchase a complete season of a favorite show. The final season of a classic show, such as *Lost,* for example, costs $32.99 in standard-def and $49.99 in high-def.

Feature films fetch prices from $9.99 to $19.99.

You can also rent some movies, typically for $2.99, $3.99, or $4.99. We're not wild about current rental restrictions — you have 30 days to begin watching a rented flick and a day to finish watching after you've started, though you can watch as often you want during the 24-hour period. But that's showbiz for you. Such films appear in their own Rented Movies section in the video list, which you get to by tapping Videos. The number of days before your rental expires displays. And you have to completely download a movie onto your iPad before you can start watching it.

As shown in Figure 9-3, by tapping a movie listing in iTunes, you can generally preview a trailer before buying (or renting) and check out additional tidbits: the plot summary, credits, reviews, and customer ratings, as well as other movies that appealed to the buyer of this one. And you can search films by genre or top charts (the ones other people are buying or renting), or rely on the Apple Genius feature for recommendations based on stuff you've already watched. (Genius works for movies and TV much the way it works for music, as we explain in Chapter 8.)

Figure 9-3: Bone up on a movie before buying or renting it.

✔ **The boatload of video podcasts, just about all free, featured in the iTunes Store:** Podcasts started out as another form of Internet radio, although instead of listening to live streams, you download files onto your computer or iPod to take in at your leisure. You can still find lots of audio podcasts, but the focus here is on video. You can watch free episodes that cover *Sesame Street* videos, sports programming, investing strategies, political shows (across the ideological spectrum), and so much more.

✔ **Videos that play via entertainment apps:** For example, Netflix offers an app that enables you to use your Netflix subscription, if you have one, to stream video on your iPad. We like it so much, it made our list of favorites in Chapter 16. Similarly, the ABC television network offers an appealing app so that you can catch up on its shows on your iPad. The Hulu Plus subscription app also lets you catch up on favorite TV.

✔ **Seminars at Harvard, Stanford, or numerous other prestigious institutions:** iTunes U boasts more than 250,000 free lectures from around the world, many of them videos. Better yet, you get no grades, and you don't have to apply for admission, write an essay, or do homework. Figure 9-4 shows the iTunes U description for Open University's The Galapagos, one of the learned videos we watched. Bring on our sheepskins.

✔ **Homegrown videos from the popular YouTube Internet site:** Apple obviously thinks highly of YouTube because it devoted a dedicated Home screen icon to the site. You can read more on YouTube's special status on the iPad in Chapter 6.

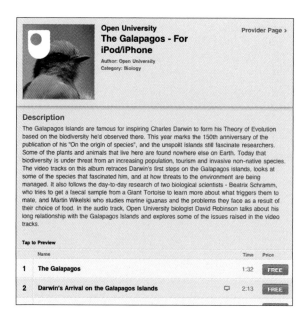

Figure 9-4: Get smart. iTunes U offers a slew of lectures on diverse topics.

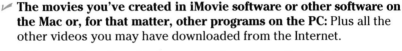

✔ **The movies you've created in iMovie software or other software on the Mac or, for that matter, other programs on the PC:** Plus all the other videos you may have downloaded from the Internet.

✔ **Videos you've given birth to using the rear- or front-facing camera on the iPad 2:** Oh, and there's now a version of iMovie made especially for the iPad 2. The optional app costs $4.99. Check out the "Shooting Your Own Videos" section, later in this chapter, for direction on creating movies with iPad 2.

You may have to prepare some videos so that they'll play on your iPad. To do so, highlight the video in question after it resides in your iTunes library. In iTunes choose Advanced⇨Create iPad or Apple TV Version. Alas, creating an iPad version of a video doesn't work for all the video content you download off the Internet, including video files in the AVI, DivX, MKV, and Xvid formats.

For a somewhat technical workaround without potential conversion hassles, try the $2.99 Air Video app from InMethod s.r.o. The utility app can deliver AVI, DivX, MKV, and other videos that wouldn't ordinarily play on your iPad. You can also check out a free version. You have to download Air Video server software on your Mac or PC to stream content to your iPad.

For more on compatibility, check out the nearby "Are we compatible?" sidebar (but read it at your own risk).

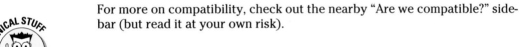

Are we compatible?

The iPad works with a whole bunch of video, although not everything you'll want to watch will make it through. Several Internet video standards — notably Adobe Flash — are not supported.

The absence of Flash is a bugaboo because Flash is the technology behind much of the video on the web.

Apple backs other standards — HTML5, CSS 3, and JavaScript — and is apparently sensitive enough to the issue that in the early days of the iPad, Apple made mention of several sites where video *would* play on the iPad. The list included CNN, The New York Times, Vimeo, Time, ESPN, Major League Baseball, NPR, The White House, Sports Illustrated, TED, Nike, CBS, Spin, and National Geographic. What's more, entertainment apps from Netflix and ABC help fill the TV/movie void as well.

With the appropriate utility software, you might also be able to convert some nonworking video to an iPad-friendly format on your computer. But if something doesn't play now, it may in the future because Apple has the capability to upgrade the iPad through software.

In the meantime, you can find a description of the video formats that iPad supports on Apple's website; point your browser to www.apple.com/ipad/specs.

Playing Video

Now that you know what you want to watch, here's how to watch it:

1. **On the Home screen, tap the Videos icon.**

   Videos stored on your iPad are segregated by category — Movies, Rented Movies, TV Shows, Podcasts, Music Videos, iTunes U, and Shared. For each category, you see the program's poster art, as shown in Figure 9-5. Categories such as Rented Movies, Podcasts, and iTunes U appear only if you have that type of content loaded on the machine. Ditto for the Shared category, which is enabled if you take advantage of iTunes Home Sharing, a feature we discuss in Chapter 8. You can use iTunes Home Sharing to watch videos that reside in the iTunes library on your Mac or PC as well.

2. **At the top of the screen, select the tab that corresponds to the type of video you want to watch.**

Movies

TV Shows

Music Videos

iTunes U

Figure 9-5: Choosing the movie, TV show, lecture, or music video to watch from Ed's Shared library.

3. **Tap the poster that represents the movie, TV show, or other video you want to watch.**

   You see a full description of the movie you want to watch, along with a listing of cast and filmmakers, as shown in Figure 9-6. Tap the Chapters tab to browse the chapters. You see thumbnail images and the length of the chapter. Tap the Info tab to return to a description.

4. **To start playing a movie (or resume playing from where you left off), tap the Play button, labeled in Figure 9-6.**

   Alternatively, from the Chapters view (see Figure 9-7), tap any chapter to start playing from that point.

   If you go to Settings from the Home screen and tap Video, you can change the default setting to start playing from where you left off to start playing from the beginning.

5. **(Optional) Rotate your iPad to landscape mode to maximize a movie's display.**

Play movie

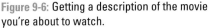
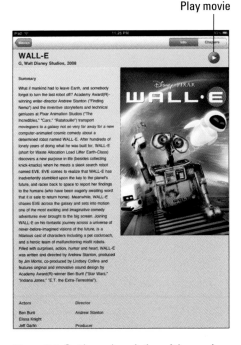

Figure 9-6: Getting a description of the movie you're about to watch.

Figure 9-7: Start playing from any chapter.

If you hold the iPad in portrait mode, you can see black bars on top of and below the screen where the movie is playing. Those bars remain when you rotate the device to its side, but the iPad plays the film in a wider-screen mode.

For movies, this is a great thing. You can watch flicks as the filmmaker intended, in a cinematic *aspect ratio*.

The iPad doesn't give you a full high-definition presentation because that requires 1280-x-720-pixel resolution and the iPad's screen is 1024 x 768, meaning that it's scaled down slightly. Having said that, we don't think too many viewers are going to complain or even notice about the quality of the images.

Finding and Working the Video Controls

While a video is playing, tap the screen to display the controls shown in Figure 9-8. Then you can tap a control to activate it. Here's what each of the controls can do:

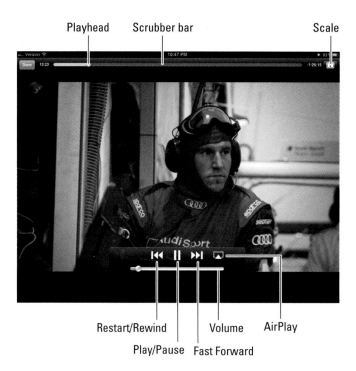

Figure 9-8: Controlling the video.

✐ **To play or pause the video,** tap the Play/Pause button.

✐ **To adjust the volume,** drag the volume slider to the right to raise the volume and to the left to lower it. Alternatively, use the physical Volume buttons to control the audio levels.

✐ **To restart or go back,** tap the Restart/Rewind button to restart the video, or tap and hold the same button to rewind.

✐ **To skip forward,** tap and hold Fast Forward to advance the video. Or, skip ahead by dragging the playhead along the Scrubber bar.

✐ **To set how the video fills the screen,** tap the Scale button, which toggles between filling the entire screen with video or fitting the video to the screen. Alternatively, you can double-tap the video to go back and forth between fitting and filling the screen. You see this button or can double-tap to change the scale only when the iPad is in landscape mode.

Fitting the video to the screen displays the film in its theatrical aspect ratio. Again, you may see black bars above or below the video (or to its sides), which some people don't like. *Filling* the entire screen with the video may crop or trim the sides or top of the picture, so you don't see the complete scene that the director shot.

✐ **To select language and subtitle settings,** tap the Audios and Subtitles button. You see options to select a different language, turn on or hide subtitles, and turn on or hide closed captioning. The control appears only if the movie supports any of these features or if you've turned on closed captioning choosing Settings⇨Video.

✐ **To make the controls go away,** tap the screen again (or just wait for them to go away on their own).

✐ **To tell your iPad you're done watching a video,** tap Done. You return to the last Videos screen that was visible before you started watching the movie.

Watching Video on a Big TV

We love watching movies on the iPad, but we also recognize the limitations of a smaller screen. For starters, friends won't crowd around to watch with you. As good as it is, the iPad screen doesn't match the HDTV in your living room, so Apple offers two ways to display video from your iPad to a TV:

✐ **AirPlay:** Through the AirPlay feature, you can wirelessly stream movies — commercial flicks or videos you shot — as well as photos and music from the iPad to an Apple TV box that's connected to an HDTV. Start watching the movie on the iPad and tap the AirPlay button that appears in the video controls (refer to Figure 9-8). You can watch only one screen at a time. Tap Apple TV to stream to the TV through the Apple TV box. Tap iPad to watch on the iPad.

You can multitask while streaming a video. Therefore, while the kids are watching a flick on the TV, you can surf the web or catch up on e-mail.

Although you can stream from an iPad to an Apple TV and switch screens between the two, you can't stream a movie that you start watching on Apple TV to the iPad.

✔ **Digital AV Adapter and HDMI cable:** Apple sells a $39 Digital AV Adapter accessory that lets you connect the iPad or iPad 2 to a high-definition television, projector, or other device that has an HDMI port. The adaptor lets you *mirror* the iPad screen on the connected TV or projector. So you can watch a movie, or for that matter, view anything else that's on the tablet screen: web pages, apps, you name it. You have to supply your own HDMI cable. For more on accessories, check out Chapter 15.

Restricting Video Usage

If you've given an iPad to your kid or someone who works for you, you may not want that person spending time watching movies or television. You might want him to do something more productive, such as homework or the quarterly budget. That's where parental restrictions come in. Please note that the use of this iron-fist tool can make you really unpopular.

Tap Settings➪General➪Restrictions➪Enable Restrictions. You're asked to establish or enter a previously established passcode. Twice. Having done so you can set restrictions based on movie ratings (PG, R, and so on) and TV shows. You can also restrict FaceTime usage or use of the camera (which when turned off also turns off FaceTime). For more on restrictions, flip to Chapter 13, where we explain the stings for controlling (and loosening) access to iPad features.

Deleting Video from Your iPad

Video takes up space — lots of space. After the closing credits roll and you no longer want to keep a video on your iPad, here's what you need to know about deleting video:

✔ To delete a video manually, tap and hold its movie poster until the small circled x shows up on the poster. To confirm your intention, tap the larger Delete button that appears or tap Cancel if you change your mind.

▶ Deleting a movie from the iPad only removes it from the iPad. It remains in the iTunes library on your Mac or PC, assuming you synced it to your computer in the first place. That means if you want to watch it on your iPad again in the future, you can do so, as long as you sync it again.

▶ If you delete a rented movie before watching it on your iPad, it's gone. You have to spend (more) loot if you hope to watch it in the future on the iPad.

Shooting Your Own Videos

The iPad 2 is the first iPad with a camera — um two cameras to be more precise. The rear camera can record video up to the high-definition techie standard of 720p and at 30 frames-per-second (fps), or *full motion video*. Come again? That's a fancy way to say the video ought to play back smoothly. The front camera can also perform at 30 fps, but the VGA (*video graphics array*) quality isn't quite as good.

Now that we've dispensed with that little piece of business, here's how to shoot video on the iPad:

1. **Tap the Camera icon on the Home screen.**

2. **Drag the little onscreen button at the bottom-right corner of the display from the camera position to the video camera position.**

   The button is labeled in Figure 9-9. The camera button is for stills, a subject we cover in Chapter 10.

   You can't switch from the front to the rear camera or vice versa while you're capturing a scene. So before shooting anything, think about which camera you want to use and then tap the front/rear camera button at the top-right corner of the screen when you've made your choice.

3. **Tap the red record bottom at the bottom center to begin shooting a scene.**

4. **Tap the red record button again to stop recording.**

   Your video is automatically saved to the Camera Roll, alongside any other saved videos and digital stills.

Editing what you shot

We assume you captured some really great footage, but you probably shot some stuff that belongs on the cutting room floor as well. No big whoop because you can perform simple edits right on your iPad 2. Remember to tap the Camera Roll at the bottom-left corner of the Camera app to find your recordings. Then:

Front/Rear Camera

Camera Roll   Start/Stop video capture   Camera/Video switch

Figure 9-9: Lights, camera, action.

1. **Tap a video recording to display the onscreen controls, as shown in Figure 9-10.**

2. **Drag the start and end points along the timeline to select only the video you want to keep.**

   Hold your finger over the section to expand the timeline to make it easier to apply your edits. Tap the Play button to preview your surgery.

3. **Choose what to do with your trimmed clip:**

   - Tap *Trim Original* to permanently remove scenes from the original clip.

   - Tap *Save as New Clip* to create a newly trimmed video clip; the original video remains intact, and the new clip is stored in the Camera Roll.

   - Tap *Cancel* to start over.

For more ambitious editing on the iPad 2, consider iMovie for iPad, a $4.99 app that resembles a bare-bones version of iMovie for Mac computers. Through iMovie, you can export your finished video to YouTube, Vimeo, and Facebook.

Figure 9-10: Getting a trim.

Sharing video

Unlike other video on your iPad, you can play back what you've just shot in portrait or landscape mode. And if the video is any good, you likely want to share it with a wider audience. To do so, display the playback controls by tapping the screen and then tap the icon that resembles an arrow trying to escape a rectangle. From here you can e-mail the video, send it to YouTube (see Chapter 6), or copy it.

Seeing Is Believing with FaceTime

We bet you can come up with a lengthy list of people you'd love to be able to eyeball in real time from afar. Maybe it's your old college roommate. Maybe it's your old college sweetheart. And maybe it's your grandparents, who've long since retired to warm climates somewhere.

That's the beauty of *FaceTime,* the video chat app on the iPad 2. FaceTime exploits the two cameras built into the device, each serving a different purpose. The front camera lets you talk face to face. The back camera shows the person you're talking to what you're seeing.

To take advantage of FaceTime, here's what you need:

- **Access to Wi-Fi:** And the people you're talking to need Internet access, too. On an iOS device, you need Wi-Fi. On a Mac, you need an upstream or downstream Internet connection of at least 128 Kbps. You also need at least a 1 Mbps upstream and downstream connection for HD-quality video calls.

- **FaceTime:** On your conversation partner's own iPad 2, on an Intel-based Mac computer, on a recent model iPod touch, or an iPhone 4 (FaceTime first appeared on Apple's prized smartphone).

The iPad's large inviting screen would seem to be made for FaceTime, but we'd be remiss if we didn't point out that some critics have been underwhelmed by the quality of the cameras. We think the cameras do just fine for FaceTime, at least with halfway decent lighting and a robust Wi-Fi connection.

Getting started with FaceTime

When you use FaceTime for the first time, after you tap the app's icon from the Home screen, you're required to sign in to FaceTime using your Apple ID, which can be your iTunes Store account, MobileMe account, or another Apple account. If you don't have an account, tap Create New Account to set one up within FaceTime. You also must supply an e-mail address that callers use to call you from their own FaceTime-capable iPads, Macs, iPhones, or iPod touches.

If this is the first time you've used a particular e-mail address for FaceTime, Apple sends an e-mail to that address to verify the account. Click (or tap) Verify Now and enter your Apple ID and password to complete the FaceTime setup. If the e-mail address resides in Mail on the iPad, you're already good to go.

If you have multiple e-mail addresses, callers can use any of them for FaceTime. To add an e-mail address after the initial setup, tap Settings⇨FaceTime⇨Add another Email.

You can turn FaceTime on or off within Settings, but if you don't turn it off, you don't have to sign back in when you launch the app.

Making a FaceTime call

Now the real fun begins — making an actual call.

Follow these steps:

1. **Start the FaceTime app from the Home screen.**

   You can check out what you look like in a window prior to making a FaceTime call. So powder your nose and put on a happy face.

2. **Choose someone to call. Pick among:**

   - *Your Contacts:* Tap a name or number, and then tap the e-mail address or phone number they have associated with FaceTime. To add a contact, tap Contacts and tap +.

   - *Your recent calls:* Tap Recents and then tap the appropriate number or name.

   - *Your favorites:* You can add frequent callers to a favorites list. Once again merely tap a name to call.

3. **Check or change what you display on the screen if needed.**

   When a call is underway, you can still see what you look like to the other person through a small picture-in-picture window that you can drag to any corner of the video call window. It's a great way to know if your mug has dropped out of sight.

4. **(Optional) To toggle among the front and rear cameras, tap the camera button that is also labeled in Figure 9-11.**

5. **Tap End when you're ready to hang up.**

While you're on a FaceTime call, the following tips are handy to know:

- ✔ **Rotate the iPad to its side to change the orientation.**

- ✔ **Silence or mute a call by tapping the Microphone icon (labeled in Figure 9-11).** Be aware that you can still be seen even if not heard (and you can still see and hear the other person).

✔ **Momentarily check out another iPad app by pressing the Home button and then tapping the icon for the app you have in mind.** At this juncture, you can still talk over FaceTime, but you can no longer see the person. Tap the green bar at the top of the iPad screen to bring the person and the FaceTime app back in front of you.

Call window shows   How you look
who you're talking to   to other person

Mute Voice   Switch Cameras

Hang up

Figure 9-11: Bob can see Ed, and Ed can see Bob in FaceTime.

Receiving a FaceTime call

Of course, you can get FaceTime calls as well as make them. FaceTime doesn't have to be open for you to receive a video call. Here's how incoming calls work:

✔ **Hearing the call:** When a call comes in, the caller's name prominently displays on the iPad's screen, as shown in Figure 9-12. You simultaneously hear the phone ring.

✏ **Accepting or declining the call:** Tap Accept to answer the call or Decline if you'd rather not. If your iPad is locked when a FaceTime call comes in, slide the green arrow button to the right to answer. To decline it, do nothing and wait for the caller to give up.

✏ **Silencing the ring:** You can press the Sleep/Wake button at the top of the iPad to silence the incoming ring. If you know you don't want to be disturbed by FaceTime calls before the phone even rings, flip the side switch on the iPad 2 to mute. Make sure you're using the side switch as a mute control rather than as a rotation lock. Otherwise head to Settings (see Chapter 13) to change the function of this switch back to mute.

Figure 9-12: Tap Accept to answer the call.

And with that, we hereby silence this chapter. But there's more to do with the cameras on your iPad 2. And we get to that in Chapter 10.

You Oughta Be in Pictures

*T*hroughout this book, we sing the praises of the iPad's vibrant multitouch display. You'd be hard-pressed to find a more appealing portable screen for watching movies or playing games. As you might imagine, the iPad you have recently purchased (or are lusting after) is also a spectacular photo viewer. Images are crisp and vivid, at least those that were properly shot by you. (C'mon, we know Ansel Adams is a distant cousin.)

What's more, if you snapped up an iPad 2, you can shoot some of those pictures directly with your prized tablet. The reasons, of course, are the front and rear cameras built into the device. If you read Chapter 9, you already know you can put those cameras to work capturing video. In this chapter, you get the big picture on shooting still images.

Okay, we need to get a couple of things out of the way: The iPad is never going to substitute for a point-and-shoot digital camera, much less a pricey digital SLR. As critics, we can quibble about the grainy images you get shooting in low light or the fact that there's no flash.

But we're here, friends, to focus on the positive. And having cameras on your iPad may prove to be a godsend when no better option is available. And we can think of certain circumstances — selling real estate, say, or shopping for a new home — where tablet cameras are quite convenient.

Meanwhile, you're in for a real treat if you're new to *Photo Booth,* a yuk-it-up Mac program that makes its way onto the iPad 2. That may be the best, or at least the most fun, use of the cameras yet.

We get to Photo Booth at the end of this chapter. But over the next few pages, you discover the best ways to make the digital photos on the iPad come alive, no matter how they managed to arrive on your machine.

Shooting Pictures

To start shooting pictures on the iPad 2, tap the Camera icon on the Home screen. The screen resembles a closed camera shutter. When that shutter opens an instant later, you're peering through one of the largest viewfinders imaginable in the near 10-inch display of the iPad 2. Here's what to do next:

1. **For the purposes of this exercise, make sure the Camera/Video switch at the bottom-right corner of the screen (and shown in Figure 10-1) is turned to Camera mode. If not, slide the switch from right to left.**

2. **Use the viewfinder to frame your image.**

3. **Tap the portion of the screen in which you see the face or object you want as the image's focal point.**

   A small square (not shown in Figure 10-1) surrounds your selection, and the iPad automatically adjusts the exposure of that part of the image.

4. **(Optional) To zoom in or out, tap the screen and drag the slider.**

   The iPad 2 has a 5X digital zoom, which basically crops and resizes an image. Such zooms are nowhere near as effective quality-wise as optical zooms on many digital cameras. Be aware that zooming works only with the rear camera still in Camera mode; it doesn't work with the front camera or when you shoot video.

5. **To toggle among the front and rear cameras, tap the front/rear camera button (see Figure 10-1) on the upper-right corner of the screen.**

6. **When you're satisfied and ready to snap an image, tap the camera button on the bottom of the screen.**

   You hear a shutter sound unless you turned the side switch to silent, as we explain in Chapter 1.

The image you shoot lands in the Camera Roll at the bottom-left corner of the screen. We explain what you can do with the images on the iPad later in this chapter.

Front/Rear camera

Camera Roll

Camera/Video switch

Figure 10-1: Using the iPad 2 as a camera.

Importing Pictures

Even in the absence of a digital camera on the original iPad, you'll discover a few ways to add pictures to the iPad. (Obviously, you can employ these strategies on the iPad 2, too.) Alas, one of the methods involves buying an accessory. We zoom in in the following sections.

Syncing pix

We devote an entire chapter (see Chapter 3) to synchronizing data with the iPad, so we don't dwell on it here. But because syncing pictures is still the most common way to import images to the iPad, we'd be remiss for not mentioning it in this chapter. (The assumption in this section is that you already know how to get pictures onto your computer.)

Quickie reminder: On a Mac, you can sync photos (and videos) via iPhoto software version 6.06 or later and Aperture 3.02 or later. On a PC, you can sync with Adobe Photoshop Elements 8.0 or later. Alternatively, with both computers, you can sync with any folder that contains pictures.

When the iPad is connected to your computer, click the Photos tab on the iPad Device page in iTunes on the Mac or PC. Then select the appropriate check boxes to specify the Albums, Events, and Faces you want to synchronize. Or, select All Photos, Albums, Events, and Faces if you have ample storage on the iPad to accommodate them all.

So what are Events and Faces anyway? Here's a quick look at these staple features in iPhoto on the Mac:

- **Events:** In their infinite wisdom, the folks at Apple figured that most pictures shot on a given day are tied to a specific occasion, such as Junior's birthday party or a wedding ceremony. So the iPhoto program on a Mac automatically groups them as such by placing all the pictures taken on that day into a single collection. Don't worry: You can split a day's worth of pictures into more than one event, if say, the birthday party was in the morning and the wedding was at night. Apple automatically names an event by its date; you can change it to something more descriptive (such as Timmy's Softball Game or Geri's Graduation).

- **Faces:** As its name implies, Faces is a collection of pictures on a single common thread: Whose mug is in them. In our experience with Faces, the technology, although pretty darn impressive, isn't perfect.

Connecting a digital camera or memory card

Almost all the digital cameras we're aware of come with a USB cable that can be used to transfer images to a computer. Of course, the iPad isn't a regular computer, and it isn't equipped with a USB port.

Instead, Apple sells an optional $29 iPad Camera Connection Kit; here's how it works:

1. **Connect your camera to your iPad using one of the two connectors in the kit.**

   Two small connectors are included, and each fits into the iPad's dock connector at the bottom of the machine. One connector has a USB port, the other an SD slot.

   If you're going the USB route, kindly use the cable that comes with your camera because no such cable comes with Apple's kit.

2. **Make sure that the iPad is unlocked.**

3. **If you haven't already done so, turn on the camera and ensure that it's set to transfer pictures.**

   Consult the manual that came with the camera if you're unsure of which setting to use.

   The Photos app on the iPad opens and displays the pictures that you can import from the camera.

4. **Tap Import All to select the entire bunch or tap the individual pictures you want to include if you'd rather cherry-pick.**

   A check mark appears next to each image you select. And that's pretty much it: The Pad organizes the pictures into albums and such, as we describe later in this chapter.

You're free at this point to erase the pictures from your camera.

The SD Card Reader connector accommodates the SD memory cards common to so many digital camera models. The procedure works almost identically to the USB connector, except you're inserting the SD gizmo into the dock connector port rather than the USB connector mentioned previously. Just be careful to insert the SD gently, to prevent any damage.

The Camera Connection Kit supports many common photo formats, including JPEG and Raw. The latter is a format favored by photo enthusiasts.

Saving images from e-mails and the web

You can save pictures that arrive in e-mails or pictures that you come across on the web very easily: Just press and hold your finger against the image, and then tap Save Image when the button pops up a second later. Pictures are stored in a Saved Photos album on the original iPad or in the Camera Roll on the iPad 2.

Where Have All My Pictures Gone?

So where exactly do your pictures hang out on the iPad? Well, we explain in the preceding section what happens to images saved from e-mails and the Internet: They reside in a Saved Photos album on the original iPad or the Camera Roll on the iPad 2. (We wanted to see whether you were paying attention.)

Other imported images are grouped in the same albums as they were on the computer, or lumped together as Events, Faces, and — when the embedded *metadata* inside an image identifies where a picture was shot — under a very cool Places feature. We have more to say about Places later in this chapter.

So now that you know where the pictures are, you're ready to discover how best to display them and share them with others — and how to dispose the duds that don't measure up to your lofty photographic standards.

Get ready to literally get your fingers on the pics (without worrying about smudging them). The following steps walk you through the basics of navigating among your pictures with the Photos app:

1. **Tap the Photos app on the Home screen.**

   The app opens with a grid of thumbnail images on top of a black background, as shown in Figure 10-2. The Photos tab at the top of the screen is highlighted because you're in the Photos view. If the thumbnail you have in mind doesn't appear on this screen, flick your finger up or down to scroll through the pictures rapidly or use a slower dragging motion to pore through the images more deliberately. So, if you have more photos than can possibly show up on the screen at any one time, which is highly probable, your flicking or dragging skills will improve quickly.

2. **Tap or pinch the photo you want to display.**

   These lead to slightly different outcomes. When you *tap* an image, the picture rapidly gets bigger, practically jumping off the screen. If you *pinch* or *unpinch* instead, by putting your thumb and forefinger together and then spreading them apart, you have more control over how the image shrinks or grows in size. You can also keep your finger pressed against the image to drag it around.

3. **To navigate through collections of images, tap Albums, Events, Faces, or Places at the top of your iPad screen. Or pinch them.**

   You see stacks or collections of pictures. Tap an album, event, or faces pile, and all the underlying pictures scatter into a mass of individual images. It's an orderly escape because the individual pictures once again appear in a grid. Most likely, you'll again have to scroll up or down to see all the pictures in the collection. As before, tap any of the individual pictures you want to focus on.

But what if you unpinch a collection instead of tapping? The answer depends on how you pinched. If you pinched just a little bit, the pictures spread out slowly enough that you can preview some of the images in the pile. Let go, and the collection opens (unless, that is, you hadn't pinched far enough, and the images retreat into a stack). If you do a *wider pinch* by spreading your fingers even more, the entire collection opens. As before, tap a picture to see a large view of it.

4. **With an individual photo on the screen, tap the picture to open the picture controls at the top and bottom of the screen.**

    These are shown in Figure 10-3. We discuss what they do later but want you to know how to summon them, because we're certain at some point or another you'll be calling on them.

5. **To make the controls disappear, tap the screen again; or just wait a few seconds, and they go away on their own.**

6. **Tap the Home button when you're finished with the Photos app.**

Figure 10-2: The landing spot for photos.

Number of photos
in current album

Tap to e-mail,
send to MobileMe,
assign to contact,
use as wallpaper,
print, or copy

Tap to return
to Album view

Tap to see
a slideshow

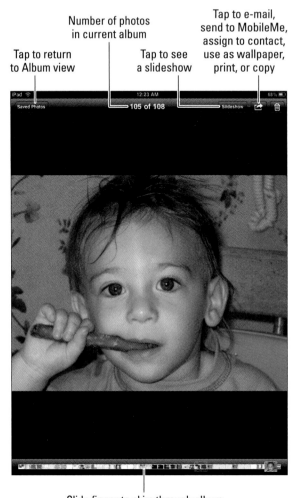

Slide finger to skim through album

Figure 10-3: Picture controls.

Admiring Pictures

Photographs are meant to be seen, of course, not buried in the digital equivalent of a shoebox. And, the iPad affords you some neat ways to manipulate, view, and share your best photos.

You've no doubt already figured out (from the preceding section) how to find a photo, view it full-screen, and display picture controls. But you can do a lot of maneuvering of your pictures without summoning those controls. Here are some options:

✓ **Skip ahead or view the previous picture:** Flick your finger left or right.

✓ **Landscape or portrait:** The iPad's wizardry (or, more specifically, the device's accelerometer sensor) is at work. When you turn the iPad sideways, the picture automatically reorients itself from portrait to landscape mode, as the images in Figure 10-4 show. Pictures shot in landscape mode fill the screen when you rotate the iPad. Rotate the device back to portrait mode, and the picture readjusts accordingly.

The screen orientation lock to the left of the iPad controls in the multitasking tray (see Chapter 2) must be switched off.

Figure 10-4: The same picture in portrait (left) and landscape (right) modes.

Show a picture to a friend by flipping the iPad over. The iPad always knows which is right side up.

✓ **Zoom:** Double-tap to zoom in on part of an image. Double-tap again to zoom out. Alternatively, spread and pinch with your thumb and index finger to zoom in and zoom out. The downside to zooming is that you can't see the entire image.

✓ **Pan and scroll:** This cool little feature is practically guaranteed to make you the life of the party. After you zoom in on a picture, drag it around the screen with your finger. Besides impressing your friends, you can bring front and center the part of the image you most care about. That lets you zoom in on Fido's adorable face as opposed to, say, the unflattering picture of the person holding the dog in his lap.

✔ **Skim:** A bar appears at the bottom of the screen when you summon picture controls. Drag your finger across the bar in either direction to quickly view all the pictures in an open album.

✔ **Map it:** If you tap the Places tab instead of an album, or event or faces collection, a map like the one shown in Figure 10-5 appears. Notice the red pins on the map shown at the left. These indicate that pictures were taken in the location shown on the map. Now tap a pin, and a stack of all the images on the iPad shot in that area appears, as shown in the image on the right. As before, you can tap or pinch the collection to open it.

The iPad 2 is pretty smart when it comes to geography. So as long as Location Services are turned on in Settings and the specific Location settings (also under Location Services in Settings) for the camera are turned on, pictures you take with the iPad 2 cameras are *geotagged*, or identified by where they were shot.

Think long and hard before permitting images to be geotagged if you plan on sharing those images with people for whom you want to keep your address and other locations private.

Figure 10-5: Mapping out your pictures.

You can spread your fingers on a map to enlarge it and narrow the pictures taken to a particular area, town, or even neighborhood. For more on Maps, flip to Chapter 6.

Launching Slide Shows

Those who store a lot of photographs on computers are familiar with running slide shows of those images. You can easily replicate the experience on the iPad, and through AirPlay, stream the slide show wirelessly to an Apple TV, or lacking that device, via an optional cable that connects to a TV or projector:

1. **Open an album by tapping it or display all your photos in the Photos view.**

2. **Tap the Slideshow button in the upper-right corner of the screen.**

   The Slideshow Options window, as shown in Figure 10-6 appears. We explore these and other options in the next section. But if you just want to start the slide show from here, continue to Step 3.

3. **Tap Start Slideshow.**

   Your only obligation is to enjoy the show.

Figure 10-6: Tap the Slideshow button to see slide show options.

Adding special slide show effects

Both the Settings options and the Slideshow button enable you to add special effects to your slide shows. Under Settings, you can alter the length of time each slide is shown, change the transition effects between pictures, and display images in random order. With Slideshow Options, you can add transitions and music.

From the Home screen, tap Settings⇨Photos. Then tap any of the following to make changes:

- **Play Each Slide For:** You have five choices (2 seconds, 3 seconds, 5 seconds, 10 seconds, and 20 seconds). When you're finished, tap the Photos button to return to the main Settings screen for Photos.

- **Repeat:** If this option is turned on, the slide show continues to loop until you stop it. The Repeat control may be counterintuitive. If Off displays, tap it to turn on the Repeat function. If On displays, tap it to turn off the Repeat function.

- **Shuffle:** Turning on this feature plays slides in random order. As with the Repeat feature, tap Off to turn on shuffle or tap On to turn off random playback.

Tap the Home button to leave Settings and return to the Home screen.

To select transitions and music for your slide shows, tap the Slideshow button to select options (refer to Figure 10-6):

- **Transitions:** You can change the effect you see when you move from one slide to the next. Again, you have five cool choices (Cube, Dissolve, Ripple, Wipe, or a personal favorite of ours, *Origami,* in which the images fold out in ways similar to the Japanese folk art of paper folding). Why not try them all to see what you like? Tap the Photos button when you're finished.

- **Music:** Adding music to a slide show couldn't be easier. From the Slideshow Options window, tap the Play Music option so that it's turned on. Then tap Music to choose your soundtrack from the songs stored on the device. Ed loves backing up slide shows with Sinatra, Sarah Vaughan, or Gershwin, among numerous other artists. Bob loves using Beatles songs or stately classical music.

Admiring pictures on the TV

The AirPlay feature that lets you stream music and videos from the iPad to an Apple TV (see Chapter 9) works with photos, too.

To watch the slide show (or view individual pictures) on a big screen TV via Apple TV, tap the AirPlay button shown in the upper-right corner of Figure 10-3 and then tap Apple TV from the list. If the AirPlay button isn't visible, make sure the iPad and Apple share the same Wi-Fi network. Tap the iPad button to view the slide show again on the iPad. We can tell you the experience is very cool.

Turning the iPad into a picture frame

Even when the iPad is locked, it can do something special — turn into a handsome animated digital picture frame, a variation on the slide show feature. To turn on this feature, tap the Picture Frame icon in the lower-right corner of the Lock screen.

Inside Picture Frame Settings, reachable like all other settings when you tap the Settings icon on the Home screen, you can choose one of two transitions (Dissolve or Origami), turn a "zoom in on faces" feature on or off, and arrange to play slides in random or shuffle mode. And, of course, you can pick the albums, faces, or events to include in your slide show.

To truly take advantage of the frame feature, prop up the iPad so that you can see it by using Apple's optional $29 iPad Dock on the original iPad or the Smart Cover accessory that's usable with the iPad 2.

You can pause or stop a slide show by tapping the Picture Frame icon or sliding the slider to unlock the iPad. To disable the feature altogether, tap General under Settings, tap Passcode Lock so that it's on (you have to enter your passcode at this point, if you have one), and tap Picture Frame so that the setting is off.

More (Not So) Stupid Picture Tricks

You can take advantage of the photos on the iPad in a few more ways. In each case, you tap the picture and make sure that the picture controls are displayed. Then tap the icon in the upper-right corner that looks like an arrow trying to escape from a rectangle. That displays the choices shown in Figure 10-3.

Here's what each choice does:

- **Email Photo:** Some photos are so precious that you just have to share them with family members and friends. When you tap Email Photo, the picture is automatically embedded in the body of an outgoing e-mail message. Use the virtual keyboard to enter the e-mail addresses, subject line, and any comments you want to add — you know, something profound, like "Isn't this a great-looking photo?" (Check out Chapter 5 for more info on using e-mail.)

- **Send to MobileMe:** If you're a member of Apple's $99-a-year MobileMe online service (formerly .Mac and before that iTools), you can publish a photo to an album in the MobileMe Gallery. Tap the Send to MobileMe control (it appears only if you've set up a MobileMe account on the iPad) and then tap the appropriate gallery album to which you want to add the picture. Enter the title of the photo and an optional description in the spaces provided on the Publish Photo screen that pops up. Tap Publish. Your photo is on its way to the Internet cloud.

✔ **Assign to Contact:** You can assign a picture to someone in your contacts list. To make it happen, tap Assign to Contact. Your list of contacts appears on the screen. Scroll up or down the list to find the person who matches the picture of the moment. You can drag and resize the picture to get it just right. Then tap Set Photo.

You can also assign a photo to a contact by starting out in Contacts, as we explain in Chapter 12. Sneak peek on that chapter: From Contacts, choose the person, tap Edit, and then tap Add Photo. At that point, you can select an existing portrait from one of your on-board picture albums.

To change the picture you assigned to a person, tap her name in the contacts list, tap Edit, and then tap the person's thumbnail picture, which also carries the label Edit. From there, you can select another photo from one of your albums, edit the photo you're already using (by resizing and dragging it to a new position), or delete the photo you no longer want.

✔ **Use as Wallpaper:** The default background image on the iPad when you unlock the device is raindrops on a gray background. But you have a sunny demeanor, and probably have an even better photograph to use as the iPad's wallpaper. A picture of your spouse, your kids, or your pet, perhaps?

When you tap the Use as Wallpaper button, you see what the present image looks like as the iPad background picture. You can move and resize the picture through the now-familiar action of dragging or pinching across the screen with your fingers. When you're satisfied with the wallpaper preview, tap the Set Home Screen button to make it your new Home background, or tap Set Lock Screen to have the image appear when the iPad is locked. Or, you can tap Set Both to make that image your Home and Locked wallpaper screens. These choices are shown in Figure 10-7. Per usual, you also have the option to tap Cancel. (You can find out more about wallpaper in Chapter 13.)

✔ **Copy Photo:** Tap this button when you want to copy a photo and paste it elsewhere.

Alternatively, you can also press and hold your finger against a photo until a Copy button appears. Tap that button, and you can paste the image into an e-mail, for example, by preparing a message, holding your finger against the screen until a Paste button appears, and then pressing the button to paste it into the body of the message.

Figure 10-7: Choose your own photo for your iPad wallpaper.

✔ **Print a Picture:** In the 21st century, people are accustomed to viewing pictures on computer screens, digital frames, smartphones, and tablets. In the last century, most viewed prints. But there's still something special about printing pictures to give away, carry around, or place in an old-fashioned photo frame. Through AirPrint, you can print photos from an iPad onto a compatible printer. Tap the icon with the arrow that's trying to escape a rectangle and then tap Print. The iPad tries to find the printer. You can select the number of copies. If your printer has a tray for photo paper in addition to plain paper, the printer may automatically switch to that tray when you try to print a picture.

In addition to the photo tricks that come ready to use on your iPad, we encourage you to check out the App Store, which we explore in greater depth in Chapter 7. As of this writing, dozens of photography-related applications, some free, are available. These come from a variety of sources and range from Photobucket for iPad, which is free, to Alterme's 99-cent Photo Splash Effects, which lets you convert a picture to black and white, except for a single object in the image that can retain a splash of color.

Deleting Pictures

We told a tiny fib by intimating that photographs are meant to be seen. We should have amended that statement by saying that *some* pictures are meant to be seen. Others, well . . . you can't get rid of them fast enough. Fortunately, the iPad makes it a cinch to bury the evidence:

- **Deleting photos in the Saved Photos or Camera Roll albums:** Some pictures, namely those you saved from an e-mail or web page and that now reside in the aptly named Saved Photos album (or Camera Roll album), are easy to dispose of. Just tap the soon-to-be-whacked picture to open it, and then tap the Trash icon that appears in the upper-right corner when you summon picture controls. To finish the job, tap the big red Delete Photo button. Or, tap anywhere else on the screen if you have second thoughts and decide to keep the picture on your iPad.

- **Deleting multiple photos in Saved Photos or Camera Roll:** When the Saved Photos or Camera Roll albums are open, tap the icon in the upper-right corner that resembles a right-pointing arrow that leans out of a rectangle. A red Delete button appears in the upper-left corner of the screen. Now tap each photo that you want to get rid of; a check mark appears on each one. When you've identified the doomed bunch, tap Delete, or tap Cancel to save them.

- **Removing synced photos:** The Trash icon appears only in the Saved Photos or Camera Roll album. That's because the other pictures on your iPad — those that you synced through your Mac or PC — must be deleted from the photo album on your computer first. Then when you resync those albums, the photos are no longer on your iPad.

Entering the Photo Booth

Remember the old-fashioned photo booths at the local 5 and Dime? Remember the 5 and Dime? Okay, if you don't remember such variety stores, your parents probably do, and if they don't, their parents no doubt do. The point is that photo booths (which do still exist) are fun places to ham it up solo or with a friend as the machine captures and spits out wallet-size pictures.

In the Photo Booth app included on the iPad 2, Apple has cooked up a modern alternative to a real photo booth. The app is a close cousin to a similar application on the Mac. Here's how Photo Booth works on iPad 2:

1. **Tap the Photo Booth icon on the iPad 2.**

   A red curtain opens, revealing the tic-tac-toe style grid, as shown in Figure 10-8.

2. **Point the front-facing camera at your face.**

   You see your mug through a prism of eight rather whacky special effects: Thermal Camera, Mirror, X-Ray, Kaleidoscope, Light Tunnel, Squeeze, Twirl, and Stretch. The center square — what is this *Hollywood Squares?* — is the only one in which you come off looking normal — or as we like to kid, like you're supposed to look.

   You can also use the rear camera in Photo Booth, to subject your friends to this form of, um, visual abuse.

3. **Choose one of the special effects (or stick with Normal) by tapping one of the thumbnails.**

   Ed chose Mirror for the example shown in Figure 10-9, because, after all, two Eds are better than one. (Sorry, couldn't resist.)

Figure 10-8: Photo Booths of yesteryear weren't like this.

4. **If you're not satisfied with the effect you've chosen, tap the icon at the bottom-left corner of the app to return to the Photo Booth grid and select another.**

5. **After choosing an effect, you can doctor things up even further by pinching or unpinching with your fingers.**

6. **When you have your bizarre look just right, tap the camera button on the screen to snap the picture.**

   Your pic lands (as do other pictures taken with the iPad 2 camera) on the Camera Roll album.

   From the Camera Roll album, pictures can be shared, or — you might want to seriously consider this given the distortions you've just applied to your face — deleted.

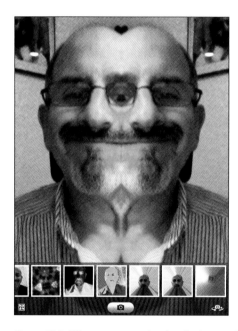

Figure 10-9: When one co-author just isn't enough.

Nah, we're only kidding. Keep the image and take a lot more. Photo Booth may be a blast from the past. But it's also a blast.

Curling Up with a Good iBook

In This Chapter

▶ Getting the skinny on e-books

▶ Opening up to iBooks

▶ Reading books

▶ Shopping for iBooks

▶ Reading electronic periodicals

Don't be surprised if you have to answer this question from an inquisitive child someday: "Is it true, Grandpa, that people once read books on paper?"

That time may still be a ways off, but it somehow doesn't seem as farfetched anymore, especially now that Apple has signed on as a major proponent in the burgeoning electronic books revolution.

Don't get us wrong; we love physical books as much as anyone and are in no way urging their imminent demise. But we also recognize the real-world benefits behind Apple's digital publishing efforts, and those by companies like Amazon, which manufactures what is, for now, the market-leading Kindle electronic reader. As you discover in this chapter, the Kindle plays a role on the iPad as well.

For its part, the iPad makes a terrific electronic reader, with color and dazzling special effects, including pages that turn like a real book.

We open the page on this chapter to see how to find and purchase books for your iPad, and how to read them after they land on your virtual bookshelf. But first we look at why you might want to read books and periodicals on your iPad.

Why E-Books?

We've run into plenty of skeptics who beg the question, "What's so wrong with the paper books that folks have only been reading for centuries that we now have to go digital?" The short answer is there's nothing wrong with physical books — except maybe that paper, over the long term, is fragile, and they tend to be bulky, a potential impediment for travelers.

On the other hand, when asked why he prefers paper books, Bob likes to drop one from shoulder height and ask, "Can your iPad (or Kindle) do that?"

Having said that, though, now consider the electronic advantages:

- **No more weighty or bulky constraints:** You can cart a whole bunch of e-books around when you travel, without breaking your back. To the avid bookworm, this potentially changes the whole dynamic in the way you read. Because you can carry so many books wherever you go, you can read whatever type of book strikes your fancy at the moment, kind of like listening to a song that fits your current mood. You have no obligation to read a book from start to finish before opening a new bestseller, just because that happens to be the one book, maybe two, that you have in your bag. In other words, weighty constraints are out the window.

- **Feel like reading a trashy novel?** Go for it. Rather immerse yourself in classic literature? Go for that. You might read a textbook, cookbook, or biography. Or gaze in wonder at an illustrated beauty. What's more, you can switch among the various titles and styles of books at will, before finishing any single title.

- **Flexible fonts and type sizes:** With e-books, or what Apple prefers to call *iBooks,* you can change the text size and fonts on the fly, quite useful for those with less than 20/20 vision.

- **Get the meaning of a word on the spot:** No more searching for a physical dictionary. You can look up an unfamiliar word on the spot.

- **Search with ease:** Looking to do research on a particular subject? Enter a search term to find each and every mention of the subject in the book you're reading.

- **Read in the dark:** The iPad has a high-resolution backlit display so that you can read without a lamp nearby, which is useful in bed when your partner is trying to sleep.

- **See all the artwork in color:** Indeed, you're making no real visual sacrifices anymore. For example, the latest iBooks software from Apple lets you experience (within certain limits) the kind of stunning art book once reserved for a coffee table. Or you can display a colorful children's picture book.

Truth is, there are two sides to this backlit story. The grayscale electronic ink displays found on Amazon's Kindle and several other e-readers may be easier on the eyes and reduce fatigue, especially if you read for hours on end. And although you may indeed have to supply your own lighting source to read in low-light situations, those screens are easier to see than the iPad screen when you're out and about in bright sunshine.

Beginning the iBook Story

To start reading electronic books on your iPad, you have to fetch the iBooks app in the App Store. (For more on the App Store, consult Chapter 7.)

As you might imagine, the app is free, and it comes with access to Apple's brand new iBookstore, of which we have more to say later in this chapter. For now just know that iBookstore is an inviting place to browse and shop for books 24 hours a day. And as a bonus for walking into this virtual bookstore, you receive a free electronic copy of *Winnie-the-Pooh*.

A.A. Milne's children's classic and all the other books you end up purchasing for your iPad library turn up on the handsome wooden bookshelf, as shown in Figure 11-1. The following basics help you navigate the iBooks main screen:

- **Change the view:** If you prefer to view a list of your books rather than use this Bookshelf view, tap the button toward the upper-right corner of the screen (labeled in Figure 11-1). In this view, you can sort the list by title, author, or category (as shown in Figure 11-2), or you can rearrange where books appear on the bookshelf.

- **Rearrange books on the bookshelf:** To perform this feat, tap Bookshelf from the List view and then tap Edit (in the upper-right corner). Press your finger against the icon to the right with the three horizontal lines of the book title you want to move. Drag the book up or down the list.

- **Remove a book from the bookshelf:** In the List view, tap Edit and then tap the red circle with the white line to the left of the book title you want to remove. Then tap Delete. In the Bookshelf view, tap Edit and then tap the black circle with the white X that appears in the upper-left corner of a book cover. Then tap Delete.

- **Organize books by collections:** If you have a vast library of e-books, you might want to segregate titles by genre or subject by creating collections of like-minded works. You might have collections of mysteries, classics, biographies, how-to's, even all the *For Dummies* books you (hopefully) own. Apple has already created two collections on your behalf: Books (for all titles) and PDFs (for the Adobe PDF files you may have on your iPad). (Apple doesn't let you edit or remove the premade Books or PDFs collections.) To create, rename, or remove a collection of your own, tap the Collections button (also labeled in Figure 11-1) to show off your current list of collections and choose from the following options:

- Tap New to add a new collection.

- Tap Edit and the red circle with the white dash to delete a collection. Tap Delete to finish the job.

- If you want to change the name of a collection, tap its name.

- If you want to move a book or PDF to a collection, go to the bookshelf, tap each work you want to move, and then tap Move. Select the new collection for these titles.

A book can reside only in one collection at a time.

Tap to open iBookstore   Bookshelf view

Tap to view books by collections   Tap a cover to open a book   List view

Figure 11-1: You can read a book by its cover.

Figure 11-2: Sort a list of your books by title, author, category, or bookshelf.

Of course, here we are telling you how to move or get rid of a book before you've even had a chance to read it. How gauche. The next section helps you start reading.

Reading a Book

To start reading a book, tap it — you can start with the Pooh book now. The book leaps off the shelf, and at the same time, it opens to either the beginning of the book or the place where you left off. (And you may have left off on an iPhone, iPod touch, or another iPad because through your Apple IDn your virtual place in a book is transported from device to device.)

Even from the very title page, you can appreciate the color and beauty of Apple's app as well as the navigation tools, as shown in Figure 11-3.

If you rotate the iPad to the side, the one-page book view becomes a two-page view, though all the navigational controls remain the same.

While lounging around reading, and especially if you're lying down, we recommend that you use the Screen Rotation Lock (shown in Chapter 1) to stop the iPad from inadvertently rotating the display.

But you can take advantage of the iPad's VoiceOver feature to have the iPad read to you out loud. It may not be quite like having Mom or Dad read you to sleep, but it can be a potential godsend to those with impaired vision. For more on the VoiceOver feature, consult Chapter 13.

Turning pages

You've been turning pages in books your entire life, so you don't want this simple feat to become a complicated ordeal just because you're now reading electronically. Fear not, it's not. You have no buttons to press.

Instead, to turn to the *next* page of a book, do any of the following:

- **Tap or flick your finger near the right margin of the page.** If you tap or flick, the page turns in a blink.
- **Drag your finger near the margin,** and the page folds down as it turns, as if you were turning pages in a real book.

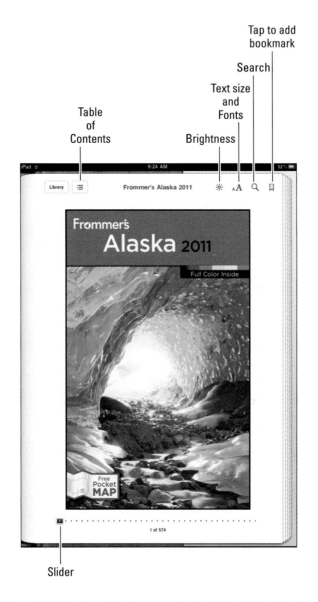

Figure 11-3: Books on the iPad offer handy reading and navigation tools.

> ✓ **Drag down from the upper-right corner of the book,** and the page curls from that spot. The effect is so dazzling, you can make out the faint type bleeding from the previous page on the next folded down page.

- **Drag up from the lower-right corner,** and the page curls up from that spot.
- **Drag from the middle-right margin,** and the entire page curls.

To turn to the *previous* page in a book, tap, flick, or drag your finger in a similar fashion, except now do so closer to the left margin. You'll witness the same cool page-turning effects.

That's what happens by default anyway. If you go into the main iPad Settings and tap iBooks under Apps on the left side of the screen, you have the option to go to the next page instead of the previous page when you tap near the left margin.

The iPad is smart, remembering where you left off. So if you close a book by tapping the Library button in the upper-left corner or by pressing the main Home button, you automatically return to this page when you reopen the book. It isn't necessary to bookmark the page (though you can, as we describe later in this chapter).

Jump to a specific page

When you're reading a book, you often want to go to a specific page. Here's how:

1. **Tap anywhere near the center of the page you're reading to summon page navigator controls, if they're not already visible.**

   The controls are labeled in Figure 11-2.

2. **Drag your finger along the slider at the bottom of the screen until the chapter and page number you want appear.**

3. **Release your finger and *voilà* — that's where you are in the book.**

Go to the Table of Contents

Most books you read on your iPad have Tables of Contents, just like many other books. Here's how you use a Table of Contents on your iPad:

1. **With a book open on your iPad, tap the Table of Contents button near the top of the screen.**

   The Table of Contents screen, as shown in Figure 11-4, appears.

2. **Tap the chapter, title page, or another entry to jump to that page.**

   Alternatively, tap the Resume button that appears at the upper-left corner of the screen to return to the previous location in the book.

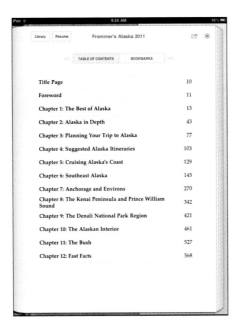

Figure 11-4: The Table of Contents for *Frommer's Alaska 2011*.

Add bookmarks

Moving around to a particular location on the iPad is almost as simple as moving around a real book, and as we explain in the earlier section "Turning pages," Apple kindly returns you to the last page you were reading when you close a book.

Still, occasionally, you want to bookmark a specific page so that you can easily return. To insert a bookmark somewhere, merely tap the Bookmark icon near the upper-right reaches of the screen. A red ribbon slides down over the top of the Bookmark icon signifying that a bookmark is in place. Tap the ribbon if you want to remove the bookmark. Simple as that.

After you set a bookmark, here's how to find it later:

1. **Tap the Table of Contents/Bookmark button.**

2. **Tap Bookmarks (if it's not already selected).**

    Your bookmark is listed along with the chapter and page citations, the date you bookmarked the page, and a phrase or two of surrounding text, as the example in Figure 11-5 shows.

3. **Tap your desired bookmark to return to that page in the book.**

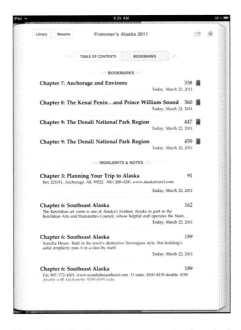

Figure 11-5: Finding the pages you bookmarked.

You can also remove a bookmark from the Bookmarks list by swiping your finger in either direction along a bookmark and then tapping the red Delete button that appears.

Add highlights and notes

Bookmarks are great for jumping to pages you want to read again and again. Of course you may instead want to highlight specific words or passages within a page. And sometimes you want to add your own annotations or comments, as well, which is handy for school assignments. Pardon the pun, but Apple is on the same page. Here's how to do both.

1. **Press your finger and hold it down against any text on a page. Then lift your finger to summon the Highlight and Note buttons.**

   These two buttons appear side-by-by side (sandwiched along with Dictionary and Search buttons that we address in a moment).

   You see grab points along the highlighted word.

2. **(Optional) Refine the highlighted section by expanding the grab points.**

3. Choose a button to add a highlight or note.

- *When you tap the Highlight button,* the word or passage you selected is highlighted in yellow. You can later read the highlight by returning to the Table of Contents page in the same way that you find a bookmark. (See the preceding section and refer to Figure 11-4.)

  - *Tap Notes,* and a post-it like note appears on the screen. Using the virtual keyboard, type your note.

After you add a highlight or note, the following tips are handy to know:

- **To remove a highlight or note:** Press and hold the word or passage, and then tap Remove Highlight or Delete Note when the respective option appears. Alternatively, from the Highlights & Notes section under the Bookmarks list, swipe your finger in either direction along an entry and tap the red Delete button that appears.

- **To change the highlighted color of a highlight or note:** You can change the color from the default yellow to green, blue, pink, or purple. Touch the highlighted selection for a moment and lift your finger. Tap the Colors button and tap to choose your new highlight color.

- **To e-mail or print notes:** From the Table of Contents page, in the upper-right corner of the screen, tap the icon that looks like an arrow trying to escape a rectangle. Tap Email to e-mail your notes, or tap Print to print them (provided you have an AirPrint printer). See Chapter 2 for details about printing.

Change the type size and font

If you want to enlarge the typeface size (or make it smaller), here's how:

1. Tap the fonts button, labeled in Figure 11-2, at the upper-right corner of the screen.

2. Tap the uppercase A.

The text swells right before your eyes so that you can pick a size that's comfortable for you.

To make the font smaller, tap the lowercase a instead.

If you want to change the fonts, tap the fonts button and then tap Fonts and the font style you want to switch to. Your choices are Baskerville, Cochin, Georgia, Palatino, Times New Roman, and Verdana. We don't necessarily expect you to know what these look like just by the font names — fortunately you get to examine the change right before your eyes. A check mark indicates the currently selected font style.

Searching inside and outside a book

If you want to find a passage in a book but just can't remember where it is, try searching for it. Here's how:

1. **Tap the magnifying glass Search icon to enter a search phrase on the virtual keyboard that slides up from the bottom.**

   All the occurrences in the book turn up in a window under the Search icon, complete with a few lines of text and a page citation.

2. **Tap one of the items to jump to that portion of the book.**

You can also search Google or the Wikipedia online encyclopedia using the corresponding buttons at the bottom of the search results. If you do so, the iBooks app closes and the Safari browser fires up Google or Wikipedia, with your search term already entered.

If you search Google or Wikipedia in this fashion, you are for the moment, closing the iBooks application and opening Safari. To return to the book you're reading, you must tap the iBooks icon again to reopen the app. Fortunately, you're brought back to the page in the book where you left off.

Shopping for E-Books

Bob and Ed love browsing in a physical bookstore. But the experience of browsing Apple's new iBookstore, although certainly different, is equally pleasurable. Apple makes it a cinch to search for books you want to read, and even lets you peruse a sample prior to parting with your hard-earned dollars. To enter the store, tap the Store button in the upper-left corner of your virtual bookshelf or your library List view.

A few things to keep in mind: The iBooks app and iBookstore, is available to U.S. customers, with versions of the store also available in the U.K., Germany, France, and Canada. Apple's iBookstore had some 150,000 titles at the time our book was being published, including some works — Jay-Z's memoir *Decoded,* for example — that are enhanced with video. Meanwhile, the store includes titles from all six major trade publishers: Hachette Book Group, HarperCollins, Macmillan, Penguin Group, Simon & Schuster, and Random House, as well as several independents. Wiley is also represented, of course. Random House had been the only holdout among big-name publishers when Apple first launched the iBookstore, but the largest trade book publisher in the U.S. finally came aboard.

Publishers, not Apple, set the prices. Many bestsellers in the joint cost $12.99, though some fetch $9.99 or less. In fact, Apple even has a $9.99-or-less section, the virtual equivalent of the bargain rack. And free selections are available. On the other hand, the Donald Rumsfeld memoir, *Known and Unknown* commands $19.99.

Just browsing iBookstore

You have several ways to browse for books in the iBookstore. The top half of the screen shows ever-changing ads for books that fit a chosen category (Children & Teens in the example shown in Figure 11-6). But you can also browse Release Date in the particular category you have in mind. The left- and right-pointing arrows indicate more recent releases to peek at. Or tap See All for many more selections.

To choose another category of books, tap the Categories button to summon the list shown in Figure 11-7; you have to scroll to see the bottom of the list.

Look at the bottom of the screen. You see the following icons:

- **Featured:** This is where we've been hanging out so far. Featured works are the books being promoted in the store. These may include popular titles from Oprah's Book Club or an author spotlight from the likes of *Twilight* writer Stephenie Meyer.

- **NYTimes:** Short for *The New York Times,* of course. These books make the newspaper's famous bestsellers lists, which are divided into fiction and nonfiction works. The top ten books in each list are initially shown. To see more titles, tap Show More at the bottom of the screen. You have to scroll down to see it.

Figure 11-6: The featured page for Children & Teens is pushing *Magic Tree House.*

Figure 11-7: So many books, so many category choices.

✏ **Top Charts:** Here Apple shows you the most popular books in the iBookstore. You find a list for Top Paid Books and Top Free Books. Once more, you can see more than the top ten shown in each category by tapping Show More.

✏ **Browse:** Tapping the Browse icon lets you find books by poring through a list of popular authors, shown in a scrollable pane on the left half of the screen. Flick your finger up or down to scroll the list, or tap one of the letters in the margin to jump to authors whose name begins with that letter. When you tap an author's name, a list of her available titles appears in a scrollable pane on the right.

✏ **Purchases:** Tapping here shows you the books you've already bought. In this area, you can also check out your iTunes account information, tap a button that transports you to iTunes customer service, and redeem any iTunes gift cards or gift certificates.

Searching iBookstore

In the upper-right corner of the iBookstore is a Search field, similar to the Search field you see in iTunes. Using the virtual keyboard, type an author name or title to find the book you seek.

If you like freebies, search for *free* in the iBookstore. You'll find tons of (mostly classic) books that cost nothing, and you won't even have to import them. See the section "Finding free books outside iBookstore," later in this chapter, for more places to find free books.

Deciding whether a book is worth it

To find out more about a book you come across in the iBookstore, you can check out the detail page and other readers' reviews, or read a sample of the book. Follow these steps to navigate the detail page:

1. **Tap its cover.**

   An information screen similar to the one shown for *I Am Ozzy* in Figure 11-8 appears. You can see when the book was published, read a description, and more.

2. **Tap Author Page to see other books by that writer or Alert Me to add the author to your custom alerts, perhaps to be notified when he writes a new book.**

3. **(Optional) Tap Tell a Friend and the iPad fires up your e-mail app, with the subject line filled in with "Check out *I Am Ozzy*" in the case of this example.**

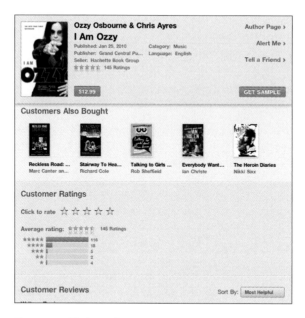

Figure 11-8: Find out all you can about a book.

A picture of the book cover, its release date and rating, and a View Item link are embedded in the body of the message.

4. **Check out the sections for Customers Also Bought, Customer Reviews, and Customer Ratings. Flick or drag to scroll down the overlay and see all the reviews.**

   You can throw in your own two cents if you've already read it by tapping Write a Review.

Of course the best thing you can do to determine whether a book is worth buying is to read a sample. Tap Get Sample, and the book cover almost immediately lands on your bookshelf. You can read it like any book, up until that juncture in the book where your free sample ends. Apple has placed a Buy button inside the pages of the book to make it easy to purchase it if you're hooked. The word *Sample* also appears on the cover, to remind you that this book isn't quite yours — yet.

Buying a book from iBookstore

Assuming that the book exceeds your lofty standards, and you're ready to purchase it, here's how to do so:

1. **Tap the price shown in the gray button on the book's information page (refer to Figure 11-8).**

   Upon doing so, the dollar amount disappears, and the button becomes green and carries a Buy Book label. If you tap a free book instead, the button is labeled Get Book.

2. **Tap the Buy Book/Get Book button.**

3. **Enter your iTunes password to proceed with the transaction.**

   The book appears on your bookshelf in an instant, ready for you to tap it and start reading.

If you buy another book within 15 minutes of your initial purchase, you aren't prompted for your iTunes password again.

Buying books beyond Apple

The business world is full of examples where one company competes with another on some level only to work with it as a partner on another. When the iPad first burst onto the scene in early April 2010, pundits immediately compared it to Amazon's Kindle, the market-leading electronic reader. Sure the iPad had the larger screen and color, but Kindle had a few bragging points too, including longer battery life (up to about a month on the latest Kindle versus about 10 hours for the iPad), a lighter weight, and a larger selection of books in its online bookstore.

But Amazon has long said it wants Kindle books to be available for all sorts of electronic platforms, and the iPad, like the iPhone and iPod touch before it, is no exception. So we recommend taking a look at the free Kindle app for the iPad, especially if you've already purchased a number of books in Amazon's Kindle Store and want access to that wider selection of titles. And you can tap a Shop in Kindle Store button inside the app, which fires up Safari on the iPad.

The Barnes & Noble NOOK app is also worth a look. Meanwhile, we haven't tried them all, and we know it's hard enough competing against Apple (or Amazon). But we'd be selling our readers short if we didn't at least mention that you can find several other e-book-type apps for the iPad in the App Store. As this book goes to press, you can have a look at the following apps, just to name a few:

- CloudReaders from Satoshi Nakajima (free)
- Free eBooks by Kobo
- Stanza from Lexcycle (free)

See Chapter 7 for details about finding and downloading apps.

Finding free books outside iBookstore

Apple supports a technical standard — *ePub,* the underlying technology behind thousands of free public-domain books. You can import these to the iPad without shopping in the iBookstore. Such titles must be *DRM-free,* which means they're free of digital rights restrictions.

To import ePub titles, you have to download them to your Mac or PC (assuming that they're not already there) and then sync them to the iPad through iTunes.

You can find ePub titles at numerous cyberspace destinations, among them

- **Feedbooks:** www.feedbooks.com
- **Google Books:** Not all the books here are free, and Google has a downloadable app. http://books.google.com/ebooks
- **Project Gutenberg:** www.gutenberg.us
- **Smashwords:** www.smashwords.com
- **Baen:** www.baen.com

Reading Newspapers and Magazines

Those in the newspaper business know that it's been tough sledding in recent years. The Internet, as it has in so many areas, has proved to be a disruptive force in media.

It remains to be seen what role Apple generally, and the iPad specifically, will play in the future of electronic periodicals or in helping to turn around sagging media enterprises. It's also uncertain which pricing models will make the most sense from a business perspective.

What we can tell you is that reading newspapers and magazines on the iPad is not like reading newspapers and magazines in any other electronic form. The experience is really slick, but only you can decide whether it's worth paying the tab (in the cases where you do have to pay).

Fine publishing apps worth checking out include USA TODAY (where Ed works), The Wall Street Journal, Time magazine, The New York Times, Reuters News Pro, BBC News, and Popular Science. We also highly recommend fetching the free Zinio Magazine Newsstand & Reader app. It's a terrific way to read magazines like *Rolling Stone, The Economist, Macworld, PC Magazine,*

Car and Driver, National Geographic, Spin, Business Week, Sporting News, and many more. You can buy single issues of a magazine or subscribe, and sample and share some articles without a subscription.

You have to pay handsomely or subscribe to some of these newspapers and magazines, which you find not in the iBookstore but in the regular App Store, which we cover in Chapter 7. You also see ads (somebody's got to pay the freight).

We want to pause a moment here in the middle of the book to thank you again for reading our book because as this chapter points out, you have a lot of rich reading to do on your iPad. And maybe you're even reading our book on it.

12

The iPad at Work

*W*e hate to break the news to you, but your iPad isn't all fun and games; it has a serious side. The iPad can remind you of appointments, help you keep all your contacts straight, and if you're willing to purchase iWork apps, deliver a first-class spreadsheet, word processor, and presentation program.

Over the next several pages, we look at some of the less sexy functions of your iPad. Indeed, we'd venture to say that no one bought an iPad because of its calendar, note-taking ability, or Address Book. Still, having these programs is awfully handy, and we're confident you'll feel the same way if you spring for some or all the optional iWork apps.

Taking Note of Notes

Notes is an application that creates text notes that you can save or send through e-mail. To create a note, follow these steps:

1. **Tap the Notes icon on the Home screen.**

2. **Tap the + button in the upper-right corner to start a new note.**

    The virtual keyboard appears.

3. **Type a note, such as the one shown in Figure 12-1.**

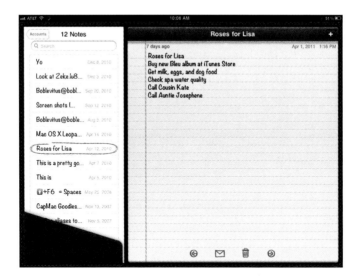

Figure 12-1: The Notes application revealed.

Other things you can do before you quit the Notes app include

 ✔ Tap the Notes button in the upper-left corner of the screen to see a list of all your notes. When the list is onscreen, just tap a note to open and view, edit, or modify it.

 ✔ Tap the left- or right-arrow button at the bottom of the screen to read the previous or next note.

 ✔ Tap the Letter icon at the bottom of the screen to e-mail the note using the Mail application (see Chapter 5 for more about Mail).

 ✔ Tap the Trash icon at the bottom of the screen to delete the note.

Like most iPad apps, your notes are saved automatically while you type them so you can quit Notes at any time without losing a single character.

We'd be remiss if we didn't remind you that you can sync notes with your computer (see Chapter 3).

And that's all she wrote. You now know everything there is to know about creating and managing notes with Notes.

Working with the Calendar

The Calendar program lets you keep on top of your appointments and events (birthdays, anniversaries, and so on). You open it by tapping the Calendar icon on the Home screen. The icon is smart in its own right because it changes daily; the day of the week and date display.

Mac users can sync their calendars with either iCal or the discontinued Microsoft Entourage (but strangely, not with Outlook 2011 for the Mac); PC users can sync calendars with Microsoft Outlook. See Chapter 3 for more info on how to sync.

You can't create new calendars on your iPad — they must be created on your Mac or PC and then synced.

You have four main ways to peek at your calendar(s): Day, Week, Month, and List views. Choosing one is as simple as tapping the Day, Week, Month, or List button at the top of the Calendar screen. From each view, you can always return to the current day by tapping the Today button in the lower-left corner.

Choosing a calendar view

From a single calendar view, you can look at appointments from an individual calendar, or consolidate several calendars — like one for home, one for your kid's activities, and one for your job — in a single view. Here's how:

To pick the calendars you want to display, follow these steps:

1. **Tap the Calendars button at the upper-left corner of the screen.**

   That summons a Show Calendars window.

2. **Tap each calendar you want to view by tapping its entry.**

   A check mark appears. Tap an entry again so that a given calendar won't appear, and the check mark disappears. To show all the calendars, tap the All option. To make them disappear, tap All again. In the example shown in Figure 12-2, all the calendars are selected.

Be careful: To-do items created on your Mac or PC calendars aren't synced and don't appear on your iPad.

Figure 12-2: Making sure that bowling night doesn't conflict with the kids' soccer game.

You can also choose to view your calendar(s) in different views:

✔ **List view:** List view isn't complicated. As its name indicates, List view, as shown in Figure 12-3, presents a list of current and future appointments on the left side of the screen, and an hour-by-hour view of the day that's highlighted on the right. About eight hours of the highlighted date are visible in landscape mode; about ten are visible in portrait mode. You can drag the list up or down with your finger or flick to rapidly scroll through the list. To switch the day shown, tap the right or left arrow on the bottom of the screen, or tap or drag the timeline.

✔ **Day view:** Day view, as shown in Figure 12-4, reveals the appointments of a given 24-hour period (though you have to scroll up or down to see an entire day's worth of entries). As in the List view, you can drag or tap the timeline to move to a new date or press the left or right arrows for the same purpose.

Figure 12-3: List view.

Figure 12-4: Day view.

✔ **Week view:** As you'd expect, the Week view displayed in Figure 12-5 shows your appointments over a seven-day period. Again, use the arrows or timeline at the bottom of the screen to change the time frame that you see. You'll notice of course that the timeline now reflects one-week intervals, which is the way it should be.

✔ **Month view:** By now, you're getting the hang of these different views. When your iPad is in Month view, as it is in Figure 12-6, you can see appointments from January to December. In this monthly calendar view, a colored dot (designating a specific calendar) and short description appear on any day that has appointments or events scheduled. Tap that day to see the list of activities the dot represents.

Searching appointments

Consider that you scheduled an appointment with your dentist months ago, but now you can't remember the date or the time. You could pore through your daily, weekly, or monthly calendars or scroll through a List view until you land on the appointment. But that is the very definition of inefficiency. The much faster way is to just type the name of your dentist in the Search box in the upper-right corner of the various Calendar screens. You're instantly transported to the date and time of the entry from your current calendar view.

Figure 12-5: Week view.

Figure 12-6: Month view.

Adding calendar entries

In Chapter 3, you discover pretty much everything there is to know about syncing your iPad, including syncing calendar entries from your Mac (using iCal or Microsoft Entourage) or PC (using Microsoft Outlook).

Of course, in plenty of situations, you enter appointments on the fly. Adding appointments directly to the iPad is easy. Follow these steps:

1. **Tap the Calendar icon at the top of the screen, and then tap the Day, Week, Month, or List button.**

2. **Tap the plus sign (+) button in the lower-right corner of the screen.**

   The Add Event screen, as shown in Figure 12-7, appears along with the virtual keyboard.

   If you use a Bluetooth keyboard (see Chapter 15), that pesky virtual keyboard stays out of your way so you see more of whatever is on the screen.

3. **Tap the Title and Location fields and finger-type as much (or as little) information as you feel is necessary.**

4. **Set the time for the entry by tapping the Starts/Ends field and then proceeding as follows:**

   If your calendar entry has a start time or end time (or both):

a. *In the Start & End screen that appears (see Figure 12-8), choose the time the event starts and then the time it ends.*

Use your finger to roll separate wheels for the date, hour, and minute (in five-minute intervals) and to specify AM or PM. It's a little like manipulating one of those combination bicycle locks or an old-fashioned date stamp used with an inkpad.

b. *Tap Done when you're finished.*

If you're entering a birthday or another all-day milestone:

a. *Tap the All-Day button so that On (rather than Off) displays.*

b. *Tap Done.*

Because the time isn't relevant for an all-day entry, note that the bottom half of the screen now has wheels for just the month, day, and year, and not hours and minutes.

5. **(Optional) If you're setting up a recurring entry, such as an anniversary, tap the Repeat window, tap to indicate how often the event in question recurs, and then tap Done.**

The options are Every Day, Every Week, Every 2 Weeks, Every Month, and Every Year.

6. **(Optional) If you want to set a reminder or alert for the entry, tap Alert, tap a time, and then tap Done.**

Figure 12-7: You're about to add an event to your iPad.

Figure 12-8: Controlling the Starts and Ends fields is like manipulating a bike lock.

Alerts can be set to arrive on the actual date of an event, 2 days before, 1 day before, 2 hours before, 1 hour before, 30 minutes before, 15 minutes before, or 5 minutes before. When the appointment time rolls around, you hear a sound and see a message like the one shown in Figure 12-9. Tap View Event to check out the details of the appointment or tap Close if you feel the reminder you just received will suffice.

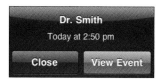

Figure 12-9: Alerts make it hard to forget.

If you're the kind of person who needs an extra nudge, set another reminder by tapping the Second Alert field, which appears only after you've set one alert.

7. **Tap Calendar to assign the entry to a particular calendar, and then tap the calendar you have in mind (Home or Work, for example), assuming that you have multiple calendars. Then tap Done.**

8. **(Optional) If you want to enter notes about the appointment or event, tap Notes, type your note on the virtual keyboard, and then tap Done to return to the Add Event screen.**

9. **Back on the Add Event screen, tap Done after you finish entering everything.**

After you create calendar entries, check out the following tips for working with your calendar:

- **Turn off a calendar alert** by tapping Settings➪General➪Sounds. Make sure that the Calendar Alerts button is turned off.

- **To modify an existing calendar entry,** tap the entry, tap Edit, and then make whichever changes need to be made.

- **To wipe out a calendar entry altogether,** tap the entry, tap Edit, and then tap Delete Event. You have a chance to confirm your choice by tapping either Delete Event (again) or Cancel. To delete an entry in the Day view, just tap the event and then tap Delete Event. There's no need to tap an Edit button as well.

- **Calendar entries you create on your iPad are synchronized with the calendar you specified in the iTunes Info pane.**

Letting your calendar push you around

If you work for a company that uses Microsoft Exchange ActiveSync, calendar entries and meeting invitations from co-workers can be *pushed* to your device so that they show up on the screen moments after they're entered, even if they're entered on computers at work. Setting up an account to facilitate this pushing of calendar entries to your iPad is a breeze, although you should check with your company's tech or IT department to make sure that your employer allows it. Then follow these steps, which are similar to adding an e-mail account, covered in Chapter 5:

Setting your default calendar and time zone

Choose a default calendar by tapping Settings➪Mail, Contacts, Calendars and then flicking the screen until the Calendar section appears. Tap Default Calendar and select the calendar you want new events you create on your iPad to appear on.

If you travel long distances for your job, you can also make events appear according to whichever time zone you selected for your calendars. In the Calendar settings, tap Time Zone Support to turn it on, and then tap Time Zone. Type the time zone location on the keyboard that appears.

When Time Zone Support is turned off, events display according to the time zone of your current location.

1. **Tap Settings⇨Mail, Contacts, Calendars.**

2. **From the Add Account list, tap Microsoft Exchange.**

3. **Fill in the e-mail address, username, password, and description fields, and then tap Next.**

4. **Enter your server address on the next screen that appears.**

   The rest of the fields are filled in with the e-mail address, username, and password you just entered.

5. **Tap Next.**

   If your company uses Microsoft Exchange 2007, you don't have to enter the address of your Exchange server — your iPad can determine it automatically.

6. **Tap the On switches for all the information types you want to synchronize using Microsoft Exchange, from among Mail, Contacts, Calendars.**

   You're good to go now, although some employers may require you to add passcodes to safeguard company secrets.

If your business-issued iPad is ever lost or stolen — or it turns out that you're a double agent working for a rival company — your employer's IT administrators can remotely wipe your device clean. You, too, can wipe the slate clean, using a free component in Apple's MobileMe (formerly .Mac) service, and take advantage of the Find My iPad feature that we explain in Chapter 13.

Responding to meeting invitations

The iPad has one more important button — but you see it only when the Exchange calendar-syncing feature is turned on (see the preceding section) and you have a supported so-called CalDAV account or a MobileMe calendar. This Invitations button to attend a meeting or event is represented by an arrow pointing downward into a half-rectangle. If you get an invitation in this manner, the listing appears in your calendar with a dotted line around it and an Invitations button appears in the upper-left corner of the Calendars screen. You need an Internet connection to respond to an invitation. The following steps walk you through the process:

1. **Tap the Invitations button to view your pending invitations.**

2. **Tap any of the items on the list to see more details.**

   For example, suppose that a meeting invitation arrives from your boss. You can see who else is attending the shindig (by tapping Invitees); send them an e-mail, if need be; and check scheduling conflicts, among other options.

3. **Tap Accept to let the meeting organizer know you're attending; tap Decline if you have something better to do (and aren't worried about upsetting the person who signs your paycheck); or tap Maybe if you're waiting for a better offer.**

You can choose to receive an alert every time someone sends you an invitation. In the Calendar settings of Mail, Contacts, Calendars, tap New Invitation Alerts so that the On button in blue displays.

MobileMe subscribers can keep calendar entries synchronized between your iPad and Mac or PC (or iPhone or iPod touch for that matter). When you make a scheduling change on your iPad, it's automatically updated on your computer and vice versa. Choose MobileMe from the Add Account screen to get started.

You can also import events from an e-mail. Open the message and tap the calendar file, which adheres to the `.ics` standard. When the events show up, tap Add All, choose the calendar you want to add it to, and then tap Done.

Subscribing to calendars

You can subscribe to calendars that meet the CalDAV and iCalendar (`.ics`) standards, which are supported by the popular Google and Yahoo! calendars, or iCal on the Mac. Although you can read entries on the iPad from the calendars you subscribe to, you can't create new entries from the iPad or edit the entries that are already present.

To subscribe to one of these calendars, follow these steps:

1. **Tap Settings⇨Mail, Contacts, Calendars⇨Add Account⇨Other.**
2. **Choose either Add CalDAV Account or Add Subscribed Calendar.**
3. **Enter the URL of the calendar you want to subscribe to.**
4. **If prompted, enter a username, password, and optional description.**

   After you subscribe to a calendar, it appears just like any another calendar on your iPad.

   Calendars you subscribe to are *read-only.* In other words, you can't change existing events or add new ones.

Sifting through Contacts

If you read the chapter on syncing (see Chapter 3), you know how to get the snail-mail addresses, e-mail addresses, and phone numbers that reside on your Mac or PC into the iPad. Assuming that you went through that drill already, all those addresses and phone numbers are hanging out in one place. Their not-so-secret hiding place is revealed when you tap the Contacts icon on the Home screen.

Adding and viewing contacts

To add contacts from within the Contacts app, tap the + button at the bottom of the screen and type as much or as little profile information as you have for the person. Tap Add Photo to add a picture from your photo albums (or to take a snapshot on the iPad 2). You can edit the information later by tapping the Edit button when a contact's name is highlighted.

A list of your contacts appears on the left panel of the screen, with one contact name, Rosemarie Hall in the example shown in Figure 12-10, highlighted in blue. On the right you can see a mug shot of Rosemarie plus her phone number, e-mail address, regular address, and birthday. You also find an area to scribble notes on a contact. We guess there was not much to say about Rosemarie.

Figure 12-10: A view of all contacts.

You have three ways to land on a specific contact:

✔ **Flick your finger so that the list of contacts on the left side scrolls rapidly up or down,** loosely reminiscent of the spinning Lucky 7s (or other pictures) on a Las Vegas slot machine. Think of the payout you'd get with that kind of power on a One-Armed Bandit.

✔ **Slide your thumb or another finger along the alphabet on the left edge of the contacts list or tap one of the teeny-tiny letters** to jump to names that begin with that letter.

> ✔ **Start to type the name of a contact in the Search field near the top of the contacts list. Or, type the name of the place your contact works.** When you're at or near the appropriate contact name, stop the scrolling by tapping the screen.

When you tap to stop the scrolling, that tap doesn't select an item in the list. This may seem counterintuitive the first few times you try it, but we got used to it and now we really like it this way.

You can change the way your contacts are displayed. Tap Settings⇨ Mail, Contacts, Calendars. Then scroll down to Contacts settings on the right side of the screen, if it's not already visible. Tap Sort Order or Display Order, and for each one, choose the First, Last option or Last, First to indicate whether you want to sort or display entries by a contact's first or last name.

Searching contacts

You can search contacts by entering a first or last name in the Search field, or by entering a company name.

You can locate people on your iPad without actually opening the Contacts app. Type a name in the Spotlight Search field (see Chapter 2), and then tap the name in the search results. If you're searching contacts with a Microsoft Exchange account, you may be able to search your employer's *Global Address List, GAL* for short. This typically works in one of two ways:

> ✔ Tap the Groups button in the upper-left corner of the All Contacts screen and tap the appropriate Exchange server name to find folks. Groups on your computer might reflect, say, different departments in your company, friends from work, friends from school, and so on.

> ✔ Or, you might search a so-called *LDAP (Lightweight Directory Access Protocol)* server. It strikes us that there's nothing "lightweight" about something called an LDAP server, but we digress. Similarly, if you have a CardDAV account, you can search for any contacts that have been synced to the iPad.

Contacting and sharing your contacts

You can initiate an e-mail from within Contacts by tapping an e-mail address under a contact's listings. Doing so fires up the Mail program on the iPad with the person's name already in the To field. For more on the Mail app, we direct you to Chapter 5.

You can also share a contact's profile with another person. Tap the Share button, and once again, the Mail program answers the call of duty. This time, the contact's vCard is embedded in the body of a new Mail message. Just address the message and send it on its merry way. A *vCard* is kind of like an electronic business card. You can identify it by its .vcf file format.

Finally, you can tap a contact's snail-mail address to launch the Maps app and see it there.

Linking contacts

There's a great chance the people you know have contact entries in more than one account, meaning you might end up with redundant entries for the same person. The iPad solution is to *link* contacts. Find the contact in question, tap Edit, and tap the silhouette icon with the + at the bottom-right corner of the entry. Choose the related contact entry and then tap Link. It's worth noting that the linked contacts in each account remain separate and are not merged.

Removing a contact

Hey, it happens. A person falls out of favor. Maybe he is a jilted lover. Or maybe you just moved cross country and no longer will call on the services of your old gardener.

Removing a contact is easy, if unfortunate. Tap a contact and then tap Edit. Scroll to the bottom of the Edit screen and tap Delete Contact. You get one more chance to change your mind.

Apps for Work

Because Apple is pretty much without equal when it comes to manufacturing beautiful-looking hardware, it's sometimes easy to overlook the fact that the company knows a thing or two about making great software, too. So although the vast majority of apps in the App Store are created not by Apple itself but by outside software developers, the gang in Cupertino knows how to pick its spots when it comes to producing its own apps. Nowhere is that truer than with the iWork software suite that Apple has completely redesigned for the iPad.

If you're unfamiliar with *iWork*, it's a "productivity" package that's popular with the Mac faithful that includes the Pages word processor, the Keynote presentation program, and the Numbers spreadsheet — in other words, the kind of programs you use for, well, work.

In the App Store, each iPad version of these programs costs $9.99. If you buy all three, you're still paying less than half the $79 it costs for the complete iWork version for Mac OS X.

Of course, iWork on the iPad, although slick and simple, isn't quite as full-featured as its Mac sibling. And we've heard the arguments, valid for some, that when it comes to doing heavy duty-work work, you might want to get a more traditional desktop or laptop computer. Still, with iWork, you can indeed do a lot, if not most, of the stuff you need to accomplish work-wise — and with the kind of style and (dare we even say it) fun that you expect from Apple products. We recommend tooling around with Keynote by touching and holding objects and moving them around.

With that, we describe an overview of each iWork app in the following sections.

The keys to Keynote

Keynote is all about producing polished business presentations for clients, customers, and would-be clients and customers.

When you initially open Keynote — and for that matter when you open the other two apps in the iWorks suite for the first time — you're treated to helpful tutorials on how to use the programs.

The basics: Down the left side of the Keynote screen is the *Navigator,* a vertical strip that contains every slide in your presentation. Flick up or down in the list to see all the slides. You can drag slides around to rearrange them in any order. You can tap them to cut, copy, paste, delete, or skip them. And just below the Navigator is the Add Slide + button that you tap — you guessed it — to add a new slide.

It's worth noting that Keynote, unlike Pages, Numbers, and most other apps for the iPad, only works in landscape mode, probably because presentations look better that way.

You find the following on the Keynote toolbar:

- **My Presentations/New Presentation button:** Tap this button in the upper-left corner of the screen to summon any presentation you've already completed or still have in progress. This button and all others are labeled in Figure 12-11.

- **Undo:** A potential lifesaver (okay, presentation saver). If you make a mistake, just tap the Undo button, and it's like whatever turned you off in the first place never happened. Don't you wish real life had an Undo button sometimes?

- **Info:** Tap here to change the properties of an object or text, with different borders and effects. For example, you might add shadows and reflections to an object.

- **Insert:** Tap this icon to insert photos, tables, charts, or shapes to a slide.

- **Animate Slides:** You have all sorts of neat choices, from a Flash Bulbs effect to twirling objects around.

- ✔ **Tools:** You find a bevy of helpful instruments. You can check spellings, number slides, turn on edge guides, print (with a compatible AirPrint printer), consult an online user guide, and use a Find function to search for words in presentations.

- ✔ **Play:** The most exciting control of all. Tap Play to watch your presentation come to life full-screen.

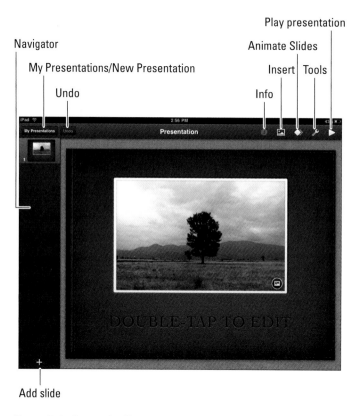

Figure 12-11: Presenting Keynote basics.

Now that you know the basics, here's how to get going:

1. Tap the New Presentation button.

2. Choose a theme.

Out of the gate, you have a dozen handsomely themed templates to choose from, including those visible in Figure 12-12. Think of themes as a great head start; they come with text and image placeholders that you can substitute with your own words and pictures.

Figure 12-12: Choose a theme.

3. **(Optional) Import a Keynote '09 or '11 or Microsoft PowerPoint presentation from your computer.**

   Connect the iPad to your computer, open iTunes, and choose iPad under Devices. On the Summary page, choose Apps, and then scroll to the bottom of the screen on your computer and select Keynote in the Apps list in the File Sharing section. Click Add and find the presentation you want to transfer to your iPad in the Choose a File: iTunes window that opens. Click Choose when you find the file in question.

In much the same way, you can also transfer iWork documents between your computer and the iPad for Pages and Numbers.

You can export iWork documents from the iPad to your computer in a similar fashion. But although Keynote documents can be exported in the Keynote or PDF file formats, you can't export a file in the Microsoft PowerPoint or PPT file format. It's too bad, given that PowerPoint remains the 800-pound gorilla of the presentation software field.

To print slides, you have to export your presentation to a computer through iTunes, e-mail, or the iWork.com public beta, which you can access using the same Apple ID and password you use to buy apps, songs, and other items in the iTunes Store.

Page me with Pages

The toolbar at the top of the Pages word processor has a similar look and feel to the Keynote toolbar and is shown in Figure 12-13. A My Documents/New Document button is in the upper-left corner, adjacent to the Undo button. At the upper right are the now-familiar Info (for changing fonts and styles), Insert (for adding pictures, tables, charts, and so on), and Tools buttons for printing and other functions. You also find a Full Screen button in the right-most corner of the screen.

Like its iWork brethren, Pages allows you to start with a custom template, though a blank page may work best for most people. Templates cover résumés, formal letters, party invites, and term papers, among others.

Figure 12-13: The Pages toolbar.

As you start working in Pages, the following tips are handy to know:

- ✔ When you double-tap text, a style ruler appears at the top, for changing paragraph and character styles (for example, bold, italic, and underline), text alignments, and page breaks.

- ✔ As with Keynote, you can move, resize, and rotate objects in a document and add your own pictures.

- ✔ Double-tap any word in a document and then tap More⇨Definition for a dictionary entry. You may not find the meaning of life here, but at least you'll find the meaning for the word in question. In other words, we think it's a nice feature.

- ✔ Tap and hold your finger along the right edge of the screen to make the Pages Navigator appear. Drag this handy tool up and down the screen to preview your document inside its transparent window. The number on the right tells you the page you're on.

- ✔ If you plan on doing a lot of writing in Pages, consider getting Apple's optional physical iPad Keyboard Dock (for the original iPad only at press time) or using a Bluetooth wireless keyboard. This is a matter of personal preference, of course.

- ✔ Tap the Share button after tapping the My Documents button to send a Pages document via e-mail, to share it at iWork.com (you have to enter your Apple ID or MobileMe credentials), or to send it to iTunes. You can also copy it to an iDisk storage locker in the cloud. Still another option is to copy the document to a so-called WebDAV server (you have to enter the server address, username, and password). You can send off your document in the Pages, PDF, or Microsoft Word `.doc` file formats.

When you import documents to work inside Pages (and for that matter, the other iWork apps), they don't always come through clean. Fonts from the original document may be missing or altered, and when that happens, you see a warning message. The same goes for headers and bookmarks. Hopefully such formatting challenges will be fixed in the future.

Playing with Numbers

Perhaps more than any other iWork app, Numbers best exploits multitouch and lets you become a whiz at number crunching in no time. As with Keynote and Pages, the Numbers spreadsheet relies on a similar button scheme at the top of the screen. The button in the upper-left corner is labeled New Spreadsheet or My Spreadsheets, depending on the view you're in.

Apple has supplied 16 useful Getting Started templates that appear when you tap the New Spreadsheet button. Your options range from Checklist and Expense Report sheets to Invoice and Employee Schedule sheets.

A few tips can help you start working with Numbers:

- You can import spreadsheets from Numbers on your Mac, or Microsoft Excel on a Mac or PC. And of course, you can start out on the iPad with a blank slate as well.

- To enter data in a spreadsheet cell, just double-tap the cell to automatically bring up the keyboard you need for the sheet you're working on (digits, duration, date and time, or text).

- Numerous functions and formulas are built into the app, in such areas as engineering, finance, and statistics.

- Tables and charts have the kind of pizzazz Apple is famous for.

- As with Keynote and Pages, you can export spreadsheets to iWork or elsewhere, or send them via e-mail. To do so, tap the icon on the My Spreadsheets page that looks like a right-pointing arrow coming out of a rectangle. It's labeled in Figure 12-14.

There you have it — your iPad at work. Okay, you can admit it now. That wasn't so bad. In fact, it was even fun!

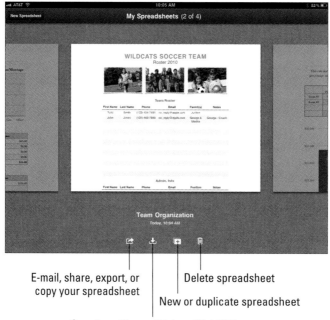

E-mail, share, export, or copy your spreadsheet

Copy from iTunes, iDisk, or WebDAV

New or duplicate spreadsheet

Delete spreadsheet

Figure 12-14: Sharing your spreadsheet.

Part IV
The Undiscovered iPad

The 5th Wave   By Rich Tennant

"What I'm doing should clear your sinuses, take away your headache, and charge your iPad."

In this part . . .

This part is where we show you what's under the hood and how to configure your iPad to your liking. Then we look at the things to do if your iPad ever becomes recalcitrant.

In Chapter 13, we explore every single iPad setting that's not discussed in depth elsewhere in the book. The iPad offers dozens of different preferences and settings to make your iPad your very own; by the time you finish with Chapter 13, you'll know how to customize every part of your iPad that can be customized.

iPads are well-behaved little beasts for the most part, except when they're not. Like the little girl with the little curl, when they're good they're very, very good, but when they're bad, they're horrid. So Chapter 14 is your comprehensive guide to troubleshooting the iPad. It details what to do when almost anything goes wrong, offering step-by-step instructions for specific situations as well as describing a plethora of tips and techniques you can try if something else goes awry. You may never need Chapter 14 (and we hope you won't), but you'll be very glad we put it here if your iPad ever goes wonky on you.

Carrying cases, physical keyboards — in Chapter 15, we take a look at some iPad accessories that we recommend. No, they're not included with your iPad purchase, but we consider them essential just the same.

Photo courtesy of
Griffin Technology

13

Setting You Straight on Settings

D o you consider yourself a control freak? The type of person who has to have it your way? Boy, have you landed in the right chapter.

Settings is kind of the makeover factory for the iPad. You open Settings by tapping its Home screen icon, and from there, you can do things like change the tablet's background or wallpaper and specify Google, Yahoo!, or Bing as the search engine of choice. You can also alter security settings in Safari, tailor e-mail to your liking (among other modifications), and get a handle on how to fetch or push new data.

The Settings area on the iPad is roughly analogous to System Preferences on a Mac and the Control Panel in Windows.

Because we cover some settings elsewhere in this book, we don't dwell on every setting here. But you still have plenty to digest to help you make the iPad your own.

Checking Out the Settings Screen

When you first open Settings, you see a display that looks something like Figure 13-1, with a scrollable list on the left side of the screen and a panel on the right that corresponds to whichever setting is highlighted in blue. We say "something like this" because the Settings on your iPad may differ slightly from those of your neighbor's.

One other general thought to keep in mind: If you see a greater-than symbol (>) appear to the right of a listing, the listing has a bunch of options. Throughout this chapter, you tap the > symbol to check out those options.

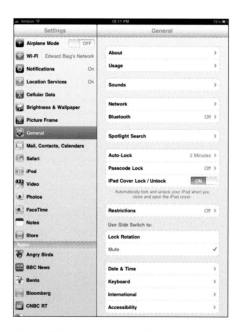

Figure 13-1: Presenting your list of settings.

As you scroll to the bottom of the list on the left, you come to all the settings that pertain to some of the specific third-party apps you've added to the iPad (see Chapter 7). Everybody has a different collection of apps on his iPad, so any settings related to those programs will also obviously be different.

Flying with Sky-High Settings

Your iPad offers settings to keep you on the good side of air-traffic communications systems. However, the settings for the iPad Wi-Fi + 3G model differ from those of the Wi-Fi-only model. The original Wi-Fi-only iPad didn't have an Airplane Mode setting that the original iPad + 3G had. Airplane mode subsequently did arrive on the first Wi-Fi-only iPad with an iOS update. And the Airplane Mode setting appears on the iPad 2 regardless of which wireless model you own.

Using a cellular radio on an airplane is a no-no. But there's nothing verboten about using an iPad on a plane to listen to music, watch videos, and peek at pictures — at least, after the craft has reached cruising altitude.

So how do you take advantage of the iPad's built-in iPod (among other capabilities) at 30,000 feet, while temporarily turning off your wireless gateway to e-mail and Internet functions? The answer is, by turning on Airplane mode.

To do so, merely tap Airplane Mode on the Settings screen to display On (rather than Off).

That act disables each of the iPad's wireless radios (depending on the model): Wi-Fi, cellular, and Bluetooth. While your iPad is in Airplane Mode, you can't surf the web, get a map location, send or receive e-mails, stream YouTube, sync contacts, use iTunes or the App Store, or do anything else that requires an Internet connection. If there's a silver lining here, it's that the iPad's long-lasting battery ought to last even longer — good news if the flight you're on is taking you halfway around the planet.

 The appearance of a tiny Airplane icon on the status bar at the top left corner of the screen reminds you that Airplane mode is turned on. Just remember to turn it off when you're back on the ground.

If you have the Wi-Fi-only model, you have to manually turn off Wi-Fi in Settings before your flight takes off, as discussed in the next section.

Controlling Wi-Fi Connections

As we mention in Chapter 4, Wi-Fi is typically the fastest wireless network you can use to surf the web, send e-mail, and perform other Internet tricks on the iPad. You use the Wi-Fi setting to determine which Wi-Fi networks are available to you and which one to exploit based on its signal.

Tap Wi-Fi so that the setting is on and all Wi-Fi networks in range display, as shown in Figure 13-2. (Alternatively, you can reach this screen by tapping the General setting⟹Network⟹Wi-Fi.)

Tap the Wi-Fi switch to off when you're on a plane or don't have access to a network and don't want to drain the battery.

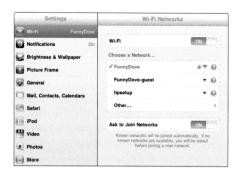

Figure 13-2: Checking out your Wi-Fi options.

A signal-strength indicator can help you choose the network to connect to if more than one is listed; tap the appropriate Wi-Fi network when you reach a decision. If a network is password-protected, you see a Lock icon.

You can also turn the Ask to Join Networks setting on or off. Networks that the iPad are already familiar with are joined automatically, regardless of which one you choose. If the Ask feature is off and no known networks are available, you have to manually select a new network. If the Ask feature is on, you're asked before joining a new network. Either way, you see a list with the same Wi-Fi networks in range.

If you used a particular network automatically in the past but you no longer want your iPad to join it, tap the > symbol next to the network in question (within Wi-Fi settings) and then tap Forget This Network. The iPad develops a quick case of selective amnesia.

In some instances, you have to supply other technical information about a network you hope to glom on to. You encounter a bunch of nasty-sounding terms: DHCP, BootP, or Static IP Addresses, Subnet Mask, Router, DNS, Search Domains, Client ID, HTTP Proxy, and Renew Lease. (At least this last one has nothing to do with renting an apartment or the vehicle you're driving.) Chances are that none of this info is on the tip of your tongue — but that's okay. For one thing, it's a good bet that you'll never need to know this stuff. What's more, even if you *do* have to fill in or adjust these settings, a network administrator or techie friend can probably help you.

Sometimes, you may want to connect to a network that's closed and not shown on the Wi-Fi list. If that's the case, tap Other and use the keyboard to enter the network name. Then tap to choose the type of security setting the network is using (if any). Your choices are WEP, WPA, WPA2, WPA Enterprise, and WPA2 Enterprise. Again, it's not exactly the friendliest terminology in the world, but we figure that someone nearby can lend a hand.

If no Wi-Fi network is available, you have to rely on 3G or a slower cellular connection if you have a Wi-Fi + 3G model. If you don't or you're out of reach of a cellular network, you can't rocket into cyberspace until you regain access to a network.

Roaming among Cellular Data Options

You see another set of settings only if you have the Wi-Fi + 3G iPad. Your options here are as follows:

- ✓ **Data Roaming:** You may unwittingly rack up lofty roaming fees when exchanging e-mail, surfing with Safari, or engaging in other data-heavy activities while traveling abroad. Turn off Data Roaming to avoid such potential charges.

- ✓ **Cellular Data Network:** If you know you don't need the cellular network when you're out and about or are in an area where you don't have access to the network, turn it off. Your battery will thank you later.

- ✓ **Account Information:** Tap View Account to see or edit your account information.

- ✓ **Add a SIM PIN (AT&T model only):** The tiny *SIM,* or *Subscriber Identity Module,* card inside your iPad holds important data about your account. To add a PIN or a passcode to lock your SIM card, tap SIM PIN. That way, if someone gets hold of your SIM, she can't use it in another iPad without the passcode.

  If you assign a PIN to your SIM, you have to enter it to turn the iPad on or off, which some might consider a minor hassle.

Turning Notifications On and Off

Through Apple's Push Notification service, app developers can send you alerts related to programs you've installed on your iPad. Such alerts are typically in text form but may include sounds as well. The idea is that you'll receive notifications even when the application they apply to isn't running. Notifications may also appear as numbered "badges" on their corresponding Home screen icon.

The downside to keeping notifications turned on is that they can curtail battery life (though honestly we've been pretty satisfied with the iPad's staying power even when notifications are active). And some may find notifications distracting at times.

To turn off all the notifications on your iPad, tap Notifications on the left side of the Settings screen and then tap the Notifications button, as shown in Figure 13-3, so that Off displays. To turn them back on, tap the Off button so that it turns blue and shows as an On button. Simple as that.

Figure 13-3: Notify the iPad of your notification intentions.

You can turn notifications on or off for specific apps, too, and you have two ways to accomplish this feat. We recommend trying both methods because different notifications are controlled in each example:

  ✔ **Method 1:** Tap to highlight Notifications on the left side of the screen and then tap an app on the right, as shown in Figure 13-3. Within that specific app, you can turn sounds, alerts, or badges on or off.

  ✔ **Method 2:** Scroll down to the Apps section on the left side of Settings and tap the app with the notifications you want to alter. Note that the app you hope to fiddle with doesn't always appear in the Apps section of Settings. For that matter, many of the apps that do appear on the list do not push notifications to you anyway.

One app that does have a variety of notifications is Facebook. You can choose to have the giant social network push notifications related to Wall posts, friend requests, photo tags, events, and more. Or, choose not to be notified about any or all of these. You can only tweak such settings under Method 2 because Method 1 lets you alter only sounds, alerts, or badges.

Location, Location, Location Services

By using the onboard Maps app or any number of third-party apps, the iPad makes good use of knowing where you are. The iPad with 3G exploits built-in GPS. The Wi-Fi-only iPad can find your general whereabouts (by *triangulating* signals from Wi-Fi base stations and cellular towers).

If that statement creeps you out a little, don't fret. To protect your right to privacy, individual apps pop up quick messages (similar to the one shown in Figure 13-4) asking whether you want them to use your current location. But you can also turn off Location Services right in Settings (refer to Figure 13-1). Not only is your privacy shielded, but you also keep your iPad battery juiced a little longer.

Figure 13-4: The AOL Radio app wants to know where you are.

Settings for Your Senses

The next bunch of settings control what the iPad looks like and sounds like.

Brightening your day

Who doesn't want a bright, vibrant screen? Alas, the brightest screens exact a trade-off: Before you drag the brightness slider shown in Figure 13-5 to the max, remember that brighter screens sap the life from your battery more quickly. The control appears when Brightness & Wallpaper is highlighted.

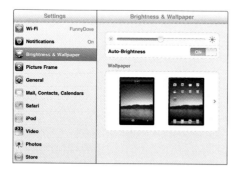

Figure 13-5: Sliding this control adjusts screen brightness.

That's why we recommend tapping the Auto-Brightness control so that it's on. The control automatically adjusts the screen according to the lighting environment in which you're using the iPad while at the same time being considerate of your battery.

Wallpaper

Choosing wallpaper is a neat way to dress up the iPad according to your aesthetic preferences. You can sample the pretty patterns and designs that the iPad has already chosen for you as follows:

1. **Tap the thumbnails shown when you highlight the Brightness & Wallpaper setting. (Refer to Figure 13-5.)**

2. **Choose an image.**

   You can choose a favorite picture from your photo albums or select one of the gorgeous images that Apple has supplied, as shown in Figure 13-6.

3. **Tap one of the following options to set where your wallpaper appears:**

   - *Set Lock Screen* makes your selected image the wallpaper of choice when the iPad is locked.

   - *Set Home Screen* makes the wallpaper decorate only your Home screen.

   - *Set Both* makes your image the wallpaper for locked and Home screens.

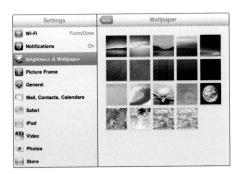

Figure 13-6: Choosing a majestic background.

From Settings, you can also turn your iPad into an animated picture frame. See Chapter 10 for more on the Picture Frame feature and the settings to get it just the way you like it.

Sounds

Consider the Sounds settings area, found after you highlight General in the Settings list to the left, the iPad's soundstage. There, you can turn audio alerts on or off for a variety of functions: new e-mail, sent mail, and calendar alerts. You can also decide whether you want to hear lock sounds and keyboard clicks.

On iPad 2, you can alter the ringtone you hear in FaceTime and tap a button to buy more tones if you're not satisfied with those that Apple supplies.

To raise the decibel level of alerts, drag the volume slider to the right. Drag in the opposite direction to bring down the noise.

An alternative way to adjust sound levels is to use the physical Volume buttons on the side of the iPad for this purpose, as long as you're not already using the iPad's iPod to listen to music or watch video.

Exploring Settings in General

Certain miscellaneous settings are difficult to pigeonhole. Apple wisely lumped these under the General settings moniker, and we've just told you about one of these, Sounds. Here's a closer look at other General options.

About About

You aren't seeing double. This section, as shown in Figure 13-7, is all about the About setting. And About is full of trivial (and not-so-trivial) information *about* the device. What you find here is straightforward:

Figure 13-7: You find info about your iPad under About.

- ✓ **Network you use:** AT&T or Verizon

- ✓ **Number of songs stored on the device**

- ✓ **Number of videos**

- ✓ **Number of photos**

- ✓ **Number of applications**

- ✓ **Storage capacity used and available:** Because of the way the device is formatted, you always have a little less storage than the advertised amount of flash memory.

- ✓ **Software version:** As this book goes to press, we're up to version 4.3. But as the software is tweaked and updated, your device takes on a new "build" identifier indicating it's just a little bit further along than some previous build. So you see, in parentheses next to the version number, a string of numbers and letters that looks like 8F191 and tells you more precisely what software version you have. The number/letter string changes whenever the iPad's software is updated and is potentially useful to some tech support person who might need to know the precise version you're working with.

- ✓ **Carrier and cellular data (Wi-Fi + 3G version only):** Yep, that's AT&T or Verizon in the United States.

- ✓ **Serial and model numbers**

- ✓ **Cellular Data Number**

- ✓ **Wi-Fi address**

- ✓ **Bluetooth address:** More on Bluetooth in an upcoming section.

- ✓ **MEID:** It's a geeky acronym for *Mobile Equipment Identifier* associated with CDMA gear. That's why you see this only on the Verizon iPad.

- ✓ **Modern Firmware:** Another geeky term; it's software programmed into the iPad's memory.

- ✓ **Legal and Regulatory:** You had to know that the lawyers would get in their two cents somehow. All the fine print is here. And *fine print* it is because you can't unpinch to enlarge the text. (Not that we can imagine more than a handful will bother to read this legal mumbo jumbo.)

Usage settings

The About setting we cover in the preceding section gives a lot of information about your device. But after you back out of About and return to the main General settings, you can find other settings for statistics on iPad usage:

- ✓ **Battery percentage:** You almost always see a little battery meter in the upper-right corner of the screen, except in those instances when you watch videos in which the whole top bar disappears. If you also want to see your battery life presented in percentage terms, make sure that the Battery Percentage setting is turned on.

- ✓ **Cellular network data:** This is the amount of network data you sent and received over the AT&T or Verizon networks, a setting that appears only if you have a Wi-Fi + 3G iPad. You can reset these statistics by tapping the Reset Statistics button.

   If you choose to pay for only 250MB per month, this is where you can check whether you're close to exceeding your data limit.

VPN settings

After you tap Network on the General settings screen, you see two controls: Wi-Fi and VPN. We address Wi-Fi earlier in this chapter, in the section "Controlling Wi-Fi Connections." We tackle VPN here.

A *virtual private network,* or *VPN,* is a way for you to securely access your company's network behind the firewall — using an encrypted Internet connection that acts as a secure "tunnel" for data.

You can configure a VPN on the iPad by following these steps:

1. **Tap Settings⇨General⇨Network⇨VPN⇨Add VPN Configuration.**

2. **Tap one of the protocol options.**

   The iPad software supports the protocols *L2TP* (Layer 2 Tunneling Protocol), *PPTP* (Point-To-Point Tunneling Protocol), and Cisco *IPSec,* which apparently provides the kind of security that satisfies network administrators.

3. **Using configuration settings provided by your company, fill in the appropriate server information, account, password, and other information.**

4. **Choose whether to turn on RSA SecurID authentication.**

   Better yet, lend your iPad to the techies where you work and let them fill in the blanks on your behalf.

After you configure your iPad for VPN usage, you can turn that capability on or off by tapping (yep) the VPN On or Off switch inside Settings.

Bluetooth

Of all the peculiar terms you may encounter in techdom, *Bluetooth* is one of our favorites. The name is derived from Harald Blåtand, a tenth century Danish monarch, who, the story goes, helped unite warring factions. And, we're told, *Blåtand* translates to *Bluetooth* in English. (Bluetooth is all about collaboration between different types of devices — get it?)

Blåtand was obviously ahead of his time. Although we can't imagine that he ever used a slate computer, he now has an entire short-range wireless technology named in his honor. On the iPad, you can use Bluetooth to communicate wirelessly with a compatible Bluetooth headset or to use an optional wireless keyboard. Such accessories are made by Apple and many others. To ensure that the iPad works with one of these devices, it has to be wirelessly *paired,* or coupled, with the chosen device. If you're using a third-party accessory, follow the instructions that came with that headset or keyboard so that it becomes *discoverable,* or ready to be paired with your iPad. Then turn on Bluetooth (under General on the Settings screen) so that the iPad can find such nearby devices and the device can find the iPad. In Figure 13-8, an Apple Wireless Keyboard and the iPad are successfully paired when you enter a designated passkey on the keyboard. Bluetooth works up to a range of about 30 feet.

You know Bluetooth is turned on when you see the Bluetooth icon on the status bar. If the symbol is white, the iPad is communicating wirelessly with a connected device. If it's gray, Bluetooth is turned on in the iPad *but* a paired device isn't nearby or isn't turned on. If you don't see a Bluetooth icon, the setting is turned off.

To unpair a device, select it from the device list, and tap Unpair. We guess breaking up *isn't* hard to do.

Figure 13-8: Pairing an Apple Wireless Keyboard with the iPad.

The iPad supports *stereo* Bluetooth headphones, so you can now stream stereo audio from the iPad to those devices.

The iPad can tap into Bluetooth in other ways. One is through *peer-to-peer* connectivity, so you can engage in multiplayer games with other nearby iPad, iPhone, or iPod touch users. You can also do such things as exchange business cards, share pictures, and send short notes. And, you don't even have to pair the devices as you do with a headset or wireless keyboard.

You can't use Bluetooth to exchange files or sync between an iPad and a computer. Nor can you use it to print stuff from the iPad on a Bluetooth printer (though the AirPrint feature added with iOS 4.2 handles that chore in some instances). That's because the iPad doesn't support any of the Bluetooth profiles (or specifications) required to allow such wireless stunts to take place — at least not as of this writing. We think that's a shame.

Spotlight Search

Tell the iPad the apps that you want to search. Touch the three horizontal lines next to an app you want to include in your search and drag it up or down to rearrange the search order.

Auto-Lock

Tap Auto-Lock in the General settings pane, and you can set the amount of time that elapses before the iPad automatically locks or turns off the display. Your choices are 15 minutes before, 10 minutes, 5 minutes, or 2 minutes. Or, you can set it so that the iPad never locks automatically.

If you work for a company that insists on a passcode (see the next section), the Never Auto-Lock option isn't on the list that your iPad shows you.

Don't worry if the iPad is locked. You can still receive notification alerts and adjust the volume.

Passcode

You can choose a 4-digit simple passcode to prevent people from unlocking the iPad. Tap Passcode Lock. Then use the virtual keypad to enter a 4-digit code. During this setup, you have to enter the code a second time before it's accepted.

You can also determine whether a passcode is required immediately, after 1 minute, after 5 minutes, or after 15 minutes. Shorter times are more secure, of course. On the topic of security, the iPad can be set to automatically erase your data if someone makes ten failed passcode attempts.

You can also change the passcode or turn it off later (unless your employer dictates otherwise), but you need to know the present passcode to apply any changes. If you forget the passcode, you have to restore the iPad software, as we describe in Chapter 14.

Cover Lock/Unlock

The iPad 2 gives you the choice to automatically lock and unlock your iPad when you close and open the clever iPad Smart Cover accessory. If you set a passcode, you still have to enter it to wake the iPad from siesta-land.

Restrictions

Parents and bosses may love the Restrictions tools, but kids and employees usually think otherwise. You can clamp down, er, provide proper parental guidance to your children, by preventing them at least some of the time from using the Safari browser, YouTube, Camera, FaceTime, iTunes, Ping, Location Services, or Game Center. Or, you might not let them install new apps or make purchases inside the apps you do allow. When restrictions are in place, icons for off-limit functions can no longer be seen. Tap Enable Restrictions, set or enter your passcode — you have to enter it twice if you are setting up the passcode — and tap the buttons next to each item in the Allow or Allowed Content lists that you plan to restrict. Their corresponding settings show Off.

Moreover, parents have more controls to work with. For instance, you can allow Junior to watch a movie on the iPad but prevent him from watching a flick that carries an R or NC-17 rating. You can also restrict access to certain TV shows, explicit songs and podcasts, and apps, based on age-appropriate ratings. In Game Center, you can decide whether your kid can play a multiplayer game or add friends. Stop feeling guilty: You have your users' best interests at heart.

If guilt gets the better of you, you can turn off Restrictions. Open the Restrictions setting by again typing your passcode. Then switch the On/ Off setting back to On for each setting you free up. Tap Disable Restrictions. You have to enter your passcode one more time before your kids and office underlings return you to their good graces.

Side Switch

You can use the side switch for one of two purposes: You can lock the rotation so that the screen orientation doesn't change when you turn the iPad to the side, or you can mute certain sounds. Here's where you get to make that choice.

Date and Time

In our neck of the woods, the time is reported as 11:32 p.m. (or whatever time it happens to be). But in some circles, it's reported as 23:32. If you prefer the latter format on the iPad's status bar, tap the 24-Hour Time setting (under Date & Time) so that it's on.

This setting is just one that you can adjust under Date & Time. You can also have the iPad set the time in your time zone.

Here's how:

1. **Tap Set Date & Time.**

   You see fields for setting the time zone and the date and time.

2. **Tap the Time Zone field.**

   The current time zone and virtual keyboard are shown.

3. **Tap the letters of the city or country whose time zone you want to enter until the one you have in mind appears. Then tap the name of that city or country.**

   The Time Zone field is automatically filled in for that city.

4. **Tap the Set Date & Time field so that the time is shown; then roll the bicycle-lock-like controls until the proper time displays.**

5. **Tap the date shown so that the bicycle-lock-like controls pop up for the date; then roll the wheels for the month, day, and year until the correct date appears.**

6. **Tap the Date & Time button to return to the main Date & Time settings screen.**

You can dispense with these settings and just have the iPad set the time automatically based on its knowledge of where you happen to be.

Keyboard

Under Keyboard settings, you have the following options:

- **Auto-Capitalization:** You can turn Auto-Capitalization on or off.

  Auto-Capitalization, which the iPad turns on by default, means that the first letter of the first word you type after ending the preceding sentence with a period, a question mark, or an exclamation point is capitalized.

- **Auto-Correction:** When turned on, the iPad takes a stab at what it thinks you meant to type.

- **Check Spelling:** When on, the keyboard can check spelling while you type.

✏ **Caps Lock:** If Caps Lock is enabled, all letters are uppercased LIKE THIS if you double-tap the Shift key. (The Shift key is the one with the arrow pointing up.) Double-tap Shift again to exit Caps Lock.

✏ **Automatic period and space:** You can also turn on a keyboard setting that inserts a period followed by a space when you double-tap the spacebar. The "." setting that permits this is turned on by default.

Additionally, you can choose to use an international keyboard (as we discuss in Chapter 2), which you choose from the International setting — the next setting after Keyboard in the General settings area. See the next section for details.

International

The iPad is an international sensation just as it is in the United States. In the International section, you can set the language you type (by using a custom virtual keyboard), the language in which the iPad displays text, and the date, time, and telephone format for the region in question. You can choose a Gregorian, Japanese, or Buddhist calendar, too.

Accessibility

The Accessibility or Universal Access Features tools on your iPad are targeted at helping people with certain disabilities. The following sections explain each one in turn.

VoiceOver

This screen reader describes aloud what's on the screen. It can read e-mail messages, web pages, and more. With VoiceOver active, you tap an item on the screen to select it. VoiceOver places a black rectangle around it, and either speaks the name or describes an item. For example, if you tap, say, Brightness & Wallpaper, the VoiceOver voice speaks the words "Brightness & Wallpaper button." VoiceOver even lets you know when you alternately position the iPad in landscape or portrait mode or when your screen is locked or unlocked.

Within the VoiceOver setting, you have several options. For instance, if you turn on Speak Hints, VoiceOver may provide instructions on what to do next, along the lines of "double-tap to open." You can drag a Speaking Rate slider to speed up or slow down the speech. You can also determine the kind of typing feedback you get, from among characters, words, characters and words, or no feedback. Additional controls let you turn on Phonetics and Pitch Change settings.

The voice you hear speaks in the language you specified in International settings, which we explain earlier.

You have to know a whole new set of finger gestures when VoiceOver is on, which may seem difficult, especially when you first start using VoiceOver. When you stop to think about it, the reason makes a lot of sense. You want to be able to hear descriptions on the screen before you actually activate buttons. Different VoiceOver gestures use different numbers of fingers. Here's a rundown on many of these:

- **Tap:** Speak the item.
- **Flick right or left:** Select the next or previous item.
- **Flick up or down:** This gesture has multiple outcomes that depend on how you set the so-called "rotor control" gesture. Think of the rotor control like you'd think about turning a dial. You rotate two fingers on the screen. The purpose is to switch to a different set of commands or features. Which leads us back to the flick up or down gestures. Say you're reading text in an e-mail. By alternately spinning the rotor, you can switch between hearing the body of a message read aloud word by word or character by character. After you set the parameters, flick up or down to hear stuff read back. The flicking up or down gestures serve a different purpose when you type an e-mail: The gestures move the cursor left or right within the text.
- **Two-finger tap:** Stop speaking.
- **Two-finger flick up:** Read everything from the top of the screen.
- **Two-finger flick down:** Read everything from your current position on the screen.
- **Three-finger flick up or down:** Scroll a page.
- **Three-finger flick right or left:** Go to the next or previous page.
- **Three-finger tap:** Lets you know which page or rows are on the screen.
- **Four-finger flick up or down:** Go to the first or last part of the page.
- **Four-finger flick right or left:** Go to the next or previous section.
- **Double-tap:** Activate a selected icon or button to launch an app, turn a switch from On to Off, and more.
- **Touch an item with one finger and tap the screen with another:** Otherwise known as *split-tapping,* when you touch an item, a voice identifies what you touched (for example "Safari button" or "Notifications on button"). A tap with the second finger selects whatever was identified with the first finger (that is, "Safari button selected," "Notifications on button selected.") Now you can double-tap to launch the button or whatever else was selected.

✔ **Double-tap, hold for a second, and then add a standard gesture:** Tell the iPad to go back to using standard gestures for your next move. You can also use standard gestures with VoiceOver by double-tapping and holding the screen. You hear tones that remind you that standard gestures are now in effect. They stay that way until you lift your finger.

✔ **Two-finger double-tap:** Play or pause. You use the double-tap in the iPod, YouTube, and Photos apps.

✔ **Three-finger double-tap:** Mute or unmute the voice.

✔ **Three-finger triple-tap:** Turn the display on or off.

After all this you may be thinking, "Geez, that's a lot to take in." It surely is. But Apple helps you practice VoiceOver gestures by tapping a Practice VoiceOver Gestures button.

Zoom

The Zoom feature offers a screen magnifier for those who are visually challenged. To zoom by 200 percent, double-tap the screen with *three* fingers. Drag three fingers to move around the screen. To increase magnification, use three fingers to tap and drag up. Tap with three fingers and drag down to decrease magnification.

When magnified, the characters on the screen aren't as crisp, and you can't display as much in a single view.

Large Text

You can make text larger in the Mail and Notes apps. You have the choice of six point sizes (from 20pt to 56pt), in addition to the default.

White on Black

The colors on the iPad can be reversed to provide a higher contrast for people with poor eyesight. The screen resembles a film negative.

Mono Audio

If you suffer hearing loss in one ear, the iPad can combine the right and left audio channels so that both can be heard in both earbuds of any headset you plug in.

The iPad, unlike its cousins the iPhone or the iPod touch, doesn't come with earbuds or headphones. You have to supply your own.

Speak Auto-Text

When this setting is on, the iPad automatically speaks auto-corrections and capitalizations.

Triple-Click Home

Set the Triple-Click Home feature to summon the following accessibility tools. Clicking Home three times rapidly can be used to toggle VoiceOver on or off, toggle White on Black on or off, or toggle Zoom on or off. You can also set up a prompt to be asked which of these functions you want to accomplish.

Closed Captioning

To turn on closed captioning subtitles for a movie or video in which they're available, tap Video Settings and turn on the feature.

Reset

As little kids playing sports, we ended an argument by agreeing to a "do-over." Well, the Reset settings on the iPad are one big do-over. Now that you're (presumably) grown up, think long and hard about the consequences before implementing do-over settings. Regardless, you may encounter good reasons for starting over; some of these are addressed in Chapter 14.

Here are your reset options:

- **Reset All Settings:** Resets all settings, but no data or media is deleted.

- **Erase All Content and Settings:** Resets all settings *and* wipes out all your data.

- **Reset Network Settings:** Deletes the current network settings and restores them to their factory defaults.

- **Subscriber Services:** Here you have options to reprovision your account and reset your authentication code.

- **Reset Keyboard Dictionary:** Removes added words from the dictionary. Remember that the iPad keyboard is intelligent. And, one reason it's so smart is that it learns from you. So when you reject words that the iPad keyboard suggests, it figures that the words you specifically banged out ought to be added to the keyboard dictionary.

- **Reset Home Screen Layout:** Reverts all icons to the way they were at the factory.

- **Reset Location Warnings:** Restores factory defaults.

Find My iPad

We hope you never have to use the Find My iPad feature — though we have to say that it's pretty darn cool. If you inadvertently leave your iPad in a taxi or restaurant, Find My iPad may just help you retrieve it. The feature used to require a MobileMe paid subscription, but now it's free on MobileMe to anyone running iOS 4.2 or later on the iPad.

To turn on Find My iPad, tap Settings⇨Mail, Contacts, Calendars and then tap the me.com e-mail account you added to the iPad. You get a me.com e-mail account when you subscribe to MobileMe. If necessary, see Chapter 5 to see how to add an e-mail account to the iPad. If you don't have a paid MobileMe account, and thus no me.com e-mail address, use your Apple ID to add a free MobileMe account. You can turn on the Find My iPad feature, but can't take advantage of other MobileMe goodies.

Now suppose that you lost your tablet — and we can only assume that you're beside yourself. Follow these steps to see whether the Find My iPad feature can help you:

1. **Log on to your MobileMe me.com account from any browser on your computer.**

2. **Click the Find My iPhone icon.**

   If you don't see it, click the icon with a cloud in it that appears in the upper-left corner of the MobileMe site. You see a panel with icons that are tied to various MobileMe services including Find My iPhone. (Yes, even though the feature is Find My iPad on the iPad, it shows up as Find My iPhone on the MobileMe site. Don't worry, it'll still locate your iPad and for that matter, a lost iPhone, too.)

   Assuming that your tablet is turned on and in the coverage area, its general whereabouts turn up on a map (as shown in Figure 13-9), in satellite view, or a hybrid of the two. In our tests, Find My iPad found our iPads quickly.

   The truth is that even seeing your iPad on a map may not help you much, especially if the device is lost somewhere in midtown Manhattan. Take heart.

3. **At the MobileMe site, click the Display Message or Play Sound button.**

4. **Type out a plea to the Good Samaritan that you hope picked up your iPad.**

   The message appears on the lost iPad's screen. Don't forget to include in the message a way for the person to reach you, such as the message displayed on the iPad in Figure 13-10.

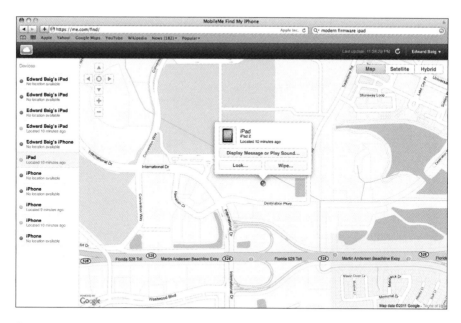

Figure 13-9: Locating a lost iPad.

Figure 13-10: An appeal to return the iPad.

To get someone's attention, you can also sound an alarm that plays for two minutes, even if the volume is off. Hey, that alarm may come in handy if the iPad turns up under a couch in your house. Stranger things have happened.

After all this labor, if the iPad is seemingly gone for good, click Wipe at the MobileMe site to delete your personal data from afar and return the iPad to its factory settings. (A somewhat less drastic measure is to remotely lock your iPad using a four-digit passcode.) And, if you ever get your iPad back, you can always restore the information from an iTunes backup on your Mac or PC.

14

When Good iPads Go Bad

*I*n our experience, all Apple's iOS devices — namely the iPad, iPhone, and iPod touch — are fairly reliable. But every so often a good iPad might just go bad. We don't expect it to be a common occurrence, but it does happen occasionally. So in this chapter, we look at the types of bad things that can happen, along with suggestions for fixing them.

What kind of bad things are we talking about? Well, we're referring to problems involving

✔ Frozen or dead iPads

✔ Wireless networks

✔ Synchronization of computers (both Mac and PC) or iTunes

After all the troubleshooting, we tell you how to get even more help if nothing we suggest does the trick. Finally, if your iPad is so badly hosed that it needs to go back to the mother ship for repairs, we offer ways to survive the experience with a minimum of stress or fuss.

Resuscitating an iPad with Issues

Our first category of troubleshooting techniques applies to an iPad that's frozen or otherwise acting up. The recommended procedure when this happens is to perform the seven *R*s in sequence:

1. Recharge

2. Restart

3. Reset your iPad

4. Remove your content

5. Reset settings and content

6. Restore

7. Recovery mode

But before you even start those procedures, Apple recommends you take these steps:

1. **Verify that you have the current version of iTunes installed on your Mac or PC.**

   You can always download the latest and greatest version here: www.apple.com/itunes/download.

2. **Verify that you're connecting your iPad to your computer using a USB 2.0 port.**

3. **Make sure that your iPad software is up to date.**

   To do so:

   a. Connect your iPad to your computer, launch iTunes (if necessary), and then click your iPad in the iTunes sidebar.

   b. Click the Summary tab and then click the Check for Update button.

If those three easy steps didn't get you back up and running and your iPad is still acting up — if it freezes, doesn't wake up from sleep, doesn't do something it used to do, or in any other way acts improperly — don't panic. The rest of this section describes the things you should try, in the order that we (and Apple) recommend.

If the first technique doesn't do the trick, go on to the second. If the second one doesn't work, try the third. And so on.

Recharge

If your iPad acts up in any way, shape, or form, the first thing you should try is to give its battery a full recharge before you proceed.

Don't plug the iPad's dock connector–to–USB cable into a USB port on your keyboard, monitor, or USB hub. You need to plug it into one of the USB ports on your computer itself. That's because the USB ports on your computer supply more power than the other ports. Although other USB ports *may* do the trick, you're better off using the built-in ones on your computer.

If your computer is more than a few years old, even your built-in USB ports may not supply enough juice to recharge your iPad. It'll sync just fine; it just won't recharge. If it says Not Charging next to the battery icon at the top of the screen, use the included USB power adapter to recharge your iPad from an AC outlet rather than from a computer.

If you're in a hurry, charge your iPad for a minimum of 20 minutes. We think a full charge is a better idea, but a 20+ minute charge is better than no charge at all.

Restart

If you recharge your iPad and it still misbehaves, the next thing to try is restarting it. Just as restarting a computer often fixes problems, restarting your iPad sometimes works wonders.

Here's how to restart:

1. **Press and hold the Sleep/Wake button.**

2. **When the red slider appears, slide it to turn off the iPad and then wait a few seconds.**

3. **Press and hold the Sleep/Wake button again until the Apple logo appears on the screen.**

4. **If your iPad is still frozen, misbehaves, or doesn't start, press and hold the Home button for 6 to 10 seconds to force any frozen applications to quit.**

5. **Repeat Steps 1 to 3 again.**

If these steps don't get your iPad back up and running, move on to the third *R,* resetting your iPad.

Reset your iPad

To reset your iPad, merely press and hold the Sleep/Wake button and then press and hold the Home button, continuing to press both for at least ten seconds. When you see the Apple logo, release both buttons.

Resetting your iPad is like forcing your computer to restart after a crash. Your data shouldn't be affected by a reset — and in many cases, it cures whatever was ailing your iPad. So don't be shy about giving this technique a try. In many cases, your iPad goes back to normal after you reset it this way.

Sometimes you have to press and hold the Sleep/Wake button *before* you press and hold the Home button. That's because if you press both at the same time, you might create a *screen shot* — a picture of whatever is on your screen at the time — rather than reset your iPad. (This type of screen picture, by the way, is stored in the Photos app's Saved Photos album in its Albums tab. Find out more about this feature at the end of Chapter 18.) A screen shot *should* only happen if you press and release both buttons at the same time, but sometimes pressing and holding both buttons triggers the screen shot mechanism instead of restarting your iPad.

Unfortunately, sometimes resetting *doesn't* do the trick. When that's the case, you have to take stronger measures.

Remove content

If you've been reading along in this chapter, nothing you've done should have taken more than a minute or two. We hate to tell you, but that's about to change because the next thing you should try is removing some of or all your data to see whether it's causing your troubles.

To do so, you need to sync your iPad and reconfigure it so that some of or all your files are *not* synchronized (which removes them from the iPad). The problem could be contacts, calendar data, songs, photos, videos, or podcasts. You can apply one of two strategies to this troubleshooting task:

 ✓ **If you suspect a particular data type** — for example, you suspect your photos because whenever you tap the Photos icon on the Home screen, your iPad freezes — try removing that data first.

 ✓ **If you have no suspicions,** deselect every item and then sync. When you're finished, your iPad should have no data on it.

   If that method fixes your iPad, try restoring your data, one type at a time. If the problem returns, you have to keep experimenting to determine which particular data type or file is causing the problem.

If you're still having problems, the next step is to reset your iPad's settings.

Reset settings and content

Resetting involves two steps: The first one, resetting your iPad settings, resets every iPad *setting* to its default — the way it was when you took it out of the box. Resetting the iPad's settings doesn't erase any of your data or media. The only downside is that you may have to go back and change some settings afterward — so you can try this step without trepidation. To reset your settings, tap the Settings icon on your Home screen and then tap General➪Reset➪Reset All Settings.

Be careful *not* to tap Erase All Content and Settings, at least not yet. Erasing all content takes more time to recover from (because your next sync takes a long time), so try Reset All Settings first.

Now, if resetting all settings didn't cure your iPad, you have to try Erase All Content and Settings. You find it in the same place as Reset All Settings (tap Settings➪General➪Reset➪Erase All Content and Settings).

The Erase All Content strategy deletes everything from your iPad — all your data, media, and settings. Because all these items are stored on your computer — at least in theory — you should be able to put things back the way they were during your next sync. But you lose any screen shots or photos you've taken (iPad 2 only), as well as e-mail, apps purchased on your iPad, contacts, calendar events, playlists, and anything else you've created or modified on the iPad since your last sync.

After using Erase All Content and Settings, check to see whether your iPad works properly. If it doesn't cure what ails your iPad, the final *R,* restoring your iPad using iTunes, can help.

Restore

Before you give up the ghost on your poor, sick iPad, you can try one more thing. Connect your iPad to your computer as though you were about to sync. But when the iPad appears in the iTunes Source list, click the Restore button on the Summary tab. This action erases all your data and media and resets all your settings.

Because all your data and media still exist on your computer (except for photos you've taken, contacts, calendar events, notes, and On-the-Go playlists you've created or modified since your last sync, as noted previously), you shouldn't lose anything by restoring. Your next sync will take longer than usual, and you may have to reset settings you've changed since you got your iPad. But other than those inconveniences, restoring shouldn't cause you any additional trouble.

Recovery mode

So, if you've tried all the other steps or you couldn't try some or all of them because your iPad is so messed up, you can try one last thing: Recovery mode. Here's how it works:

1. **Disconnect the USB cable from your iPad, but leave the other end of the cable connected to the USB port on your computer.**

2. **Turn off the iPad by pressing and holding the Sleep/Wake button for a few seconds until the red slider appears onscreen, and then slide the slider.**

Wait for the iPad to turn off.

3. **Press and hold the Home button while you reconnect the USB cable to your iPad.**

When you reconnect the USB cable, your iPad should power on.

If you see a battery icon with a thin red band and an icon of a wall plug, an arrow, and a lightning bolt, you need to let your iPad charge for at least 10 or 15 minutes. When the battery picture goes away or turns green instead of red, go back to Step 2 and try again.

4. **Continue holding the Home button until you see the Connect to iTunes screen, and then release the Home button.**

If you don't see the Connect to iTunes screen on your iPad, try Steps 1–4 again.

If iTunes didn't open automatically already, launch it now. You should see a Recovery Mode alert on your computer screen telling you that your iPad is in Recovery mode and that you must restore it before it can be used with iTunes.

5. **Use iTunes to restore the device, as we describe in the preceding section.**

Okay. So that's the gamut of things you can do when your iPad acts up. If you tried all this and none of it worked, skim through the rest of this chapter to see whether anything else we recommend looks like it might help. If not, your iPad probably needs to go into the shop for repairs.

Never fear, gentle reader. Be sure to read the last section in this chapter, "If Nothing We Suggest Helps." Your iPad may be quite sick, but we help ease the pain by sharing some tips on how to minimize the discomfort.

Problems with Networks

If you're having problems with Wi-Fi or your wireless carrier's data network (Wi-Fi + 3G models only), this section may help. The techniques here are short and sweet — except for the last one, restore. Restore, which we describe in the previous section, is still inconvenient and time-consuming, and it still entails erasing all your data and media and then restoring it.

First, here are some simple steps that may help:

✓ **Make sure you have sufficient Wi-Fi or 3G signal strength, as shown in Figure 14-1.**

Figure 14-1: Wi-Fi (top) and 3G (bottom) signal strength from best (left) to worst (right).

✔ **Try moving around.** Changing your location by as little as a few feet can sometimes mean the difference between great wireless reception and no wireless reception at all. If you're inside, try moving around or even a step or two in one direction. If you're outside, try moving 10 or 20 paces in any direction. Keep an eye on the cell signal or Wi-Fi icon as you move around, and stop when you see more bars than you saw before.

✔ **Restart your iPad.** If you've forgotten how, refer to the "Restart" section, earlier in this chapter. As we mention, restarting your iPad is often all it takes to fix whatever is wrong.

If you have a Wi-Fi + 3G iPad, try the following two bullet points.

✔ **Make sure that you haven't left your iPad in Airplane mode, as we describe in Chapter 13.** In Airplane mode (Wi-Fi + 3G models only), all network-dependent features are disabled, so you can't send or receive messages, or use any of the applications that require a Wi-Fi or data network connection (that is, Mail, Safari, Maps, YouTube, and the iTunes and App Store apps).

✔ **Toggle Airplane mode on/off.** Turn on Airplane mode by tapping Settings on the Home screen and then tapping the Airplane mode On/Off switch to turn it on. Wait 15 or 20 seconds, and then turn it off again.

Toggling Airplane mode on and off like this resets both the Wi-Fi and wireless data-network connections. If your network connection was the problem, toggling Airplane mode on and off may correct it.

Apple offers two very good articles that may help you with Wi-Fi issues. The first offers some general troubleshooting tips and hints; the second discusses potential sources of interference for wireless devices and networks. You can find them here:

```
http://support.apple.com/kb/TS3237
```

and here:

```
http://support.apple.com/kb/HT1365
```

If none of the preceding suggestions fixes your network issues, try restoring your iPad, as we describe previously in the "Restore" section.

Performing a restore deletes everything on your iPad — all your data, media, and settings. You should be able to put things back the way they were with your next sync. If that doesn't happen, for whatever reason, you can't say we didn't warn you.

Sync, Computer, or iTunes Issues

The last category of troubleshooting techniques in this chapter applies to issues that involve synchronization and computer–iPad relations. If you're having problems syncing or your computer doesn't recognize your iPad when you connect it, here are some things to try.

Once again, we suggest that you try these procedures in the order they're presented here:

1. **Recharge your iPad.**

   If you didn't try it previously, try it now. Go back to the "Resuscitating an iPad with Issues" section, at the beginning of this chapter, and read what we say about recharging your iPad. Every word there also applies here.

2. **Try a different USB port or a different cable if you have one available.**

   It doesn't happen often, but occasionally USB ports and cables go bad. When they do, they invariably cause sync and connection problems. Always make sure that a bad USB port or cable isn't to blame.

   If you don't remember what we said about using USB ports on your computer rather than the ones on your keyboard, monitor, or hub, we suggest that you reread the "Recharge" section, earlier in this chapter.

3. **Restart your iPad and try to sync again.**

   We describe restarting in full and loving detail in the "Restart" section, earlier in this chapter.

4. **Reinstall iTunes.**

   Even if you have an iTunes installer handy, you probably should visit the Apple website and download the latest-and-greatest version, just in case. You can find the latest version of iTunes at `www.apple.com/itunes/download`.

More Help on the Apple Website

If you try everything we suggest earlier in this chapter and still have problems, don't give up just yet. This section describes a few more places you may find help. We recommend that you check out some or all of them before you throw in the towel and smash your iPad into tiny little pieces (or ship it back to Apple for repairs, as we describe in the next section).

First, Apple offers an excellent set of support resources on its website at www.apple.com/support/ipad/getstarted. You can browse support issues by category, search for a problem by keyword, read or download technical manuals, and scan the discussion forums.

Speaking of the discussion forums, you can go directly to them at http://discussions.apple.com. They're chock-full of useful questions and answers from other iPad users, and our experience has been that if you can't find an answer to a support question elsewhere, you can often find it in these forums. You can browse by category (Syncing, for example, as shown in Figure 14-2) or search by keyword.

Figure 14-2: Page 1 of 18 pages of discussions about syncing your iPad.

Either way, you find thousands of discussions about almost every aspect of using your iPad. Better still, you can frequently find the answer to your question or a helpful suggestion.

Now for the best part: If you can't find a solution by browsing or searching, you can post your question in the appropriate Apple discussion forum. Check back in a few days (or even in a few hours), and some helpful iPad user may well have replied with the answer. If you've never tried this fabulous tool, you're missing out on one of the greatest support resources available anywhere.

Last, but certainly not least, before you throw in the towel, you might want to try a carefully worded Google search. It couldn't hurt, and you might just find the solution you spent hours searching for.

If Nothing We Suggest Helps

If you tried every trick in the book (this one) and still have a malfunctioning iPad, consider shipping it off to the iPad hospital (better known as Apple, Inc.). The repair is free if your iPad is still under its one-year limited warranty.

You can extend your warranty for as long as two years from the original purchase date, if you want. To do so, you need to buy the AppleCare Protection Plan for your iPad. You don't have to do it when you buy your iPad, but you must buy it before your one-year limited warranty expires. The retail price is $99, but we've seen it for a lot less, so it might pay to shop around.

Here are a few things you need to know before you take your iPad in to be repaired:

- *Your iPad may be erased during its repair,* so you should sync your iPad with iTunes before you take it in, if you can. If you can't and you entered data on the iPad since your last sync, such as a contact or an appointment, the data may not be there when you restore your iPad upon its return.

- Remove any third-party accessories, such as a case or screen protector.

Although you may be able to get your iPad serviced by Best Buy or another authorized Apple reseller, we recommend that you take it to your nearest Apple Store, for two reasons:

✔ **No one knows your iPad like Apple.** One of the geniuses at the Apple Store may be able to fix whatever is wrong without sending your iPad away for repairs.

✔ **The Apple Store will, in some cases, swap out your wonky iPad for a brand new one on the spot.** You can't win if you don't play, which is why we always visit our local Apple Store when something goes wrong (with our iPads, iPhones, iPods, and even our laptops and iMacs).

And that retires the side. If you've done everything we've suggested, we're relatively certain you're now holding an iPad that works flawlessly. Again.

Accessorizing Your iPad

*A*nyone who has purchased a new car in recent years is aware that it's not always a picnic trying to escape the showroom without the salesperson trying to get you to part with a few extra bucks. You can only imagine what the markup is on roof racks, navigation systems, and rear-seat DVD players.

We don't suppose you'll get a hard sell when you snap up an iPad or iPad 2 at an Apple Store (or elsewhere). But Apple and several other companies are all too happy to outfit whichever iPad model you choose with extra doodads from wireless keyboards and stands to battery chargers and carrying cases. So just as your car might benefit from dealer (or third-party) options, so too might your iPad benefit from a variety of spare parts.

The iPad features the standard 30-pin dock connector that's familiar to iPod and iPhone owners. If you own either or both of these products, you also know that a bevy of accessories fit perfectly into that Dock connector. Heck, you might even try to plug the battery chargers or other iPod/iPhone accessories you have laying around into the iPad. No guarantee these will work, but they probably will. And you have nothing to lose by trying.

One thing is certain: If you see a Made for iPad label on the package, the developer is certifying that an electronic accessory has been designed to connect specifically to the iPad and meets performance standards established by Apple.

We start this accessories chapter with the options that carry Apple's own logo and conclude with worthwhile extras from other companies.

Accessories from Apple

You've come to expect a certain level of excellence from Apple hardware and software, so you should expect no different when it comes to various Apple-branded accessories. That said, you will find a variety of opinions on some of these products, so we recommend a visit to http://store.apple.com, where you can read mini-reviews and pore over ratings from real people just like you. They're not shy about telling it like it is.

Casing the iPad

The thing about accessories is that half the time, you wish they weren't accessories at all. You wish they came in the box. Among the things we would have liked to have seen included with the iPad was a protective case.

Alas, it wasn't to be — neither the iPad nor the iPad 2 comes with a case, but you can find cases aplenty just the same. You read about Apple's here and other cases a bit later in this chapter.

Apple's entry in this category for the original iPad carries the most straightforward of names: Apple iPad Case. It's a lightweight $39 soft black microfiber case that we both think is kind of classy looking (though nothing like the brown crocodile-skin iPad and iPad 2 cases from Orbino, which at $689 will take quite a bite out of your paycheck).

Apple's case-like offering for the iPad 2, shown in Figure 15-1, is more cover than case, which is probably why it's called a *Smart Cover* instead of a *Smart Case*. Made specifically for the iPad 2, it's ultra-thin and attaches magnetically. Flip the cover open (even just a little), and your iPad 2 wakes up instantly; flip it shut, and your iPad 2 goes right to sleep. Available in ten bright colors in polyurethane ($39) or leather ($69). Bob says the aniline-dyed Italian leather on his PRODUCT RED Smart Cover is gorgeous and soft as butter.

Both the iPad Case and Smart Cover can be configured so your iPad rests at about a 30-degree angle, which makes it much easier for typing on its virtual keyboard. And both can also be folded into pseudo iPad stands that prop up the iPad for hands-free movie watching or slide-show viewing.

Courtesy of Apple

Figure 15-1: Apple's Smart Cover for iPad 2.

The Apple iPad Case has a very snug fit, which we generally consider a positive. Not always. If you want to use Apple's iPad Keyboard Dock that we discuss in the next section (and certain other peripherals that use the Dock connector), you have to remove the Apple case to do so. Because of that tight fit, sliding the iPad in and out of the case is a bit of a nuisance.

Exploring virtual keyboard alternatives

We think the various virtual keyboards that pop up just as you need them on the iPad are perfectly fine for shorter typing tasks, whether it's composing e-mails or tapping a few notes. For most longer assignments, however, we writers are more comfortable pounding away on a real-deal physical keyboard, and we suspect you feel the same way.

Fortunately a physical keyboard for the iPad is an easy addition. Apple sells two alternatives as follows, each for $69.

The Apple iPad Keyboard Dock

The Apple iPad Keyboard Dock combines a full-size anodized aluminum keyboard with a built-in Dock you can use to sync, charge, or connect other accessories to the iPad. Actually this keyboard has a pair of Dock connectors, one in the front just above the top row of keys that you use to slide and connect the iPad itself, and the other on the rear for hooking up those other accessories. You also find a standard-sized 3.5mm jack on the rear for connecting powered speakers with an optional audio cable.

This keyboard is a decent option for people who want to listen to music in stereo without donning headphones. Remember, the iPad has only a single built-in mono speaker.

The easy-to-type-on keyboard has dedicated one-touch function keys along the top row to summon the Home screen, open Spotlight search, increase or decrease brightness, initiate a Picture Frame slide show (see Chapter 10), call upon the virtual keyboard, and lock or unlock the screen. You also find playback, mute, and volume controls for the iPod.

We've already pointed out one drawback to the Keyboard Dock: having to remove the optional Apple iPad Case before sliding in the iPad.

Another drawback: Despite being lightweight, the keyboard's design makes traveling with it a little awkward because the Dock on the rear sticks out in a triangular fashion. In any event, it's just one more piece to account for.

And another drawback: You can only prop up the iPad in portrait mode when connected to the keyboard. You can't connect it in landscape mode and type.

Oh, and this keyboard is for the original iPad only. An iPad 2 just won't fit.

You can purchase an iPad Dock from Apple without a keyboard for $29. The Dock is virtually identical to the one on the Keyboard Dock minus the aforementioned keyboard. In other words, it has the same audio cable jack and Dock connectors and the same drawbacks: You still can't slide the iPad into the Dock when it's outfitted in Apple's Case, and you still can't stand it up in the landscape mode. Plus we're obliged to point out that early reviews for the Dock without the keyboard on Apple's website have been mixed.

The Apple Wireless Keyboard

The Apple Wireless Keyboard, as shown in Figure 15-2, is a way to use a top-notch aluminum physical keyboard without tethering it to the iPad. It operates from up to 30 feet away from the iPad via Bluetooth, the wireless technology we spend time with in Chapter 13. Which begs us to ask, can you see the iPad screen from 30 feet away?

As with any Bluetooth device that the iPad makes nice with, you have to pair it to your tablet. Pairing is also discussed in Chapter 13.

The Bluetooth keyboard takes two AA batteries. It's smart about power management, too; it powers itself down when you stop using it to avoid draining those batteries. It wakes up when you start typing.

Courtesy of Apple

Figure 15-2: The Apple Wireless Keyboard.

The Wireless Keyboard doesn't do any of the docking tricks, of course, that are possible with the iPad Keyboard Dock. On the other hand, it's very thin, so it's easier to take with you than the Apple Keyboard Dock. If you use a backpack, briefcase, messenger bag, or even a large purse, there's almost certainly room for the Apple Wireless Keyboard.

Though we have tested only a few third-party Bluetooth keyboards, the iPad ought to work fine with any keyboard that supports Bluetooth 2.1 + EDR technology. Bob is currently using a Verbatim Wireless Bluetooth Mobile Keyboard ($80 at Amazon; $104 on the Verbatim website) that includes iPad- and iPhone-specific keys, folds in half, and includes a nice leather carrying case.

Connecting a camera

The iPad doesn't include a USB port or SD memory card slot, which happen to be the most popular methods for getting pictures (and videos) from a digital camera onto a computer.

All the same, the iPad delivers a marvelous photo viewer. That's why if you take a lot of pictures, Apple's $29 iPad Camera Connection Kit, which we also discuss in Chapter 10, is worth considering. As a reminder, the Kit consists of the two components shown in Figure 15-3, either of which plugs into the 30-pin dock connector at the bottom of the iPad. One sports a USB interface that you can use with the USB cable that came with your camera to download pictures. The other is an SD Card Reader that lets you insert the memory card that stores your pictures.

Though the official line from Apple is that this USB adapter is meant to work with the USB cable from your digital camera, we tried connecting other devices. We got an old Dell USB keyboard to work with it. There's a possibility other devices will work, too, including readers for non-SD type memory cards, USB speakers, and more. But don't expect all your USB devices to be compatible because of the power requirements of those devices, and the fact that the requisite software drivers and such aren't loaded on the iPad.

Figure 15-3: You have two ways to import images using the iPad Camera Connection Kit.

We only hope that despite this helpful accessory, Apple will get around to adding USB and an SD slot, but it didn't happen on iPad 2. Of course, Apple did add two cameras.

Connecting an iPad to a TV or projector

The iPad has a pretty big screen for what it is, a tablet computer. But that display is still not nearly as large as a living room TV or a monitor you might see in a conference room or auditorium. To send iPad content to a bigger screen, you can choose from three connectors:

 ✔ **VGA Adapter cable:** Projecting what's on the iPad's 1024 x 768 screen to a larger display is the very reason behind the iPad Dock Connector to VGA Adapter cable that Apple is selling for $29. You can use it to connect your iPad to TVs, projectors, and VGA displays. What for? To watch videos, slide shows, and presentations on the big screen.

VGA (video graphics array) delivers, by today's standards, low-resolution video output, compared, say to the more advanced HDMI (High-Definition Multimedia Interface).

✔ **Component AV Cable:** You may otherwise have decent results playing movies off iPad to a TV using yet another cable that Apple sells. It's the $39 Apple Component AV Cable. The hookup is from the Dock connector on the iPad to the so-called component video ports of your home theater or stereo receiver; such component connectors are red, blue, and green. As part of this setup, you also need to hook up red and white audio connectors to analog ports on the receiver.

Some buyers of the Apple Component AV Cable have been disappointed, however, because the product doesn't exactly mirror the iPad display at all times. In fact it all-too-frequently doesn't. The app you're trying to project must support playing video to an external display, and only some do such as

- Videos, Photos, and YouTube among the iPad's built-in apps

- The optional Keynote, Netflix, and Air Video programs

- Safari, which works for some videos, but not everything you're viewing through the browser

✔ **Digital AV Adapter cable:** Finally, there's the newest addition to the Apple adapter family, the $39 Apple Digital AV Adapter. If you have an original iPad, this cable does what the other two adapters do, but instead of using VGA or Component video connectors, it uses HDMI. If you have an iPad 2, however, this adapter includes a nice bonus: It lets you mirror the display on your iPad on a big screen TV, which is great for demos and presentations. Ed has used this adapter to, among other things, to play *Angry Birds* on the bigger TV screen.

Keeping a spare charger

With roughly ten hours of battery life, a single charge can more than get you through a typical work day with your iPad. But why chance it? Having a spare charger at the office can spare you (!) from having to commute with one. The Apple iPad 10W USB Power Adapter goes for $29 and includes a lengthy 6-foot cord.

Listening and Talking with Earphones, Headphones, and Headsets

You've surely noticed that your iPad did not include earphones or a headset. That's probably a blessing because the earphones and headsets Apple has included with iPods and iPhones since time immemorial aren't all that good.

In fact, Bob refers to them as, "mediocre and somewhat uncomfortable" in almost every article he's written about the iPod or iPhone.

Without an included pair of earphones, you can select a pair of headphones, earphones, or a headset that suits your needs and your budget.

Wired headphones, earphones, and headsets

Search Amazon for *headphones, earphones,* or *headsets* and you'll find thousands of each are available at prices ranging from around $10 to more than $1,000. Or, if you prefer to shop in a brick-and-mortar store, Target, Best Buy, and the Apple Store all have decent selections, with prices starting at less than $20.

Much as we love the shopping experience at Apple Stores, you won't find any bargains there. Bargain-hunting doesn't matter that much for Apple-branded products because they're rarely discounted. However, you can almost always find widely available non-Apple items such as headphones, earphones, and headsets cheaper somewhere else.

With so many brands and models of earphones, headphones, and headsets available from so many manufacturers at so many price points, we can't possibly test even a fraction of the ones available today. That said, we've probably tested more of them than most people, and we have our favorites.

When it comes to headphones, Bob is partial to his Grado SR60i's, which are legendary for offering astonishingly accurate audio at an affordable price (around $80). He's tried headphones that cost twice, thrice, or even more times as much that he didn't think sounded nearly as good. Find out more at www.gradolabs.com.

Ed goes with sweet-sounding, albeit pricey, (about $350) Bose QuietComfort 3 acoustic noise-canceling headphones.

For earphones and earphone-style headsets, Bob likes the Klipsch Image S4 Headphones and S4i In-Ear Headset with Mic and 3-Button Remote. At around $79 and $99, respectively, they sound better than many similarly priced products and better than many more expensive offerings.

Bluetooth stereo headphones, earphones, and headsets

Neither of us has much experience with Bluetooth (wireless) stereo headphones and headsets, but we thought we'd at least plant the seed. The idea is that with Bluetooth stereo headphones/earphones/headsets, you can listen to music wirelessly up to 33 feet away from your iPad. If this sounds good to you, we suggest that you look for reviews of such products on the web before you decide which one to buy. A search of Amazon for *stereo Bluetooth headset* brought up over 300 items, with prices starting as low as $15.

Earphones? Headphones? Headsets?

We have referred to headphones and headsets several times and thought you might be wondering whether there's a difference, and if so, what it is. When we talk about *headphones* or *earphones,* we're talking about the things you use to listen to music. A *headset* adds a microphone so that you can use it for voice chatting, recording voice notes, and (in the case of the iPhone or Internet VoIP services such as Skype) for phone calls. So headphones and earphones are for listening, and headsets are for both talking and listening.

Now you may be wondering whether earphones and headphones are the same. To some people they may be, but to us, headphones (shown on the left in the figure) have a band across the top (or back) of your head, and the listening apparatus is big and covers the outside of your ears. Think of the big fat things you see covering a radio disk jockey's ears. Earphones (sometimes referred to as *earbuds* and shown on the right in the figure), on the other hand, are smaller, fit entirely in your ear, and have no band across the top or back of your head.

Photos courtesy of iStockPhoto.com

Headsets can be earphone style or, less commonly, headphone style. The distinguishing factor is that headsets always include a microphone. And some headsets are designed specifically for use with Apple i-products (iPhone, iPod, iPad) and have integrated Play/Pause and volume control buttons.

One last thing: Some companies refer to their earbud products as headphones, but we think that's confusing and wrong. So in this book, headphones are those bulky, outside-the-ear things and earphones are teeny-tiny things that fit entirely in your ear canal.

For what it's worth, Bob has a Cardo S-2 Bluetooth stereo headset that he occasionally uses with his iPhone when he walks his dog. He tested it with his iPad, and it worked just fine. The only problem is that the model he has is apparently discontinued. On the other hand, you can find them occasionally on the web for around $70, and Bob says they perform well and sound better than you might expect for a wireless headset. On the other hand, his are over three years old, so you can probably find something better that costs less by now.

Listening with Speakers

You can connect just about any speakers to your iPad, but if you want decent sound, we suggest you look only at *powered* speakers and not *passive* (unpowered) ones. The difference is that powered speakers contain their own amplification circuitry and can deliver much better (and louder) sound than unpowered speakers.

Prices range from well under $100 to hundreds (or even thousands) of dollars. Most speaker systems designed for use with your computer, iPod, or iPhone work well as long as they have an auxiliary input or a Dock connector that can accommodate your iPad. (We haven't seen any with the Dock connector yet, but surely some will be available soon.)

Desktop speakers

Logitech (www.logitech.com) makes a range of desktop speaker systems priced from less than $25 to more than $300. But that $300 system is the Z5500 THX-certified 505-watt 5.1 digital surround system — surely overkill for listening to music or video on your iPad, which doesn't support surround sound anyway. The point is that Logitech makes a variety of decent systems at a wide range of price points. If you're looking for something inexpensive, you can't go wrong with most Logitech-powered speaker systems.

Bob is a big fan of Audioengine (www.audioengineusa.com) desktop speakers. They deliver superior audio at prices that are quite reasonable for speakers that sound this good. Audioengine 5 is the premium product priced at $349 a pair; Audioengine 2 is its smaller but still excellent-sounding sibling priced at $199 a pair. They're available only direct from the manufacturer, but the company is so confident you'll love them that it offers a free audition for their speaker systems. If you order a pair and don't love them, return them within 30 days for a full refund. Bob knows a lot of people who have ordered them, and so far no one has sent them back.

Bluetooth speakers

Like Bluetooth headsets, Bluetooth speakers let you listen to music up to 33 feet away from your iPad. They're great for listening by the pool or hot tub or anywhere else you might not want to take your iPad.

Bob recently reviewed the Tenqa SP-109 Stereo Bluetooth Speaker ($49.99) and said it was "easy to set up and simple to use at a reasonable price," though he did also say he thought the sound quality was okay at best. Bob uses the soundmatters' foxL v2 ($199) regularly; it's a palm-sized travel speaker with some spiffy advanced technology that makes it sound noticeably better than any other ultra-portable speakers he's tested (and he's tested a lot). foxL v2 also serves as a nifty wireless speakerphone with his iPhone 4, but should work equally well with most other mobile phones and smartphones.

Ed gave a favorable review to the $199.99 wireless JAMBOX by Jawbone, which offers good sound despite being able to fit into the palm of your hand. You can connect via Bluetooth or an auxiliary stereo jack. Added bonus: JAMBOX doubles as a speaker phone. Again, neither one of us has much experience with Bluetooth (wireless) stereo speakers, but we'd be remiss if we didn't at least mention them.

Docking your iPad with an extender cable

Because the iPad is much larger than an iPod or iPhone, you can't just dock the iPad into a speaker system designed for the smaller devices. All is not lost if you're partial to those speakers and still want to connect the iPad. CableJive (`http://cablejive.com`) sells Dock Extender cables that let you dock your iPad from a distance; it's described as a 30-pin Male to Female Extension cable.

Versions come in black or white and two standard lengths, $25.95 for a 2-foot length and $31.95 for 6 feet.

The cable doesn't work with S-video output, component video, and audio in for recording.

Wrapping Your iPad in Third-Party Cases

Much as we like the Apple iPad Case, other vendors offer some excellent options:

- **Abas:** Abas (`www.abas.net`) offers very nice leather cases that won't set you back $689 like the Orbino crocodile-skin case we mention earlier in the chapter.

- **Targus:** Targus (`www.targus.com`) has a full line of iPad cases in a variety of material and prices. The nice part is that none of them, including the leather portfolio, costs more than $60.

- **Griffin Technology:** Griffin Technology (`www.griffintechnology.com`) also has a pretty good selection of iPad cases at reasonable prices (that is, none more than $50).

- **iLuv:** iLuv (`www.i-luv.com`) is yet another case maker with a range of affordable cases fabricated from leather, fabric, and silicone, none of which costs more than $40.

- **Vario:** ZeroChroma (`www.zerochroma.com`) has Bob's current favorite Vario iPad (and iPhone) case ($69.95). The big attraction is the 16-angle rotating theatre-stand on the back that folds flush when not in use. Sweet!

✔ **BookBook for iPad/iPad 2:** The BookBook case from Twelve South looks like a fine vintage hardbound book but is actually a very handsome iPad case and stand.

✔ **The iPad Bubble Sleeve:** From Hard Candy Cases (www.hardcandy cases.com), the iPad Bubble Sleeve ($49.95) offers significantly better protection against bumps and scratches than any other case we've seen. If we expected our iPads to be exposed to moderate impacts, this case's rigid exterior and additional shock-absorbing rubber bumpers for the screen make it the case we'd choose.

But Wait . . . There's More!

Before we leave the topic of accessories, we think you should know about a few more products, namely film protection products that guard your iPad's exterior (or screen) without adding a bit of bulk: the Griffin Technology A-Frame tabletop stand for your iPad, and 2-into-1 stereo adapters.

Protecting the screen with film

Some people prefer not to use a case with their iPad, and that's okay, too. But if you're one of those people (or even if you're not), you might want to consider protective film for the iPad screen or even the whole device. We've tried these products on our iPhones in the past and have found them to perform as promised. If you apply them properly, they're nearly invisible and protect your iPad from scratches and scrapes without adding any bulk.

Bob has tested film products from invisibleShield by ZAGG (www.zagg.com), BodyGuardz (www.bodyguardz.com), and Best Skins Ever (www.bestskins ever.com) and says, in a nutshell, they're more similar than they are different. invisibleShield is the most expensive and possibly the best-quality film. BodyGuardz products are roughly 25 percent cheaper than invisibleShield and of comparable quality. Both invisibleShield and BodyGuardz offer free lifetime replacement of their products. Best Skins Ever products are 25–55 percent less expensive than invisibleShield or BodyGuardz, yet the product is, if not just as good, darn close to it. The difference is that Best Skins Ever has minimal packaging, and rather than including the "special liquid" you need to apply it (like invisibleShield and BodyGuardz), Best Skins Ever includes instructions for making it yourself. And unlike the others, Best Skins Ever has no free replacement policy, though it does offer a 30-day money-back guarantee. Finally, all three offer total protection (front, back, and sides) as well as separate products for the front or back.

Which one to choose? If you think you might take advantage of the lifetime replacement policy, you want either invisibleShield or BodyGuardz. If you want a good product at the lowest price but with a 30-day money-back guarantee instead of lifetime replacement, look at Best Skins Ever.

Any or all of the "skins" can be tricky to apply. Follow the instructions closely, watch videos on the vendors' websites and YouTube, and take your time. If you do, you'll be rewarded with clear film protection that's nearly invisible yet protects your iPad from scratches, nicks, and cuts.

One last thing: RadTech (`www.radtech.us`) offers two types of Mylar screen protectors — clear transparent, and antiglare. These screen protectors are somewhat stiffer than the film products, and unlike film, they can be cleaned and reapplied multiple times with no reduction in performance. They effectively hide minor scratches, surface defects, and abrasions, and the hard Mylar surface not only resists scratches and abrasions but is also optically correct. Finally, they're reasonably priced at $19.95 for a pair of protectors of the same type.

Standing up your iPad with Griffin A-Frame

The Griffin A-Frame ($39.99) is so unusual we just had to include it. As you can see in Figure 15-4, it's a dual-purpose Desktop stand made of heavy-duty aluminum. You can open it to hold your iPad in either portrait or landscape mode for video watching, displaying pictures (a great way to exploit the Picture Frame mode, as we describe in Chapter 10), or even reading. In this upright mode, it's also the perfect companion for the Apple Wireless Keyboard (or any other Bluetooth keyboard for that matter). Or, close the legs and lay it down, and it puts your iPad at the perfect angle for using the onscreen keyboard.

Photos courtesy of Griffin Technology

Figure 15-4: The Griffin A-Frame is a unique, dual-purpose tabletop stand for your iPad.

Soft silicone padding keeps your iPad from getting scratched or sliding around, and the bottom lip is designed to accommodate the charging cable in portrait mode. Furthermore, it works with many third-party cases, including Griffin's flexible and hard-shell cases, among others.

Bob says, "I really, really like this thing; it's where my iPad resides pretty much anytime it's not in my backpack."

Sharing your iPad with a 2-into-1 stereo adapter

A *2-into-1 stereo adapter* is a handy little device that lets two people plug their headphones/earphones/headsets into one iPad (or iPod or iPhone for that matter). They're quite inexpensive (less than $10) and extremely useful if you are traveling with a friend by air, sea, rail, or bus. They're also great when you want to watch a movie with your BFF but don't want to risk waking the neighbors or roommates.

We call 'em *2-into-1 stereo adapters,* but that's not the only name they go by. Other names you might see for the same device are as follows:

- ✐ 3.5mm stereo Y-splitter

- ✐ ⅛-inch stereo 1-plug to 2-jacks adapter

- ✐ ⅛-inch stereo Y-adapter

- ✐ 3.5mm dual stereo headphone jack splitter

- ✐ And many others

You really only need to know two things. The first is that ⅛-inch and 3.5mm are used interchangeably in the adapter world (even though they're not really the same).

Some measurements to keep in mind: ⅛ of an inch = 0.125 inch, whereas 3.5mm = 0.1378 inch. Not the same, but close enough for rock 'n' roll.

The second is that you want to make sure that you get a *stereo* adapter. Some monaural adapters work but pump exactly the same sound into both ears, instead of sending the audio information for the left stereo channel to your left ear and the right stereo channel to your right.

In other words, you need a ⅛-inch or 3.5mm stereo adapter that has a single stereo plug on one end (to plug into your iPad) and two stereo jacks on the other (to accommodate two sets of headphones/earphones/headsets).

Part V
The Part of Tens

The 5th Wave
By Rich Tennant

©RICHTENNANT

Accessories

iPadPad

"It's a docking system for the iPad that comes with 3 bedrooms, 2 baths, and a car port."

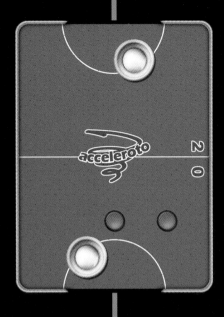

In this part . . .

1 t's written in stone somewhere at Wiley world headquarters that we *For Dummies* authors must include a Part of Tens in every single *For Dummies* book we write. It is a duty we take quite seriously. So in this part, you'll find a list of ten of our favorite free applications plucked from the iPad App Store. These include a couple of really addictive games and even an app to help you find a recipe for your favorite dish. We then move on to our diverse collection of ten fabulous apps every user should consider buying including an art studio, a database, and a piano for your iPad.

We close the show with one of our favorite topics: hints, tips, and shortcuts that make life with your iPad even better. Among the ten, you discover how to look at the capacity of your newly favored device in different ways, find out how to share Web pages, and pick up another trick or two on using the iPad's virtual keyboard.

Ten Appetizing (and Free) Apps

*K*iller app is familiar jargon to anyone who has spent any time around computers. The term refers to an application so sweet or so useful that just about everybody wants or must have it.

You could make the argument that the most compelling killer app on the iPad is the very App Store we expound on in Chapter 7. This online emporium has an abundance of splendid programs — dare we say killer apps in their own right? — many of which are free. These cover everything from food (hey, you gotta eat) to show biz. Okay, so some rotten apples (aren't we clever) are in the bunch, too. But we're here to accentuate the positive.

With that in mind, in this chapter, we offer ten of our favorite free iPad apps. In Chapter 17, we tell you about our favorite iPad apps that aren't free but are worth every penny.

We show you ours, and we encourage you to show us yours. If you discover your own killer iPad apps, by all means, let us know — our e-mail addresses are at the end of the intro to this book — so that we can check them out.

Pocket Legends

If you're a fan of MMORPG-style gaming, we're happy to inform you that *Pocket Legends* for iPad is an incredibly cool 3D MMO game that doesn't (or at least doesn't have to) cost you a cent.

For those who aren't already fans of the genre, MMORPG is the acronym for Massively-Multiplayer Online Role-Playing Game.

What that means is that you can join thousands of players from all over the world when you play. You begin by choosing one of three character classes to play as: an archer, an enchantress, or a warrior. Then, you (and, optionally, other players) wander around dungeons, forests, and castles killing zombies, skeletons, demons, and other bad guys and collecting gold pieces. Every so often, your character finds weapons, armor, and shields, or you can buy them with the gold you find. The longer you play, the more powerful your character becomes and the more powerful the weapons, armor, and shields you can use.

Figure 16-1 shows a character (Doc) in a forest shooting fireballs at a bad guy.

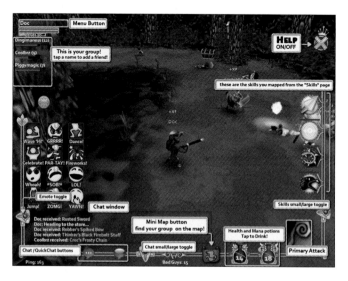

Figure 16-1: The in-game help system shows you pretty much everything you need to know to play *Pocket Legends.*

Did you notice we said "doesn't have to cost you money" rather than the more absolute "doesn't cost you money" back in the first paragraph? The reason: If you enjoy playing (as we do), you'll probably want to purchase additional dungeon campaigns ($1.99 each), platinum (30 pieces for $4.99), additional characters (just $0.99 each), or one of the other goodies that are available for in-app purchase. You can have a lot of fun for a good long time without laying out a dime — but if you like playing, you'll probably find yourself considering a purchase or two.

Here is one last thing: Bob's character is an archer named Doc. So, if you happen to run into him in a dungeon or forest, use the chat system to give him a shoutout.

Shazam

Ever heard a song on the radio or television, in a store, or at a club and wondered what it was called or who was singing it? With the Shazam app, you may never wonder again. Just launch Shazam and point your iPad's microphone at the source of the music. In a few seconds, the song title and artist's name magically appear on your iPad screen as shown in Figure 16-2.

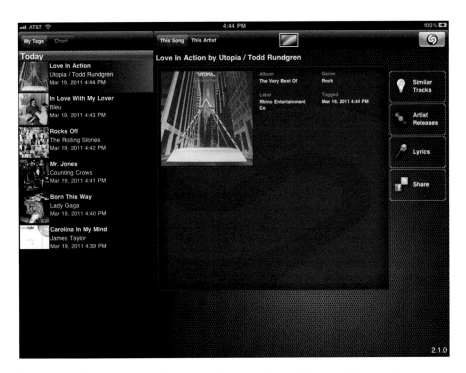

Figure 16-2: After listening for 15 seconds, Shazam told us all this about the song that was playing.

In Shazam parlance, that song has been *tagged*. Now if tagging were all Shazam could do, that would surely be enough. But wait, there's more. After Shazam tags a song you can

- Buy the song at the iTunes Store.
- Watch related videos on YouTube.
- Tweet the song on Twitter.
- Read a biography, a discography, or lyrics.
- Take a photo and attach it to the tagged item in Shazam.
- E-mail a tag to a friend.

Shazam isn't great at identifying classical music, jazz, or opera, nor is it adept at identifying obscure indie bands. But if you use it primarily to identify popular music, it rocks (pun intended). It has worked for us in noisy airport terminals, crowded shopping malls, and even once at a wedding ceremony.

ABC Player

Do you watch any ABC-TV shows like *Grey's Anatomy, Dancing with the Stars,* or Bob's favorite, *Lost,* or Ed's fave, *Modern Family?* If so, grab your copy of the free ABC Player now. Go ahead; we'll wait.

With this app and a Wi-Fi connection, you can watch complete episodes of your favorite ABC TV shows anytime you like. You can find the shows and episodes you want to watch in lots of ways.

And (not to repeat ourselves) it's *all free*! Yes, the shows do have commercials, but would you rather pay $1.99 (the average cost of an episode of a TV show in the iTunes Store) for the commercial-free version?

We thought not.

Flixster

We like movies, so we both use the Flixster app a lot. Feed it your zip code, and then browse local theaters by movie, show time, rating, or distance from your current location. Or browse to find a movie you like and then tap to find theatres, show times, and other info, as shown in Figure 16-3. Another nice feature is the ability to buy tickets to most movies from your iPad with just a few additional taps.

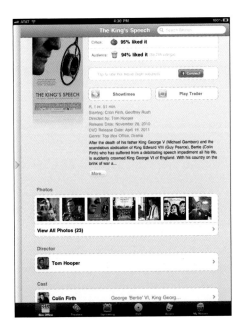

Figure 16-3: Find out show times, watch the trailer, or get more info on the director or cast with a single tap.

We appreciate that we can read reviews, play movie trailers, and e-mail movie listings to others with a single click. We also enjoy the movie trailers for soon-to-be-released films and DVDs. Other free movie showtime apps are out there, but we like Flixster best.

IMDb

While we're on the subject of the silver screen, we couldn't resist opening *IMDb*, shorthand for *Internet Movie Database.* And what a database it is, especially for the avid filmgoer. This vast and delightful repository of all things cinema is the place to go for complete cast/crew listings, actor/filmmaker bios, plot summaries, movie trailers, critics' reviews, user ratings, parental guidance, famous quotations, and all kinds of trivia.

You can always search for movies, TV shows, actors, and so on by typing a name in the search box in the upper-right corner of the screen. Or tap Browse at the lower left to find current movies by showtimes, what's coming soon, or box office results. You can browse TV recaps, too, or find people born on the day you happen to be looking and poking around the app. It's also fun to check out the most-viewed celebs on IMDb. The recent roster included Charlie Sheen, Natalie Portman, Olivia Wilde, Amber Heard, and Mila Kunis, among others.

One piece of advice to movie buffs: Avoid the IMDb if you have a lot of work to do. You'll have a hard time closing the curtain on this marvelous app.

Netflix

Flixster, IMDb, and now Netflix. You've no doubt detected a real trend by now — and that is indeed our affection for movies. If you love movies, too, you're sure to be a fan of the Netflix app. Over time, *Netflix,* the company that built its reputation by sending DVDs to subscribers through the mail, started streaming movies over the Internet to computers, TVs, and other consumer electronics gear. You can now add the iPad to that list.

From the iPad, you have more or less instant access to more than 20,000 movies on demand, including 1,000 or so from the Starz movie service. And although these titles aren't exactly current blockbusters, we know you'll find plenty of films worth seeing. You can search by *genre* (classics, comedy, drama, and so on) and *subgenre* (courtroom dramas, political dramas, romantic dramas, and so on). Figure 16-4 shows a small sample of the movies and shows you can watch instantly.

Figure 16-4: Stream a movie instantly through Netflix.

Although the app is free, as are the movies you choose to watch on the fly, you have to pay Netflix subscription fees that start at $8.99 a month. You also need an Internet connection, preferably through Wi-Fi, though Netflix works on 3G models as well.

Comics

Comics is actually three apps rolled into one. First and foremost, it's a fantastic way to read comic books on a 9.7-inch touchscreen. Second, it's a comic bookstore with hundreds of comics and comic series from dozens of publishers, including Arcana, Archie, Marvel, Devil's Due, Digital Webbing, Red 5, Zenescope, and many more (see Figure 16-5).

Finally, it's a great way to organize the comics you own on your iPad so that you can find the one you want quickly and easily.

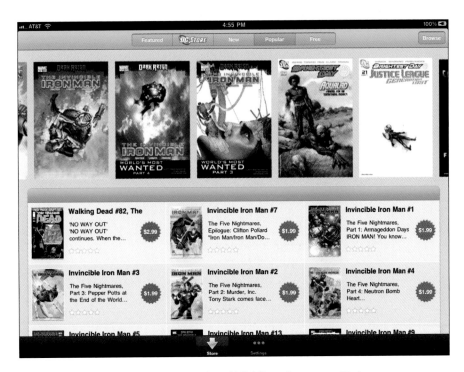

Figure 16-5: Comics lets you shop for and read (d'oh!) comics on your iPad.

The free Comics app gives you access to hundreds of free comics, or you can use the built-in store to purchase comics, usually 99 cents to $1.99 per issue.

New releases are available every Wednesday, so visit the store often to check out the latest and greatest offerings. Both the store and your personal comic collection are well organized and easy to use. And reading comics in Comics is a pleasure you won't want to miss if you're a fan of comics or graphic novels.

Epicurious Recipes & Shopping List

We love to eat. But we're writers, not gourmet chefs, so we'll take all the help we can get when it comes to preparing a great meal. And we get a lot of that culinary assistance from Epicurious, which easily lives up to its billing as the "Cook's Companion." This tasty recipe app comes courtesy of Condé Nast Digital.

Tap the Control Panel button in the upper-left corner of the screen to get started, and you can find a yummy recipe in no time. Tap Featured inside the Control Panel (if it's not already highlighted) to find recipes that have been lumped into categories, often timed to the season. Around the time we were writing this book, recipe collection categories included Spring Dinner, Mother's Day, Graduation Party, and Grilling Entrees.

If you tap Search inside the Control Panel instead, you can fine-tune your search for a recipe by food or drink, by main ingredient (banana, chicken, pasta), cuisine type, and dietary consideration (low-carb, vegan, kosher, and so on), among other parameters.

When you discover a recipe you like, you can add it to a collection of Favorites, e-mail it to a friend, pass along the ingredients to your shopping list, or summon nutritional information. Some recipes also carry reviews.

Bon appétit.

Flipboard

The media stars of today aren't necessarily those employed by old fashion publications. Nope. The stars of today are you and all your buddies on Twitter, Facebook, Flickr, and lots of other places. Flipboard transforms the social web into a gorgeous digital magazine. And you're the editor who gets to customize the content. Add Facebook pals, the folks you follow on Twitter, stuff from your Google Reader account, Instagram photos, and photos uploaded to Flickr. You can request nuggets from more traditional media too, including outlets *CNN, The Economist, The Huffington Post, Fox News, BBC World News, NPR, USA TODAY,* and many more. Figure 16-6 provides a glimpse of what your tweets and feeds can look like through Flipboard.

Figure 16-6: We think you'll flip over Flipboard.

Pandora Internet Radio

We've long been fans of Pandora on other computers and mobile devices. So we're practically delirious that this custom Internet radio service is available *gratis* on the iPad. Moreover, the addition of multitasking means you can play Pandora music in the background while doing other stuff.

Pandora works on the iPad in much the same way that it does on a Mac or PC. In the box at the upper left, type the name of a favorite artist, song title, or composer via the iPad keyboard, and Pandora creates an instant personalized radio station with selections that exemplify the style you chose. Along the left panel of Figure 16-7, you see some of the eclectic stations Ed created. Tapping QuickMix at the top of the list plays musical selections across all your stations.

Suppose that you type **Beatles**. Pandora's instant Beatles station includes performances from John, Paul, George, and Ringo, as well as tunes from other acts.

And say that you type in a song title, such as *Have I Told You Lately*. Pandora constructs a station with similar music after you tell it whether to base tunes on the Van Morrison, Rod Stewart, or another rendition.

Search for artist, song, or composer

Station list   Bookmark or buy a song

Figure 16-7: Have we told you lately how much we like Pandora?

Pandora comes out of the *Music Genome Project,* an organization of musicians and technologists who analyze music according to hundreds of attributes (such as melody, harmony, and vocal performances).

You can help fine-tune the music Pandora plays by tapping the thumbs-up or thumbs-down icon at the top of the screen above the album covers associated with the music you've been listening to during the current session.

Pandora also takes advantage of the generous screen real estate of the iPad to deliver artist profiles. (Refer to Figure 16-7.)

If you tap the Menu button below an album cover of the currently playing song, you can bookmark the song or artist that is playing, or head to iTunes to purchase the song or other material from the artist directly on the iPad (if available).

Ten Apps Worth Paying For

*I*f you read Chapter 16, you know that lots of great free applications are available for your iPad. But as the old cliché goes, some things are worth paying for. Still, none of the ten for-pay apps we've chosen as some of our favorites are likely to break the bank. As you're about to discover, some applications on this list are practical and some are downright silly. The common theme? We think you'll like carrying these apps around on your iPad.

Bill Atkinson PhotoCard

Who is Bill Atkinson? He had a hand (or both hands) in the first Macintosh computer, as well as the MacPaint and HyperCard Mac applications. Today he's a world-renowned nature photographer, which brings us to his app. Bill Atkinson PhotoCard is an inexpensive ($4.99) app that lets you create gorgeous high-resolution postcards and send them via either e-mail or the U.S. Postal Service. E-mail is, of course, free. And though sending by USPS costs between $1.50 and $2.00 per card depending on how many print-and-mail credits you purchase, the 8.25-x-5.5-inch postcards are stunning. Printed on heavy glossy stock and on a state-of-the-art HP Indigo Digital Press, they're as beautiful as any postcard you've ever seen.

You can use 1 of the 150 included Bill Atkinson nature photos, as shown on the left in Figure 17-1), or you can use any picture in your Photos library. You can add stickers and stamps, as shown in Figure 17-1, and you can even add voice notes to e-mailed cards.

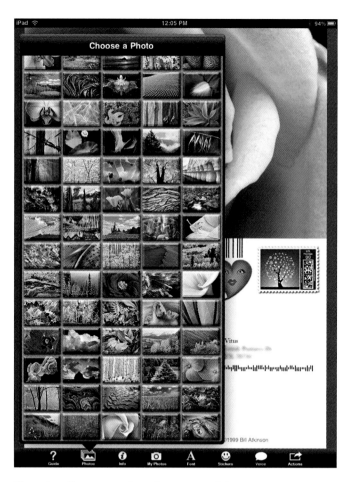

Figure 17-1: Your postcard can feature one of the gorgeous nature photos on the left, or you can use your own image (not shown here).

You get the first USPS card free, so the effective price of the app is only around $3 (and worth every penny). Or if you're still uncertain, download Bill Atkinson PhotoCard Lite, which has fewer included photos and no free print-and-mail credit.

Words with Friends HD

This brings us to perhaps the only time in this whole book that your authors had a disagreement. Both of us love word games and puzzles, but Bob loves *Words with Friends HD* whereas Ed prefers the real thing, namely *Scrabble*. Because neither of us wanted to eliminate our favorite word game from this chapter, we decided it would be best if each of us wrote about our fave. So the description of *Words with Friends* here was written by Bob, and the write-up of *Scrabble* later in the chapter is all Ed.

Social media is all the rage these days, but most multiplayer iPad games are either boring or not particularly social. *Words with Friends HD* ($2.99), on the other hand, is the most social game I've found and a ton of fun, too. It's kind of like playing *Scrabble* with a friend, but because it's turn-based, you can make a move and then quit the app and do other stuff. When your friend makes his next move, you can choose to be notified that it's your turn by sound, onscreen alert, and/or a number on the Words with Friends icon on your Home screen. Figure 17-2 shows a game I'm currently winning 299 to 242, as you can see near the top of the figure.

Try the free version *(Words With Friends HD Free),* and I'm sure you'll be hooked. Then challenge me if you like; my username is `boblevitus` (although I often have the maximum 20 games going, so keep trying if I don't accept your challenge right away).

Scrabble

You already know we work with words for a living — and that we have a (slight) disagreement about favorite apps for playing such games. Ed appreciates a good game of *Scrabble,* whereas Bob, as we told you earlier in this chapter, prefers the virtual knock-off *Words with Friends HD*.

Playing the $9.99 iPad version of *Scrabble* (from Electronic Arts and Hasbro) is the closest thing yet to replicating the experience of the famous crossword board game on an electronic device. For starters, check out the gorgeous high-definition graphics, as shown in Figure 17-3. The sounds of tiles placed on the virtual board are realistic, too.

Figure 17-2: It's my (Bob's) move in five games, as you see in the overlay.

Figure 17-3: Ed says it's hard to top *Scrabble* on the iPad.

In fact, you can build a decent case that *Scrabble* on the iPad even beats the original board game. Consider the following:

- ✔ You can play up to 25 multiplayer games at a time. Challenge word-smiths on Facebook or play over the same home network (as we have) against someone with another iPad, an iPod touch, or an iPhone. Or play against the computer and choose your level of difficulty (easy, normal, hard).

- ✔ Through Party Play mode, you can manage your private tile rack on your iPhone or iPod touch and seamlessly place tiles onto the iPad *Scrabble* game board. Works with up to four devices. You have to download the Tile Rack app from the App Store, but it's free.

- ✔ You can play iTunes music in the background for inspiration.

- ✔ A Scrabble Teacher Feature lets you see the best available word choice from your previous moves.

- ✔ Personal stats are kept on the iPad. You don't need to keep score.

- ✔ You won't lose any letter tiles or have to fret that your small child or pet will swallow any.

 Though I'm an obvious fan of this app, I did experience one quandary playing over a home network — I wanted to use the word *quandary* because the letter *Q* is worth ten points in Scrabble. The app did crash on that occasion.

ArtStudio

Do you fancy yourself an artist? We know our artistic talent is limited, but if we were talented, ArtStudio for iPad is the program we'd use to paint our masterpieces. Even if you have limited artistic talent, you can see that this app has everything you need to create awesome artwork.

We were embarrassed to show you our creations, so instead we whipped up a composite illustration (see Figure 17-4) that shows all the ArtStudio for iPad's tools and palettes at once.

Here are just some of ArtStudio for iPad's features:

- ✔ Offers 25 brushes, including pencils, a smudge tool, bucket fill, airbrush, and more. Brushes are resizable and simulate brush pressure.

- ✔ Up to five layers with options, such as delete, reorder, duplicate, merge, and transparency.

- ✔ Filters, such as blur, sharpen, detect edges, sepia, and more.

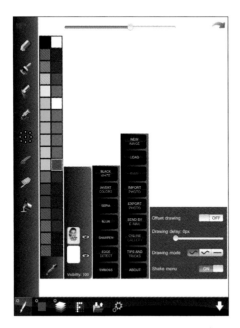

Figure 17-4: ArtStudio for iPad's tools from left to right: brushes, colors, layers, special effects, file management options, and settings.

Don't believe us? AppSmile.com (www.appsmile.com) rated it 5 out of 5, saying, "This is what Photoshop Mobile wishes it had been." SlapApp.com (www.slappapp.com) also rated it 5 out of 5 and said, "I've dabbled in quite a few painting and drawing apps and this one has 'em all beat by a long shot." And by all means, check out what talented artists can do with ArtStudio for iPad at www.flickr.com/groups/artstudioimages and www.artistinvermont.com.

One last thing: The app was only $0.99 when we bought our copies — a "special launch sale" price. Even if the price has gone up, we think this app is easily worth $5 or even $10 if you like to draw or paint.

The Pinball

Good pinball games require supremely realistic physics, and *The Pinball* ($2.99) nails it. The way the ball moves around the tables and interacts with bumpers and flippers is so realistic you'll think you're at an arcade. It's so realistic, in fact, that you can "shake" the table to influence the ball's movement.

Another hallmark of a great pinball game is great sound effects, and *The Pinball* doesn't disappoint. The sounds the ball makes when it bounces off a bumper, is hit with a flipper, or passes through a rollover are spot-on and totally authentic.

One thing that takes some getting used to is the moving camera used by the game in portrait mode. Although it occasionally pulls back to reveal the entire table at once, most of the time, it's zoomed in on the action and following the ball while showing only part of the table.

 Fortunately, if you rotate your iPad a quarter turn to landscape mode, you get to play in the "full table" view. We prefer this view but encourage you to try it both ways and see whether you like the moving camera view better than we do.

If you like pinball, we think you'll love *The Pinball* on your iPad.

Art Authority for iPad

We've already admitted to being artistically challenged. But that only applies to making art. But we both appreciate good art as much as the next person or even more. That's why we're so enthusiastic about Art Authority ($9.99).

Art Authority is like an art museum you hold in your hand; it contains over 40,000 paintings and sculptures by more than 1,000 of the world's greatest artists. The works are organized into eight period-specific rooms, such as Early (up to 1400s), Baroque, Romanticism, Modern, and American. In each room, the artworks are subdivided by movement. The Modern room, for example, has works of surrealism, cubism, Fauvism, Dadaism, sculpture, and several more.

You find period overviews, movement overviews, timelines, and slide shows, plus a searchable index of all 1,000+ artists and separate indices for each room.

Since we first wrote about this app, Open Door Networks has added an Art Near Me feature that lets you search for art in your vicinity.

Magic Piano

Smule's 99-cent Magic Piano app transforms your iPad into just that, an entrancing *magic piano* that is already among the iPad's most popular third-party programs.

Magic Piano is an oddly soothing app that presents you with a few ways to masquerade as Mozart. You can pound away on spiral or circular onscreen piano keyboards, play on a linear keyboard, or play by following beams of light with your fingers. Tap, drag, or pinch: Each gesture produces real notes. The generous-sized iPad screen means that you can play with all your fingers. You can freelance, that is, play notes at will. Or, you can select the *Nutcracker March, Eine Kliene Nachtmusik,* or (as this book was being published) more than three-dozen other gems from a classic songbook.

What's more, you can perform in a solo act or play in a duet with a stranger halfway around the world. Choose a name for your piano and a tagline to identify yourself.

You can listen to other people play, too, without performing with them, by traveling through what Smule describes as a *warp hole.* A 3D representation of a globe shows you where on Earth the music is coming from.

Had he been around today, we're sure that Mozart would have made wondrous magic on the iPad.

The Elements: A Visual Exploration

Think back to chemistry class when you first learned about the periodic table of the elements. Many probably found it rather dull. And even if the subject got you jazzed in your school days, we'd venture to say it was completely dissimilar to the treat of exploring the elements through this $13.99 app of pure gold. In fact, to call it an app is a bit of a misnomer because it has more — forgive the pun — elements of an e-book than a traditional app. It's based on the best-selling hard-cover edition of *The Elements,* by Theodore Gray. But the program is sold in the App Store, not the iBookstore.

Launch the app, and it starts with a 1959 song by Harvard mathematician and musical humorist Tom Lehrer about each of the chemical elements that were known back then. When you tap an element — iodine in the example shown in Figure 17-5 — a stunning photograph takes over a huge portion of the screen, adjacent to such statistics as atomic weight, density, and boiling point. Now tap the right-pointing arrow to bring up the next iodine page. You see a complete text explanation of the element, along with additional pictures, such as iodine-based chewing gum and vintage bottles.

You pay a price for all this stunning detail, beyond the $13.99 tab in the App Store. At around 1.8 gigabytes, The Elements is a sizable app, nearly as large, in fact, as a high-definition movie you may have loaded on your iPad. So it hogs a lot of space, is slow to load, and sometimes crashes, though the developer has improved stability in subsequent versions.

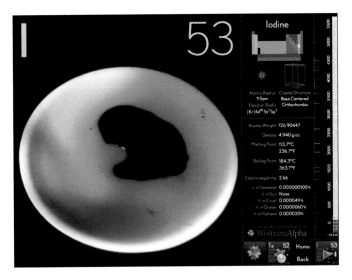

Figure 17-5: A chosen element up close.

All that said, even when we weren't rediscovering the elements ourselves, we used this app to show off the dazzling beauty of the iPad to friends. And if you, or perhaps your kids, are really into the science, you're especially going to be blown away.

Bento for iPad

Full-featured database programs have traditionally been the province for professionals and employees in a variety of job types and industries. FileMaker's Bento "personal database" programs for the Mac and iPhone, however, tend to be more inviting for mainstream consumers. The same goes for the iPad version, which, at $4.99, strikes a real bargain.

Indeed, Bento should appeal not only to salespeople, marketers, and field workers but also to students and pretty much anyone who wants to keep on top of hobbies, projects, lists, events, and then some.

The simple-to-use app comes with a variety of premade templates, covering exercise logs, vehicle maintenance, donations, recipes, expenses, and so on. It contains a gaggle of "field types" for such things as text, numbers, ratings, durations, currency, and phone numbers. And Bento is tightly integrated with the iPad's Contacts, Mail program, Safari (you can view web pages without leaving the app), and Google Maps. You can even record Voice Memos.

If you have a recent version of Bento for the Mac, you can sync the two programs so that any changes you make to a database on one machine are reflected in the corresponding database on the other machine. You need a Wi-Fi connection to sync the iPad version with the Mac version. However, because of memory constraints, Bento for iPad may not be able to handle the largest databases that you created for Bento on the Mac.

Bento for iPad makes good use of the tablet's large screen. In portrait mode, you can zero in on a single record. Rotate the iPad to landscape mode for a split-view listing of records on the left next to the details of a selected record on the right. Other neat stunts include text fields that expand and shrink when you tap them, visual check boxes, and the ability to admire photos, dispatch e-mails, and watch videos.

It's rather easy to get going with Bento. You can start out by tapping the Libraries button in the upper-left corner of the screen. As shown in Figure 17-6, *libraries* are groups of records you might want to track: Address Book, To Do Items, Projects, Inventory, Notes, Expenses, and so on. Tap the + button to add a new library with one of the aforementioned (or other) templates or create one of your own.

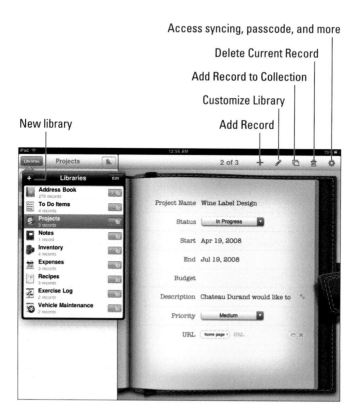

Figure 17-6: Keeping track of your wine collection in Bento.

TIP

Bento is particularly smart about the Address Book library. It lifts all the names in your iPad contacts and automatically prepopulates them in your Bento Address Book. (Don't worry; they remain in contacts, too.)

From the Library window, you can remove an already created library, rename a library, or change the order in which a library appears on the list. Start by tapping the Edit button in the Libraries window. And then:

- ✓ **To remove a library,** tap the white dash in the red circle next to the item in question. Then tap the Delete button that appears.

- ✓ **To rename a library,** tap the library listing and type a new name. It's that easy.

- ✓ **To reorder the way in which a library is organized,** press and hold your finger against the three horizontal lines to the right of the library whose order you want to change and then drag it up or down in the list to a slot you prefer.

It's a breeze to move from record to record inside the app. Double-tap the right side of a record to advance to the next record, or double-tap the left side to go to the previous record. You can also swipe right to left or left to right to move in either direction. Or, tap left/right arrows to advance or go back.

Customizing records is also a cinch. Take note of the labels in Figure 17-6 for an overview on how to add a new record, add new fields, add records to collections, delete records, and more.

ZAGAT TO GO

Hey, you have to eat sometime (and we're especially hungry after writing this book). ZAGAT TO GO from Handmark lets you access the popular Zagat ratings for restaurants, hotels, nightspots, and shopping locales around the world — you find more than 40,000 listings.

You can search and filter results by cuisine and food, décor, cost, and service ratings, and read Zagat's famous thumbnail commentaries. Foodies can tap into GPS to find decent restaurants when they're traveling and overlay the results on an integrated Google Map. Tap a Zagat pin, and the ratings and restaurant summaries appear, as shown in Figure 17-7. As you drag a map around, restaurant pins pop up in real time. Moreover, you can tap inside a listing to make it a Favorite, reserve a table online (through OpenTable), or save it to your contacts. Zagat also lets you download a database that lets you tap into ratings when you're offline.

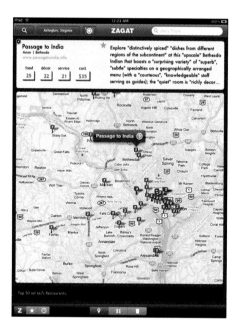

Figure 17-7: Finding an upscale Indian restaurant.

The $9.99 price (for annual up-to-date listings) is less than the print version of a local Zagat edition. We should point out that iPhone owners who purchase the app can also use the iPad app for no extra charge. It works the other way too, so if you buy the app first for the iPad, you can also have a version of it on an iPhone.

Ten Hints, Tips, and Shortcuts

After spending a lot of quality time with our iPads, it's only natural that we've discovered more than a few helpful hints, tips, and shortcuts. In this chapter, we share some of our faves.

Sliding for Accuracy and Punctuation

Our first tip can help you type faster in two ways. One, it helps you type more accurately; two, it lets you type punctuation and numerals faster than ever before.

Over the course of this book, you find out how to tap, how to double-tap, and even how to double-tap with two fingers. Now we want to introduce you to a new gesture we like to call the *slide*.

To do the slide, start by performing the first half of a tap. That is, you touch your finger to the screen but don't lift it. Now, without lifting your finger, slide it onto the key you want to type. You know you're on the right key because it changes from one shade of gray to another.

First, try the slide during normal typing. Stab at a key and if you miss, rather than lifting your finger, backspacing, and trying again, do the slide onto the proper key. After you get the hang of it, you'll see that it saves a lot of time and improves your accuracy as well.

Now here's the best part: You can use the slide to save time with punctuation and numerals, too. The next time you need to type a punctuation mark or number, try this technique:

1. **Start a slide action with your finger on the 123 key (the key to the left of the Space key when the alphabetical keyboard is active).**

   This is a slide, not a tap, so don't lift your finger just yet.

2. **When the punctuation and numeric keyboard appears onscreen, slide your finger onto the punctuation mark or number you want to type.**

3. **Lift your finger.**

The cool thing is that the punctuation and numeric keyboard disappears and the alphabetical keyboard reappears — all without tapping the 123 key to display the punctuation and numeric keyboard and without tapping the ABC key (the key to the left of the Space key when the punctuation and numeric keyboard is active).

Practice the slide for typing letters, punctuation, and numerals, and we guarantee that in a few days, you'll be typing faster and more accurately.

If you're an iPhone or iPad touch user, you may not have noticed that four frequently used punctuation marks — comma, period, exclamation point, and question mark — appear on the iPad alphabetical keyboard in the lower-right corner. There's also a fifth very useful punctuation mark — the apostrophe — hidden on your alphabetical keyboard, but you have to read the next tip to find out exactly where it's hidden.

Auto-Correction Is Your Friend

Here are two related tips about Auto-Correction that can also help you type faster and more accurately.

Autoapostrophes are good for you

First, before moving on from the subject of punctuation, know that you can type **dont** to get to *don't,* and **cant** to get to *can't.* We've told you to put some faith in the iPad's Auto-Correction software. And that applies to contractions. In other words, save time by letting the iPad's intelligent keyboard insert the apostrophes on your behalf for these and other common words.

We're aware of at least one exception. The iPad can't distinguish between *it's,* the contraction of *it is,* and *its,* the possessive adjective and possessive pronoun. So if you need, say, e-mails to important business clients to be grammatically correct, remember that Auto-Correction doesn't get it (or *it's* or *its*) right all the time.

In a similar vein, if you ever *need* to type an apostrophe (for example, when you want to type *it's*), you don't need to visit the punctuation and numeric keyboard. Instead, press the Exclamation Mark/Comma key for at least one second, and an apostrophe magically appears. Slide your finger onto it and then lift your finger, and presto — you've typed an apostrophe without touching the punctuation and numeric keyboard.

Make rejection work for you

Along those same lines, if the Auto-Correction suggestion isn't the word you want, instead of ignoring it, reject it. Finish typing the word and then tap the *x* to reject the suggestion before you type another word. Doing so makes your iPad more likely to accept your word the next time you type it and less likely to make the same incorrect suggestion again.

If you're using a real keyboard (either Apple's Keyboard Dock or any Bluetooth wireless one), you can reject an autosuggestion by pressing the Esc key.

Here you thought you were buying a tech book, and you get grammar and typing lessons thrown in at no extra charge. Just think of us as full-service authors.

Viewing the iPad's Capacity

When your iPad is selected in the sidebar in iTunes, you see a colorful chart at the bottom of the screen that tells you how your media and other data use your iPad's capacity.

By default, the chart shows the amount of space that your audio, video, and photo files use on your iPad in megabytes (MB) or gigabytes (GB). But you knew that. What you probably don't know is that when you click the colorful chart, it cycles through two more slightly different displays. The first click changes the display from the amount of space used to the number of items (audio, video, and photos) you have stored. Click once more, and the display changes to the total playing time for audio and video, as shown in Figure 18-1.

The total playing time display is particularly helpful before you go on a trip. Knowing that you have 8.2 days of audio and 13.7 hours of video is far more useful than knowing how many gigabytes you're packing.

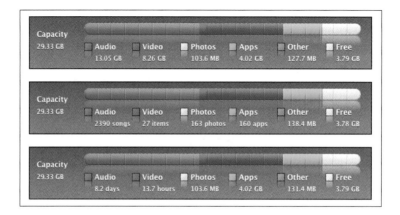

Figure 18-1: Click the colorful chart, and what's stored on your iPad is expressed in different ways.

The Way-Cool Hidden iTunes Scrub Speed Tip

Here's the situation: You're listening to a podcast or audiobook and trying to find the beginning of a specific segment by moving the Scrubber left and right. The only problem is that the Scrubber isn't very precise and your fat finger keeps moving it too far one way or the other. Never fear — your iPad has a wonderful (albeit somewhat hidden) fix. Just press your finger on the Scrubber (that little round dot on the Scrubber bar), but instead of sliding your finger to the left or right, slide it downward toward the bottom of the screen (see Figure 18-2). As you slide, the scrubbing speed changes like magic and the amount of change displays below the Scrubber bar. The default (normal) speed is hi-speed scrubbing. When you slide your finger downward an inch or two, the speed changes to half-speed scrubbing. Drag another inch or two, and it changes to quarter-speed scrubbing. Drag downward to near the bottom of the screen, and it changes to fine scrubbing.

While you're sliding, keep an eye on the elapsed time and remaining time indicators because they provide useful feedback on the current scrubbing speed.

This scrub trick is easier to do than to explain, so give it a try.

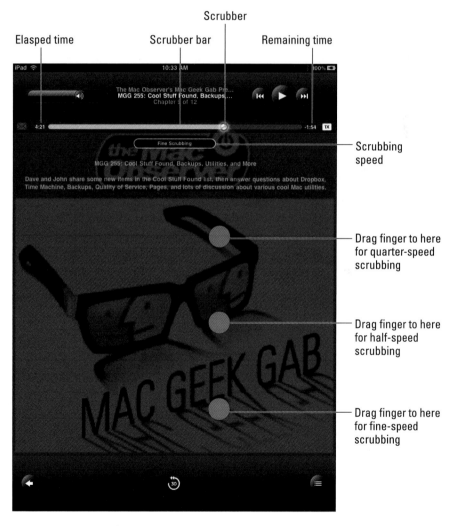

Figure 18-2: Press the Scrubber and slide your finger downward to change the scrubbing rate.

Assault on batteries

Because this is a chapter of tips and hints, we'd be remiss if we didn't include some ways that you can extend your battery life. First and foremost: If you use a carrying case, charging the iPad while it's in that case may generate more heat than is healthy. Overheating is bad for both battery capacity and battery life. So take the iPad out of the case before you charge it. The Smart Cover available for the iPad 2 isn't actually a case, so if you use one of those, you're good to go.

If you're not using power-thirsty 3G or Wi-Fi networks, or a Bluetooth device (such as a headset), consider turning off the features you don't need in Settings. Doing so could mean the difference between running out of juice and seeing the end of a movie.

Activate Auto-Brightness to enable the screen brightness to adjust based on current lighting conditions. Using this setting can be easier on your battery. Tap Settings on the Home screen, tap Brightness, and then tap the On/Off switch, if necessary, to turn it on.

Turning off Location Services (tap Settings⇨General⇨On/Off switch to turn off Location Services) and Push (tap Settings⇨Fetch New Data⇨On/Off switch to turn off Push) can also help to conserve battery life.

Finally, turning on EQ (see Chapter 8) when you listen to music can make it sound better, but it also uses more processing power. If you've selected an equalizer preset for a track in the iTunes Track Info window and you want to retain the EQ from iTunes when you listen on your iPad, set the EQ on your iPad to flat. Because you're not turning off EQ, your battery life will be slightly worse, but your songs will sound just the way you expect them to sound. Either way, to alter your EQ settings, tap Settings⇨iPod⇨EQ.

Tricks with Links and E-Mail Addresses

The iPad does something special when it encounters an e-mail address or a URL in e-mail messages. The iPad interprets character sequences that look like web addresses (URLs), such as `http://www.websitename.com` or `www.websitename.com`, and any sequences that look like e-mail addresses, such as *yourname@yourmailhost*`.com`. When the iPad sees what it assumes to be a URL or e-mail address, it appears as a blue link on your screen.

If you tap a URL or e-mail address like the ones just shown, the iPad launches Safari, takes you to the appropriate web page for a URL, and starts a new e-mail message for an e-mail address. So don't bother with copy and paste if you don't have to — tap those blue links, and the right thing will happen every time.

Here's another cool Safari trick, this time with links. If you press and hold a link rather than tapping it, a little floating text bubble appears and shows you the underlying URL. In addition it offers three options:

⮕ **Open:** Opens the page.

⮕ **Open in New Page:** Opens the page while stashing the current page in one of the nine slots available through the Bookmarks icon, as we describe in Chapter 4.

⮕ **Copy:** Copies the URL to the Clipboard (so that you can paste it into an e-mail message, save it in Notes, or whatever).

You also see the underlying URL if you press and hold a URL in Mail with buttons to open or copy it. Having this information in Mail is even more useful because it enables you to spot bogus links without switching to Safari or actually visiting the URL.

Finally, here's one last Safari trick. If you press and hold most images, Save Image and Copy buttons appear. Tap Save Image, and the picture is saved to the Saved Photos album (Camera Roll on an iPad 2) in the Albums tab of the Photos app; tap Copy, and it's copied to the Clipboard so that you can paste it into an e-mail message or document created in another app (such as Apple's Pages or Keynote).

Share the Love

Ever stumble onto a web page you just have to share with a buddy? The iPad makes it dead simple. From the site in question, tap the + button at the bottom of the browser. Then tap the Mail Link to This Page button that appears onscreen. A mail message appears with the subject line prepopulated with the name of the website you're visiting and the body of the message prepopulated with the URL. Just type something in the message body (or don't), supply your pal's e-mail address, and then tap the Send button.

Choosing a Home Page for Safari

You may have noticed that there's no home page website on the iPad version of Safari as there is in the Mac and PC versions of the browser (and for that matter, every other web browser in common use today). Instead, when you tap the Safari icon, you return to the last site you visited.

The trick is to create an icon for the page you want to use as your home page. This technique is called creating a *web clip* of a web page. Here's how to do it:

1. **Open the web page you want to use as your home page and tap the +
   button.**

2. **Tap the Add to Home Screen button.**

An icon that will open this page appears on your Home screen (or one of your Home screens if you have more than one).

3. **Tap this new Web Clip icon instead of the Safari icon, and Safari opens to your home page instead of the last page you visited.**

You can even rearrange the icons so that your Home Page icon, instead of or in addition to the Safari icon, appears in the Dock (the bottom row that appears on every Home screen), as shown in Figure 18-3.

See the tip in Chapter 1 for rearranging icons if you've forgotten how. And consider moving the Safari icon to a different Home screen so you never tap it by accident. Finally, remember that the Dock has room for six icons even though it only has four by default. So you could, if you like, have both Safari and your new Web Clip icon in the Dock so you can tap either one depending upon your needs.

Figure 18-3: The B.L. Dot Com icon appears where Safari usually appears in the Dock.

Storing Files

A tiny Massachusetts software company — Ecamm Network — sells an inexpensive piece of Mac OS X software, PhoneView ($19.95), which lets you copy files from your computer to your iPad and copy files from the iPad to a computer. (No Windows version is available.) Better still, you can try the program for a week before deciding whether you want to buy it. Go to www. ecamm.com to fetch the free demo.

In a nutshell, here's how PhoneView works. After downloading the software to your Mac, double-click the program's icon to start it. Then do one of the following:

✒ **To transfer files and folders to the iPad** (assuming that you have room on the device), click the Copy to iPad button on the toolbar and then select the files you want to copy. The files are copied into the appropriate folder on the iPad. Alternatively, you can drag files and folders from the Mac Desktop or a folder into the PhoneView browser.

✒ **To go the other way and copy files from your iPad to your computer,** highlight the files or folders you want to be copied and then click the Copy from iPad button on the toolbar. Select the destination on your Mac where you want to store the files and then click Save. You can also drag files and folders from the PhoneView file browser onto the Mac Desktop or folder. Or, you can double-click a file in the PhoneView browser to download it to your Mac's Documents folder.

If you need access to the files on your iPad or if you want to use your iPad as a pseudo–hard drive, PhoneView is a bargain.

Making Phone Calls on the iPad

Many people, including us, have compared the iPad to an iPhone on steroids. Only the iPad isn't actually a phone.

Don't let that stop you from making or even receiving phone calls on the tablet.

Come again?

You read right. You *can* make and even receive phone calls on your iPad. After all, two of the key components to calling are built into the iPad: a speaker and microphone. Now all you'll have to do is head to the App Store to fetch a third, an app that takes advantage of *VoIP,* or *Voice over Internet Protocol.* In plain-speak, that means turning the iPad into a giant iPhone. And yes, you can find more than one app to do the trick.

We've checked out Skype and Line2 (both iPhone apps as this book went to press), along with Truphone, which has a version for the large iPad screen. The apps themselves are free, although you have to pay for calls to regular phones.

✒ **Line2:** We especially like Line2, although it costs $9.95 a month. It can receive calls through Wi-Fi or cellular data network (if you have the iPad with 3G). It boasts such features as visual voice mail (like the iPhone) and conference calling. And it taps right into your iPad contacts list.

  ✔ **Skype:** Skype's app permits free Skype-to-Skype calls, instant messages, and video chats; calls to regular phones around the world cost pennies per minute.

  ✔ **Truphone:** This app permits free Wi-Fi calls to Truphone and Google Talk users. Other rates are cheap.

Taking a Snapshot of the Screen

True confession: We threw in this final tip because, well, it helps people like *us*.

Permit us to explain. We hope you've admired the pictures of the iPad screens that are sprinkled throughout this book. We also secretly hope that you're thinking what marvelous photographers we must be.

Well, the fact is, we couldn't take a blurry picture of the iPad using its built-in (and undocumented) screen-grab feature if we wanted to.

Press the Sleep/Wake button at the same time you press the Home button, but just for an instant. The iPad grabs a snapshot of whatever is on the screen.

The picture lands in the Saved Photos album (original iPad) or Camera Roll (iPad 2) in the Albums tab of the Photos app; from there, you can synchronize it with your Mac or PC, along with all your other pictures, or e-mail it to yourself or anyone else. And from there, the possibilities are endless. Why, your picture could wind up just about anywhere, including in a *For Dummies* book.

If you have an iPad 2, you can show what's happening on your iPad's screen on an HDTV in real time. All you need is a television that has at least one HDMI port and the $39 Apple Digital AV Adapter to connect your iPad to the TV.

By the way, although the original iPad (and the iPhone and iPod touch for that matter) can't mirror their screen on an HDTV with this cable, you can use it to show video playing in certain apps — such as Videos and YouTube — on an HDTV.

Index